.

THE ECONOMIES OF CENTRAL ASIA

THE ECONOMIES OF
CENTRAL ASIA

Richard Pomfret

PRINCETON UNIVERSITY PRESS   PRINCETON, NEW JERSEY

Library of Congress Cataloging-in-Publication Data
Pomfret, Richard W. T.
The economies of Central Asia / Richard Pomfret.
p.   cm.
Includes bibliographical references (p.   ) and index.
ISBN 0-691-04375-2 (cloth)
1. Asia, Central—Economic conditions.   2. Former Soviet
Republics—Economic conditions.   I. Title.
HC420.3.P76   1995
330.958—dc20   95-6829

Contents

List of Illustrations

FIGURE

MAPS

List of Tables

FOR CENTURIES the Silk Road passed through Central Asia, and Bukhara and Samarkand became great cities and centers of Islamic civilization. In 1961 Yuri Gagarin was launched from Baiyonkur to become the first cosmonaut. Images of Central Asia are anecdotal and disconnected, largely because for seventy years foreigners' access to Soviet Central Asia was tightly controlled. Then in late 1991 the USSR disintegrated and five Central Asian countries emerged as sovereign nations receiving international recognition and seeking economic links with the outside world. Now, Bukhara and Baiyonkur are being promoted as tourist destinations.

What are the characteristics of these new countries' economies? Should they be treated as a single regional entity or do they have strong differences? What policies have they pursued since independence and how have their economies performed? Where will this all lead?

This book attempts to answer these questions. It is based upon my experience as a UN regional adviser to the newly independent economies of Central Asia between December 1992 and December 1993. My base was the UN Economic and Social Commission for Asia and the Pacific (ESCAP), and I am grateful for its support, and especially to my colleagues Azizul Islam, Eugene Gherman, and Joop Theunissen.

Because of the lack and unreliability of secondary sources, I have relied heavily on personal observation for information. Partly for this reason, the cutoff date for the sections dealing with recent events is the end of 1993. In a crucial respect this is appropriate: it coincides with the final collapse of the ruble zone, which ended the first phase of the Central Asian republics' postindependence economic history. In other respects, however, it is as arbitrary as most cutoff dates, and many of the reform processes described in Part Two were still unfolding. Any predictions are even less reliable than the average economist's predictions.

Especially in Part Two, information constraints have influenced my ability to deal with some topics. In addition, the five governments were not equally cooperative, and field trips to Tajikistan were forestalled by the security situation. Thus, while I have tried to allocate space and provide data in accordance with a topic's importance, this was not always possible.

The University of Adelaide provided me with a year's leave of absence in which to carry out my UN work, and also provided support facilities for completing the manuscript. I am grateful to Ian McLean for his comments on the early draft and to Jonathan Pincus for his support, even though my absence increased his burdens. The maps were drawn by Chris Crothers and the index was prepared by Jodie Nelson.

List of Abbreviations

CAR	Central Asian republic
CIA	Central Intelligence Agency (of the United States)
CIS	Commonwealth of Independent States
CMEA	Council for Mutual Economic Assistance (Comecon)
DDR	Deutsche Demokratische Republik (former East Germany)
DFI	Direct foreign investment
EBRD	European Bank for Reconstruction and Development
ECO	Economic Cooperation Organization
GBAO	Gorno-Badakhshan autonomous oblast (eastern Tajikistan)
GDP	Gross domestic product
GNE	Gross national expenditure
GNP	Gross national product
IMF	International Monetary Fund
IPF	Investment Privatization Fund
ISI	Import-substituting industrialization
KGB	Committee for State Security (of the former USSR)
NIEs	Newly industrializing economies
NMP	Net material product
OECD	Organization for Economic Cooperation and Development
SDR	Special Drawing Right
STF	Systemic Transformation Facility (of the IMF)
STTPC	South Tajikistan Territorial Production Complex
VAT	Value-added tax

All references to dollars are to U.S. dollars.

THE ECONOMIES OF CENTRAL ASIA

CHAPTER 1

Introduction

NINETEEN NINETY-ONE was a momentous year for Central Asia. In March all of the Central Asian republics (CARs) of the Soviet Union voted in favor of a renewed Union treaty. In August the failure of the coup in Moscow signaled the end of the USSR as it had been, and the Central Asian republics began to declare independence. In December, following the decision of the three Slavic republics to form a new union, the CARs initiated the negotiations that led to the creation of the Commonwealth of Independent States (CIS). By the end of the year, the CIS was in place, the USSR had ceased to exist, and the CARs were all independent countries.

The next years were crucial because the governments were making decisions that would mold the new countries' futures in a once-in-a-lifetime situation. Although constrained by past development and external conditions, the governments had a wide range of options to choose from as they set out in novel political and economic directions. By 1993, it was already evident that the CARs were establishing different political and economic structures. The analytical aim of this book is to determine the main reasons for the different outcomes.

The book is about the economies of the CARs. Table 1.1 provides basic data on these countries' size, income levels, and life expectancies. Part One describes the historical background, which is best seen from a regional perspective. Part Two considers the countries individually, with emphasis on their post-1991 policy decisions and development. Part Three reverts to the regional perspective to analyze some common issues facing the CARs during the 1990s.

THE CONCEPT OF CENTRAL ASIA

Kazakhstan, Kyrgyzstan, Tajikistan, Turkmenistan, and Uzbekistan form a natural unit because of their common history and geography. Other neighboring countries share some of these characteristics, but differ in vital respects: the population of Mongolia is primarily Buddhist and the country has been formally independent since 1921, Afghanistan has never been part of Comecon, and the Caucasus countries differ significantly in their pre-Soviet history and in their resource base. Some parts of the Rus-

TABLE 1.1
Central Asian Republics: Basic Data, 1991–1992

	Population, mid-1992 (millions)	Area (thousands of sq km)	GNP per Capita, 1991 (U.S. $)	Life Expectancy (years)
Kazakhstan	17.1	2,717	2,470	69
Kyrgyzstan	4.6	199	1,550	66
Tajikistan	5.6	143	1,050	69
Turkmenistan	3.9	488	1,700	66
Uzbekistan	21.4	447	1,350	69

Sources: ESCAP, Population Data Sheet, August 1992; World Bank, World Development Report 1993, 238–39.

sian Federation (for example, Tatarstan) have an affinity with Central Asia, but are difficult to analyze as separate economic units.[1] Xinjiang (eastern Turkestan) has many similarities, especially to Kazakhstan and Kyrgyzstan, and at times its history has been closely linked to that of the five CARs, although it has now been under continuous Chinese rule for roughly as long as Kazakhstan was under Russian and Soviet rule; thus Xinjiang will be covered in Chapter 2 and in the discussion of China's relations with the CARs in Chapter 12, but will not feature in the main body of the book.

The dominant physical feature of Central Asia is its aridity; on physical maps it is the brown splotch in the middle of Eurasia, which continues northeast to the Gobi and southwest to Mesopotamia. Annual rainfall never exceeds twenty-five centimeters, and this evaporates in the long hot summers; the continental climate also features cold winters, during which the Aral Sea freezes for four to five months. In this arid area the great river system that flows from the high mountains on the northwestern frontier of the Indian subcontinent into the Aral Sea is of fundamental importance; in the past it has sustained pockets of high civilization based upon irrigation and upon location along the overland route across Asia, and even today much of the region's population is concentrated in the oases along the river system. In the east and north of Central Asia, where rainfall is slightly higher, the mountains and steppelands supported nomadic pastoralism, with quite different economic conditions from those of the sedentary agriculturalists and city dwellers of the south.

Despite the split between sedentary and nomadic lifestyles, the region has always had a unity. The cities flourished when the nomads were militarily strong and unified enough to provide peace in the region. In recent centuries the riverine areas were mostly settled by Turkic, formerly nomadic groups; linguistically, the Turkmen, Uzbeks, Karakalpak,

TABLE 1.2

Ethnic Interpenetration of Central Asian Republics, 1989 (thousands)

	Kazakhstan	Kyrgyzstan	Tajikistan	Turkmenistan	Uzbekistan
Kazakhs	6,535	37	11	88	808
Kyrgyz	14	2,230	64	1	175
Tajiks	25	34	3,172	3	934
Turkmen	4	1	20	2,537	122
Uzbeks	332	550	1,198	317	14,142
Russians	6,228	917	388	334	1,653
Ukrainians	896	108	41	36	153
Byelorussians	183	9	7	9	29
Germans	958	101	33	4	40
Tatars	328	70	72	39	657
Karakalpaks	—	—	—	—	412
Koreans	103	18	13	—	183
Uigurs	185	37	—	—	36
Total	16,563	4,290	5,109	3,534	19,905

Source: Friedman 1993, 59, quoting 1989 census.

Note: Friedman comments that "the data on the number of Tajiks [in Uzbekistan] is not found accurate— since many of them had to register as Uzbeks"(p. 57).

Kazakhs, Kyrgyz, and Tatars are closely related. The Tajiks, with their Persian language, and more recent Slavic, German, or Korean immigrants are the main non-Turkic groups. Table 1.2 illustrates the cultural mosaic and location of ethnic groups in the Central Asian countries.

The region has a unity, but its boundaries are not easily defined by the usual geographical features of rivers, seas, and mountains. In the west and southwest the Caspian Sea and the Kopet Dag Mountains dividing Turkmenistan from Iran provide clear boundaries, but the physical boundary between Central Asia and Afghanistan is less distinct. In the southeast and east the Pamir and Tianshan mountains divided Russian from Chinese Turkestan, but since the major ranges run east-west rather than north-south, these inhospitable regions provided a natural buffer, split by several access routes, rather than a well-defined border. To the north, the limit of Central Asia is even vaguer as the Kazakhstan steppes fade imperceptibly into the Siberian steppes.

Since the creation of the USSR, the Central Asian republics have been closely integrated. Although the CARs each had separate republic status, the planners in Moscow treated the USSR as a single unit in determining location of economic activity, transport networks, and water policy. Formal Soviet definitions, however, excluded Kazakhstan from Central Asia, in recognition of its more diversified economic (and ethnic) base. Ka-zakhstan is included in this book because its similarities to the other four countries outweigh the differences, and in particular its post-1991 history has evolved under similar conditions.

TRANSITION AND DEVELOPMENT

In the 1990s the CARs face two major economic challenges simultane-ously: transition and development. Both of these terms have become widely accepted, although neither is a precisely defined concept and there is no unanimity about the best approach to either transition or develop-ment (although there is greater agreement over what constitute false steps).

Transition is the shorthand term for the process of moving from a centrally planned economy to a market-oriented economy. The precise starting point varies, as not all centrally planned economies had identical systems, and the endpoint will vary, as all market-oriented economies are mixed economies with varying degrees of government involvement. Nevertheless, there is some agreement over what constitutes the set of transition economies, and all of the former Soviet republics certainly be-long to it.

The major debates in the literature on transition have been over the speed of economic reform and the sequencing of individual reforms.[2] Western economists have advocated a Big Bang approach to reform, em-phasizing the interrelatedness of the components of a market economy and the potential for resource misallocation in a partially reformed econ-omy. The paradigm for Big Bang reforms was the Polish package intro-duced in January 1990. Policymakers elsewhere in Eastern Europe were initially more cautious, fearing the disruption and especially the unem-ployment associated with drastic reform, but in some countries (the Czech Lands and Hungary), they have come to accept the logic of the Big Bang argument.

Even a government committed to rapid reform will take time to formulate and implement its program, so the question of priorities is al-ways relevant. Where policymakers are committed to gradualism, the se-quencing of reforms is even more critical. The theoretical literature on sequencing is diffuse, but the majority view favors early emphasis on macroeconomic stabilization and on liberalizing transactions in the cur-rent account of the balance of payments (Fischer and Gelb 1991). In practice there have been many varieties: agriculture-first in China, imme-diate adoption of world prices (or at least West German prices) in the former German Democratic Republic, privatization-first in Mongolia, and so on.

A major difficulty in evaluating the transition debates is the paucity of empirical evidence. The reform measures introduced in Eastern Europe since 1989 have been in place for too short a period to make a complete judgment of success or failure in individual cases, while the pre-1989 reforms there or in the USSR were too limited to provide lessons for the 1990s. The longest-running reform program is that of China, which began with the agricultural reforms and open door policy introduced in the late 1970s, but there is little agreement over the lessons from China's experience for Eastern Europe or the former USSR.[3] In Chapter 10 I will argue that the lessons from China are about development rather than transition, and have limited relevance to the CARs' situation.

"Economic development" is also a term that everybody understands, but is imprecisely defined. It encapsulates the idea of long-term economic change, usually with a positive connotation. It is closely related to economic growth, but also implies some structural changes in the economy.

The literature on economic development is far more extensive than that on transition, and includes a substantial body of empirical work.[4] The subject originated during the 1940s and 1950s, and initially came close to equating development with industrialization. Early development economists also tended to distrust the market mechanism, especially in international markets, whose operation was seen as often working against the less developed countries.

The conventional wisdom on economic development underwent a major revision during the 1970s, largely based on the evidence of shortcomings in inward-oriented industrialization strategies and the economic success of the export-oriented economies of East Asia. The new orthodoxy reemphasized the role of the price mechanism as the best method of allocating resources among productive activities. For most economies the appropriate relative prices are world prices, so trade policy is important because a neutral trade policy will lead to appropriate domestic prices rather than the distorted prices resulting from the discredited protectionist policies. Associated with this has been a general rehabilitation of more market-friendly policies, and distrust of government intervention at the microeconomic level. The remaining role for government in the economic sphere is to provide a framework within which market activities can flourish (including appropriate macroeconomic policies) and direct action in some social spheres (particularly in targeting assistance to people in poverty).

The new orthodoxy in the development literature involves considerable overlap in the policy implications of transition and development. Both require greater openness to the world economy and more reliance on market mechanisms, but they are not synonymous. Transition is a short- to medium-term task, and the challenge is to achieve this transformation of the economy and to set in place new governmental functions, without undermining long-run economic development.

ECONOMICS AND POLITICS

This is a book about economics, but politics cannot be excluded. Domestic politics interact with economics in a two-way causality. This interaction was highlighted by the power struggles in the USSR and Russia in the early 1990s, as debates over the role of the Communist party, the existence of the Soviet Union, and so forth were played out simultaneously with debates over economic policy. Similarly, in the CARs the personalities of the presidents, who came to power for reasons unrelated to economics, have played a significant role in determining (and differentiating) economic policy. Political considerations, especially fears of creating unaccustomed unemployment and income inequality, have also restrained policymakers who recognize the economic logic of more thoroughgoing or faster economic reforms.

Internationally the new states enjoy sovereignty, but they cannot avoid being the object of great power competition. During the nineteenth century Central Asia was where spheres of influence clashed, and although the CARs were firmly within the Russian sphere from the 1870s until 1991, they are once more the board upon which a Great Game will be played. The outcome of this game will undoubtedly influence their economic future. Incorporation into the tsarist Russian Empire inevitably oriented Central Asian trade northwards, but unpredictably led to the collectivization of agriculture and central planning sixty years later. In the 1990s outside advisers encourage diversification of the CARs' trade, and neighboring countries vie for this new trade, but Russia views such talk with a jaundiced eye.

OUTLINE OF THE BOOK

This book seeks to achieve a balance between treating Central Asia as an economic unit with common features and identifying distinctive characteristics of the individual countries (and in some cases, of regions within countries). Part One analyzes the regional economy up to the collapse of the USSR. Part Two describes each Central Asian national economy separately, focusing on their history (emphasizing national heritage and divergences from the general picture presented in Chapter 2), economic structure, economic performance in the late 1980s and early 1990s, and economic policies since independence. Part Three reverts to the regional perspective in order to analyze some common problems and to assess future prospects.

Chapter 2 surveys Central Asia's pre-Gorbachev history, emphasizing the fundamental determinants of the region's economic development. The first section takes up the theme of the sedentarists and nomads, relating the rise and fall of the great cities (Bukhara, Samarkand, Khiva) to the symbiotic relationship between the nomad warriors and the merchants; when the nomads acted as bandits, trade declined, but when they established large unified empires, trade flourished. The overland route was, however, doomed after the discovery of ocean routes from Europe to China and Central Asia went into long-term economic decline.

The region was brought back to international attention in the nineteenth century, when expanding European empires (and stagnant Asian empires) clashed in what was known as the Great Game. The outcome for Central Asia was absorption into the Russian Empire. This reoriented the region's trade northward, and in the twentieth century led to the establishment of Soviet central planning. The role of Central Asia in the Soviet division of labor was primarily as a supplier of cotton, and much of the region became devoted to monoculture based on irrigation systems.

Chapter 3 takes a structural rather than historical view of the regional economy. The main section analyzes the nature of the irrigation economy and its wide-reaching consequences, including such dramatic environmental disasters as the drying up of the Aral Sea. Major environmental problems also are associated with the space center and the nuclear testing facility in Kazakhstan, and systemic environmental problems have been experienced throughout the USSR.

Chapter 4 analyzes the demise of the USSR, emphasizing the economic forces behind the collapse. The Soviet economy was in decline by the late 1970s, and neither Brezhnev nor his caretaker successors did anything to reverse the decline. Gorbachev was more dynamic, but ultimately failed on the economic front. A key question is whether he failed because he adopted the wrong policies or whether the Soviet economy was unsalvageable; my argument is that it probably was unsalvageable, but Gorbachev did not adopt useful economic policies. Chapter 4 also describes the economic performance of the CARs during the early 1990s and analyzes the main issues facing them in the transition to more market-oriented economic systems.

Chapters 5 through 9 emphasize the differentiating features of the individual economies. The most important forces are resource endowment and the policy choices made since independence. Kazakhstan has a diversified resource base, and Turkmenistan is rich with natural gas, but Kyrgyzstan and Tajikistan have little in the way of readily exploitable resources. The postindependence government of Turkmenistan is highly personalized and authoritarian, and Uzbekistan appears to be headed in the same direction, while Kyrgyzstan and Kazakhstan are more open politically; Tajikistan has had a civil war since independence.

Chapter 10 takes up the distinction between development and transition made in Chapter 1. Policymakers in Central Asia frequently refer to South Korea as a model, but still instinctively want to protect their uncompetitive industries from international competition. This chapter highlights the dangers of not learning the lessons from failed strategies of import—substituting industrialization and discusses appropriate development strategies, especially the role of the government in such strategies.

The most pressing macroeconomic problem facing the Soviet republics after the disintegration of the USSR was accelerating inflation. Chapter 11 analyzes why the ruble zone had become inflationary and the arguments for and against introducing independent national currencies. Failure to achieve macroeconomic stabilization hampers the transition to a market-oriented economy and prevents pursuit of the appropriate development strategies, while the arguments for remaining in the ruble zone centered on short-term benefits. All of the CARs adopted national currencies in 1993: Kyrgyzstan in May, Turkmenistan, Kazakhstan, and Uzbekistan in November, and Tajikistan by default (because it continued to use pre-1993 rubles, which were no longer legal tender in Russia).

Chapter 12 turns from monetary issues to trade-related issues. Existing trade relations were strongly skewed toward intra-USSR trade. Trade patterns will become more diversified, but that is likely to have political implications, especially as the region is once again becoming the setting for great power conflicts over spheres of influence. Conversely, the outcome of the many-sided (Russia, the United States and the "West," China, Iran, Turkey) struggle for influence will have an impact on future trade patterns and the economic system.

Chapter 13 will offer some conclusions about the nature of the Central Asian economies and their future prospects.

Appendix 1 discusses the various estimates of the Central Asian countries' total output and national income in the USSR and since independence. These estimates vary widely, and the appendix explains why, in a situation of rapidly changing prices and output mix, it is impossible to produce time series of national accounts aggregates. Nevertheless, we do want to know how an economy is faring, both over time and in comparison with other countries, so it is desirable to know what are the "best" estimates for each purpose.

Appendix 2 draws ten lessons from the early independence years of the former Soviet republics.

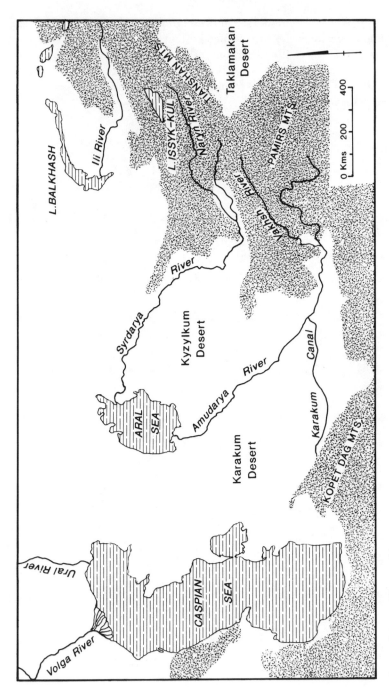

Central Asia: Physical

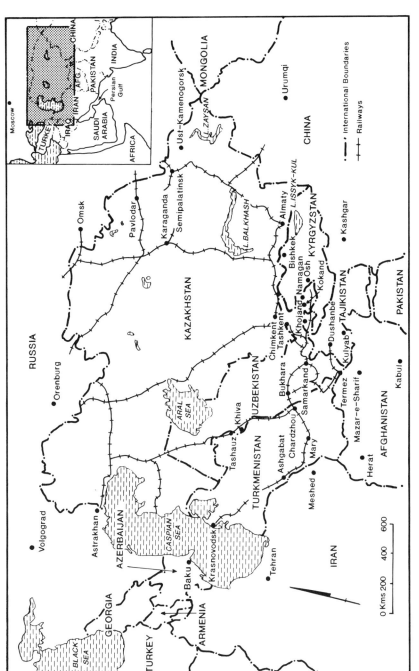

Central Asia: Political Boundaries and Railways

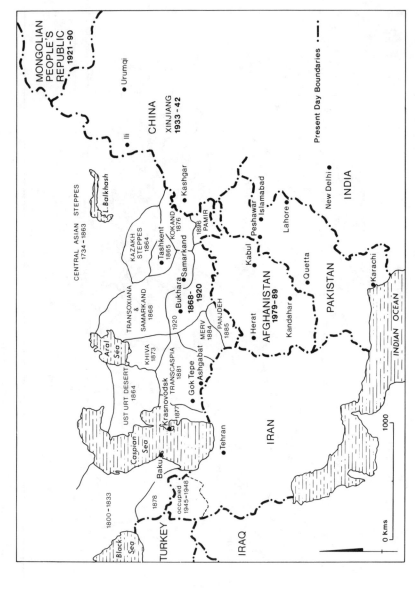

MONGOLIAN
PEOPLE'S
REPUBLIC
1921-90

• Urumqi

CHINA

XINJIANG
1933-42

CENTRAL ASIAN STEPPES
1734-1863

• Ili

L. Balkhash

• Kashgar

Present Day Boundaries ·—··—

KAZAKH
STEPPES
1864

• Tashkent
1865

KOKAND
1876

TRANSOXIANA
&
SAMARKAND
1868

• Samarkand

1896
PAMIR

Aral
Sea

• Bukhara
1920

1868-
1920

Peshawar •
• Kabul

Islamabad •

• New Delhi

INDIA

KHIVA
1873

1920

PANJDEH
1885

Lahore •

UST URT DESERT
1864

TRANSCASPIA
1881

MERV
1884

• Herat

AFGHANISTAN
1979-89

Kandahar •

• Quetta

PAKISTAN

Caspian
Sea

• Gok Tepe

• Ashgabat

Krasnovodsk
1877

• Karachi

• Baku

1878

• Tehran

IRAN

INDIAN OCEAN

1800-1833

occupied
1945-1948

TURKEY

IRAQ

Black
Sea

0 Kms   1000

Russian/Soviet Expansion in Central Asia. Dates in bold indicate periods of strong influence.

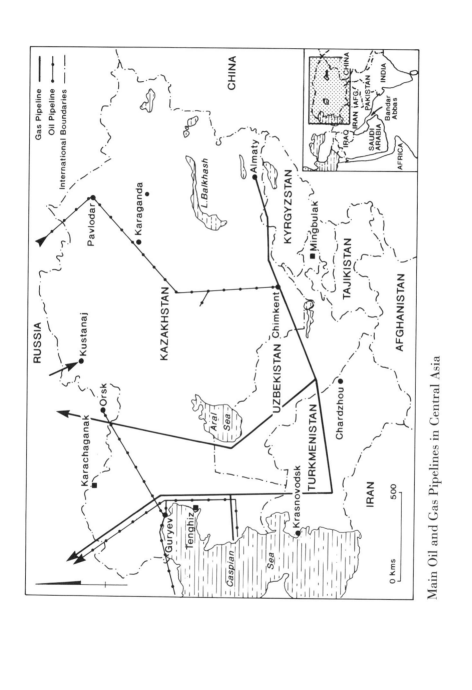

Main Oil and Gas Pipelines in Central Asia

Part One

THE BACKGROUND

CHAPTER 2

History: From Silk Road to Cotton Fields

THE POLITICAL boundaries in Central Asia are fairly arbitrary. Clear dividing lines between states were absent in many parts of the region two centuries ago, and the modern borders have been drawn by outsiders, often with
only rough approximation to cultural or natural boundaries. The southern
border of the USSR had been set in the late nineteenth century when Russia occupied Turkestan and Britain and China established the limits of this
expansion. The borders between the Soviet republics in Central Asia were
drawn more or less arbitrarily by Stalin in the 1920s and 1930s. Nevertheless, the post-1991 states are identified with specific nationalities, and
history is being invoked to provide legitimacy.

The region's more recent history is more crucial to its economies. The
campaigns of Chinggis Khan and Tamerlane or the wealth of the silk traders have little to do with the modern economy. The seventy years as part
of the USSR, on the other hand, almost completely shaped the economies
of the former Soviet republics at the time of their independence.

MERCHANTS AND NOMADS

The unity of the region is broken by several nonidentical dividing lines:
between religions, ethnic groups, and ecological regions. Historically an
important distinction is between the sedentary populations based in the
oases and valleys and the nomadic populations of the steppe. Over two
thousand years ago trade routes from the eastern Mediterranean and
Mesopotamia to China had been established with way stations at oases
and strategic points on the two great river systems of Central Asia.[1] The
nomadic people from the north frequently disrupted what later became
known as the Silk Road in their search for plunder, and control over the
region changed over time, with some rulers leaving a more lasting impact.

Arabs conquered the key towns in 751, bringing Islam and an alphabet
to Central Asia. When their power crumbled a century later, the Persian
Samanid successor state made its capital, Bukhara, into one of Islam's
greatest cultural and scientific centers. The end of Samanid rule in 999
was followed by several centuries of disruption from Turkic invaders,
until in the thirteenth century Chinggis Khan united most of Eurasia into

the world's largest-ever land empire, and the Silk Road thrived again. After Chinggis's successors fell into dispute and the empire fragmented, the final flourish came at the end of the fourteenth century, when Timur (Tamerlane) created a new empire, stretching from Egypt to India, and made his capital, Samarkand, a new center of Islamic culture and scientific learning.

The nomadic Uzbeks began to take over the remnants of Tamerlane's empire in the late fifteenth century. By then, with the discovery of cheaper ocean routes, the overland Silk Road from Europe to Asia was dwindling in importance, and the great cities of Merv, Bukhara, Samarkand, and Kashgar were in decline. When Central Asia again attracted outside attention in the nineteenth century, three Uzbek emirates, based in Khiva, Bukhara, and Kokand, ruled most of the towns, but much of the region was outside their control, especially in the southwest, where Turkmen clans dominated.

The nomadic peoples, such as the Kazakhs, Kyrgyz, Karakalpak, and Mongols, lived further north. Their empires rose and fell, as their horsemen conquered large areas rapidly, but then failed to establish the administrative structure to maintain a large empire (or did so only by losing their nomadic character, as in the case of Kublai Khan in China). Changes in military technology over the last half-millennium permanently ended the threat of nomadic hordes sweeping through rich, settled areas. Political independence was lost in the late seventeenth and early eighteenth centuries, when Xinjiang, Mongolia, and Tibet came under Chinese rule and most of the Kazakh clans accepted Russian protection. In the twentieth century the economic basis of the nomadic lifestyle has been practically destroyed, as Soviet and Chinese communists forced the nomads to settle on state farms.

The correspondence between economic basis and cultural characteristics is close in some respects. The nomads are primarily Turkic/Mongol-speaking groups. The cities have been dominated by Persian-speaking Tajiks, Han Chinese, and more recently Russians. The religious division differs, however, in that most of the population from the Caspian Sea east as far as Xinjiang is Sunni Moslem, but in Mongolia (and Tibet) the dominant religion is Lama Buddhism.

In practice, ethnic groups have become intermixed with few clear-cut ethnic boundaries. The pre-1800 groups had little sense of national identity, and political organization bore no relation to the modern nation-state. Local strongmen ruled on the basis of clan loyalties and a feudal system of vassalage. During the nineteenth century they were no match for the military power of a modern nation-state, and the emirates disappeared as independent units (see the next section). The converging of the Russian, Persian, British, and Chinese empires by the beginning of the twentieth century established international boundaries. The only area of Central Asia to escape conquest was Afghanistan, but it was included in the line-drawing, as a narrow strip of land was declared Afghan territory in order to prevent the contiguity of the Russian and British empires. The great nineteenth-century empires were multicultural, and their collapse would lead to subdivision, just as with the Hapsburg Empire in Europe. Dividing the spoils looked set to be a messy business in all cases.

The ethnic situation in Central Asia has been further complicated by large population movements in the twentieth century. During World War II Stalin moved millions of people considered security risks from border areas of the USSR to Central Asia (for example, a million Germans and a large number of Koreans). Kazakhstan was also part of the gulag to which political undesirables were assigned (Trotsky is Almaty's most famous resident—Lenin never set foot in Central Asia, despite the ubiquitous statues erected in his honor). The Virgin Lands campaign initiated by Khruschev to make Kazakhstan a major grain-growing area led to large-scale immigration of Russians, to the point that they outnumbered Kazakhs in Kazakhstan from the 1960s through the 1980s. Especially since the establishment of the People's Republic of China in 1949, the government in Beijing has sponsored large movements of Han Chinese to border areas, such as Xinjiang, Tibet, and Inner Mongolia, in order to reaffirm their status as integral parts of China (the alternative Chinese government in Taipei still claims Mongolia as part of China). In Xinjiang the 1953 population of 4.9 million included 3.6 million Uygurs and few Han Chinese, but by the 1980s the 6 million Uygurs accounted for less than half of the province's population. In Inner Mongolia in the 1980s the 2 million Mongols were far outnumbered by over 16 million Han Chinese. There has also been some emigration from China's border regions since 1949; many Tibetans fled after the Chinese military takeover in 1950, and a large emigration of Kazakhs from Xinjiang to the USSR occurred in the 1960s. The most recent mass movement of Central Asian people involves the hundreds of thousands of refugees from the postindependence civil war in Tajikistan.

THE GREAT GAME

At the start of the nineteenth century, the emirs and khans of Central Asia exercised despotic rule over their domains. Although military technology had long ago made their mud-brick defenses inadequate against modern artillery, they were protected by mountains from the military might of Britain to the south and by deserts from the growing power of Russia to the north. Tsarist Russia had been preoccupied since the 1550s with extending its empire east to the Pacific (including taking most of the Kazakhs under its protection) and south through the Caucasus.

Once the two great powers had ended the Napoleonic threat, both turned their attention to Central Asia. Russian armies had already subdued much of the Caucasus, and by 1813 they had reached the Persian Empire and agreed upon a border at the Aras River. Central Asia was the obvious next acquisition. The British had no ambition to extend their empire into Central Asia, but they feared the Russian advance and feared that the tsar's ultimate goal was India. For most of the nineteenth century, British policymakers debated whether to occupy forward positions against the expected Russian advance or whether to pursue a policy of masterly inaction behind the natural mountain defenses. The first step for both sides was to explore the region and establish which deserts were impassible and which mountain passes impregnable, and which local despots could be bought over. The missions by Muraviev to Khiva in 1819 and by Moorcroft, Trebeck, and Guthrie to Bukhara in 1820 were the opening moves in what became known in both English and Russian as the Great Game (or Bolshaya Igra).[2]

The Great Game was played by colorful players. On both sides it provided an opportunity for young officers to gain rapid fame and fortune, but behind the personalities lurks a large element of historical inevitability. The backward emirates of Central Asia were no match militarily for Russian armies, and their only natural defenses were the huge deserts, which had foiled early Russian moves against Central Asia; in 1717 a Russian expedition of four thousand men had marched to Khiva, only to arrive exhausted and be slaughtered, with just some forty survivors. Once the Russians had overcome the logistical problems of getting troops and their equipment into Central Asia in good shape, military victory would be easy; this they did gradually, a process culminating in the complete subjugation of the region after the construction of railways in the 1880s.

Initial Russian moves were unsuccessful. In 1838 an attack by Russia's ally Persia on the strategic city of Herat in Afghanistan was repulsed by Afghan forces with British help, and the shah of Persia withdrew in the face of British threats in the gulf. Britain followed up by establishing a puppet regime in Afghanistan, supported by a large British garrison. In response to this success of the British forward school, Russia sent a force of five thousand men from Orenburg to take Khiva, but devastated by a harsh winter, the troops turned back after three months, losing a thousand men without engaging the enemy.

Nemesis for Britain quickly followed. Demonstrations in Kabul in the winter of 1841–1842 forced the British garrison to withdraw; of sixteen thousand people who set out through the Khyber Pass, only one made it to the safety of Jalalabad, completing one of the British Empire's worst-ever military disasters. Symbolic of the British decline was the public behead-ing in 1842 of two British agents in Bukhara, whose emir clearly no longer feared retribution. A decade of Anglo-Russian detente followed these mu-tual disasters in Central Asia, until events elsewhere and botched diplo-macy triggered the 1853–1856 Crimean War.

The Great Game revived when the 1860 Treaty of Peking allowed Rus-sia to consolidate its Far Eastern possessions and to open consulates in Urga (modern Ulaanbaatar) and Kashgar. The American Civil War fur-thered the ascendancy of the forward school in Russia, as the cutting off of the main source of cotton increased the attractiveness of annexing the Kokand region, which contained the Fergana valley known to be suitable for cotton growing. After annexing the small oasis towns of Chimkent and Turkestan in the northern part of the Kokand khanate in 1864, in the next year nineteen hundred Russian soldiers with twelve artillery guns defeated a defending force of thirty thousand to capture Tashkent, the largest town in Central Asia. General Kaufman was appointed governor-general of Tashkent, and from there he masterminded the Russian conquest of Cen-tral Asia. In 1868 Samarkand was captured, and the emir of Bukhara accepted a treaty making him a Russian vassal.

In late 1869 Russia began construction of a fort at Krasnovodsk, on the eastern shore of the Caspian Sea. The fort provided one base for a three-pronged attack on Khiva in 1873, with two other forces coming from Tashkent and Orenburg. This time, the Russian troops reached Khiva, and after a few artillery rounds, the defenders fled, and the khanate be-came a Russian protectorate, which Kaufman integrated into the empire in 1875. Meanwhile, at the other end of Central Asia, an Islamic uprising had led to the establishment of an independent state centered on Kashgar, and the Russians took advantage of the situation to annex Ili in northern Xinjiang in 1871. Thus, in about a decade, the Russian Empire had incor-porated most of Central Asia, coming to within two hundred miles of Brit-ish India and eating into Chinese Turkestan.

During the second half of the 1870s both Britain and China responded more actively. Britain mobilized diplomatically to ensure that Russia would gain little from the 1877–1878 war with Turkey, and then pun-ished the Afghan ruler for friendship with Russia by invading and then imposing an unequal treaty. Although British occupation was again un-popular and led to another military defeat during the withdrawal, the Second Afghan War ended successfully insofar as Britain established a strong ruler over a unified Afghan state, who remained within the British sphere of influence for the remainder of the Great Game. China put down the rebellion and recaptured Kashgar in 1878, thwarting Russian ambi-tions to eventually take the town. The 1881 Treaty of St. Petersburg es-tablished the Russo-Chinese border in Central Asia, returning Ili to Chinese rule; Russian hawks criticized the treaty as a climbdown, but since 1949 China has denounced it as an unequal treaty imposed on China and does not formally recognize the current border with Tajikistan, Kyrgyzstan, and Kazakhstan.

The final Russian advance came against the Turkmen. In 1879 a Russian attack on the stronghold of Gok Tepe had failed when the commander overconfidently resorted to an infantry attack rather than relying on superior firepower. In 1881 a second attack succeeded when artillery and sappers destroyed the defenses, after which defending soldiers and civilians were massacred. The Trans-Caspian railway, begun in Krasnovodsk in 1880, followed the military advance westward. In 1884 the Turkmen capital, Merv (Mary), submitted to Russian rule, and the railway reached Merv the following year. By 1888 the railway reached Samarkand. The Russian army moved south towards Herat, but threatened by war with Britain, halted at the oasis of Pandjeh. A border commission established Russia's southern international boundary, which was not crossed until 1979.

The last episode in the Great Game took place in the high Pamir Mountains in the 1890s. Russia claimed the Pamir region, but Britain resisted this advance by conquering or reducing to dependence the local fiefdoms and thus plugging the last holes in India's northern defenses.

After the turn of the century, the Great Game between Russia and Britain wound down. In 1903–1904 a British force invaded Tibet, convinced it would uncover evidence of Russian plotting in Lhasa, but found nothing and retired. Meanwhile, in 1904–1905 Russia was unexpectedly defeated by Japan, reinforcing the view in Britain that Germany was now the real rival. Russia had its internal problems, too, with the 1905 abortive revolution. The 1907 Anglo-Russian Convention formalized the end of the Great Game, establishing frontiers and spheres of influence.

Surprisingly, the collapse of the tsarist regime in 1917 and the establishment of the Soviet Union had no impact on international boundaries in Central Asia. The Bolsheviks tore up all Russia's treaties and Anglo-Russian confrontation revived in the Caucasus and Central Asia. British troops occupied Baku and Ashgabat, and British politicians (among the most vocal was Winston Churchill) argued for taking advantage of the widespread internal opposition to communist rule to push back the frontiers of the Soviet empire. The forward school lost the debate, and British troops withdrew. By the mid-1920s Central Asia had been pacified and anachronisms, such as the emir of Bukhara, abolished. The old international borders remained in place until the disintegration of the USSR.

The only real change during the decade of 1911–1921 was that Outer Mongolia slipped out of China's sphere of influence and was subsequently consolidated into the Soviet sphere. Although it remained independent, the Mongolian People's Republic was closely tied to the Soviet Union and was often referred to as the sixteenth republic of the USSR. China, despite its chronic weakness from the 1911 revolution until the creation of the People's Republic in 1949, managed to hang on to the rest of its western empire. Tibet's independence lasted from 1911 to 1950, and the Eastern Turkestan Republic, established in 1945, was reconquered and reintegrated into Xinjiang in 1950.

Xinjiang, although nominally under Chinese rule, was practically independent from 1912 through 1928 under the autocratic governor Yang Cengxin. Yang's successor, Jin Shuren (r. 1928–1933), was equally autocratic but his reign collapsed after a series of rebellions beginning in 1931. Attempts by the Chinese government to install a successor to Jin were thwarted because Sheng Shicai already controlled the situation. Under Sheng, Xinjiang became "a nominally Chinese province under Soviet protection" (Nyman 1977, 130). In 1942 Sheng tried to switch masters, and ordered the Soviet advisers to withdraw. The Chinese government replaced him as governor in 1944. There is debate over whether the 1944–1945 East Turkestan uprising was fomented by the USSR (the official Chinese view at the time) or was a nationalist response to decades of autocratic and oppressive Chinese rule (Benson 1990). Only after the suppression of the uprising in 1949–1950 did Xinjiang come effectively under the control of the central government of China. The Chinese-controlled parts of Central Asia will not be dealt with in the remainder of this book, as they are being rapidly Sinicized and their historical experience differs from that of the former Soviet republics, but in the longer sweep of history the Uygurs belong to the same story as the Kazakhs and separatist tendencies have not been eliminated in Xinjiang.

SOVIET CENTRAL ASIA

The Central Asian economy did not undergo fundamental economic transformation during the half-century of tsarist rule. The railway network was built slowly; the Trans-Caspian line from Krasnovodsk reached Tashkent in 1908, the Turksib line connecting Central Asia to the Trans-Siberian network would not be completed until the 1930s, and the rail link to Xinjiang in the late 1980s. Substantial migration from the Slavic areas of the empire into northern Kazakhstan took place before the revolution, but elsewhere in Central Asia, Slavic immigrants were limited to the cities.[3] Cotton growing expanded, but in the early twentieth century, the Fergana valley remained the richest agricultural area, and its agriculture was based on diversified grain, fruit, and vegetable production. Tashkent increased in size, but as an administrative and military center rather than an industrial city. Indeed, there was practically no modern industry in Central Asia before the 1917 revolution.

Once the Bolshevik regime had consolidated its political control in Central Asia, it moved to change the economic structure.[4] In the Five Year Plans, which began in 1928, investment was directed to industrial development, especially in Tashkent as the main urban center. Agriculture was forcibly collectivized, in the face of strong resistance, especially from the livestock farmers of the steppes. In the river systems of the south, once the traditional agricultural organization had been destroyed, the economic base was quickly changed from diversified farming to cotton.

The Great Patriotic War of 1941–1945 interrupted the economic transformation. The main impact on Central Asia was the transfer of factories and equipment from vulnerable positions, especially in the European republics, to the security of Central Asia. A large part of this industrial activity was relocated to Tashkent, the only city already having a sizable industrial base. Stalin also shipped out large numbers of people who were considered potential security risks in front-line republics, notably Germans from the west and Koreans from the east; they mostly ended up in Kazakhstan, and never received permission to leave after 1945.

After the war Central Asia was further incorporated into the Soviet division of labor, primarily as a producer and processor of raw materials. The major product, especially for Uzbekistan and Turkmenistan, was cotton. Cotton was important as an input into Russian textile mills and also as a potential hard currency export. In typical Soviet fashion, the policy was pushed to extremes with little assessment of costs. During the 1960s and 1970s political pressure to increase cotton output led to an average hundred thousand hectares a year being brought under irrigation, almost all for cotton growing. This is when the Aral Sea began to shrink, although there was little official concern for the environmental consequences of ever-increasing land under irrigation; the problem was initially ignored, and then addressed by grandiose plans to divert water to Central Asia from Siberian rivers flowing into the Arctic Ocean. No one knows what environmental consequences those schemes would have entailed; they were shelved by Gorbachev in 1986, and are truly dead with the disintegration of the USSR.

Some of the planners' decisions paid even less attention to costs. Kyrgyzstan, for example, imported Cuban sugarcane (equal to 3 percent of GDP in the late 1980s) for refining and reexporting within the USSR. Tajikistan imported alumina, refined in Odessa from Guinean bauxite, to be smelted for sale within the USSR. Neither of these production chains made economic sense, but Soviet planners faced with raw material inputs from a Third World client and regional underdevelopment in the mountainous part of Central Asia decided to solve both problems together.

These activities made the poorer republics seem relatively industrialized for their income levels, but in fact the two industrial activities just described probably had negative value added at world prices and are better described as make-work projects.

Mining was developed in Central Asia. Again, however, Soviet mines were developed without concern for production costs or ore quality, and some were surely uneconomic at world prices. The Eastern Kalimansur mine in Tajikistan, for example, contained a huge estimated reserve of over 1 billion tons of ore, but with an ore grade of 0.6 percent combined lead-zinc, it would never have been touched by a commercial mining company. Nevertheless, a start was made in exploiting the mineral resources of the region. Kazakhstan in particular became a major producer of oil, coal, lead, silver, chrome, and other minerals, while Uzbekistan was the Soviet Union's second-largest gold producer.

Kazakhstan also developed a more diversified agricultural sector. During the 1950s the Virgin Lands campaign turned large areas of steppeland in northern Kazakhstan into grain farms. Kazakhstan became a net exporter of grain, unlike the other Central Asian republics, which became increasingly dependent upon grain imports. The Kazakhstan economy was also diversified by the location of two high-tech activities in its wide-open spaces: the Soviet space center (from whence Yuri Gagarin became the first person in space), and the nuclear-testing facilities around Semipalatinsk (Kazakhstan is the only Central Asian republic to be a nuclear power in the post-Soviet world). A feature of these developments, however, was the immigration of Russians to farm the Virgin Lands or as technicians; as a result, Kazakhstan became ethnically as well as economically diversified, with more Russians than Kazakhs from the 1960s until the 1980s.

CHAPTER 3

Common Economic Features of the Region

SOME ECONOMIC features of Central Asia cross national boundaries. The most important, determined by geography, is the irrigation-based agriculture, drawing on the waters of the two great rivers. All five Central Asian republics have at least part of this drainage system in their territory, although the irrigation system is most crucial to Uzbekistan and to Turkmenistan. Other agricultural activities are mentioned briefly in the discussion of the structure of production in this chapter, but they can best be dealt with in the individual-country chapters of Part Two, as can primary products, such as energy and mining, even though gas and oil fields or mineral deposits do not always end at national borders.

A second important common economic feature, determined by history, is the integration of the Central Asian republics into the Soviet economic system during seventy years of membership in the USSR.[1] The Central Asian republics shared with the rest of the USSR the general inefficiencies of central planning, and the drawbacks of poor quality and obsolescence in industry and lack of concern for environmental costs. Distinctive to the Central Asian republics, and partly reflecting their lack of pre-Soviet industrial development, was their extreme specialization within the Soviet system, which left them especially susceptible to economic disruption when the Soviet Union disintegrated.

WATER RESOURCES

The dominant water system of Central Asia is formed by the Amudarya (Oxus) and Syrdarya rivers and their tributaries. Both originate in the high mountains in the southeast of the region and drain into the Aral Sea. They drain the whole territory of Uzbekistan, large parts of Kyrgyzstan and Tajikistan (where they originate), and areas of Afghanistan, Kazakhstan, and Turkmenistan. Turkmenistan's agriculture is dependent upon the river system, because it is mainly irrigated from the Karakum Canal, which draws from the Amudarya.

The major water use is for irrigation, although a majority of the region's inhabitants rely on the rivers for their drinking water supply and there are some industrial users. The easily tilled soils are suitable for irrigation, and this has been a feature of the region's agriculture for several millennia. By 1900 over 3 million hectares were under irrigation. This had reached 5 million by 1960 and 8 million in the 1980s, with a large part of the twentieth century increase devoted to growing cotton, one of the most water-consuming crops.

Since 1960 the hydrological balance has been adversely affected. Of the two rivers' combined annual average runoff of around 115 cubic kilometers, about half reached the Aral Sea in the years before 1960, which was sufficient to offset the lake's high net evaporation and keep the lake's size stable. Between 1981 and 1985, however, only 5.2 cubic kilometres a year were reaching the Aral Sea (that is, less than a tenth of the pre-1960 average), and in the dry year of 1986, virtually no river water reached the lake. By 1990 the volume of the Aral Sea had fallen to less than a third of its 1960 volume and the surface area had declined by 45 percent, while the salinity of the water had almost tripled. Under present conditions, the Aral Sea will disappear entirely within the first two decades of the next century, but already its shrinking has been environmentally catastrophic.

The fishing industry has almost disappeared, as twenty of the lake's twenty-four species of fish have become extinct. Similarly, many of the flora and fauna that thrived in the river deltas have disappeared as the deltas have dried up and the wildlife habitat has been degraded. Exposure of the former lake bottom with a concentration of toxic salts in the upper layers has made it difficult to establish a plant cover, and has led to increasingly frequent dust storms. These storms transport an estimated 43 million metric tons of salts per year over vast areas. Salinization is the major cause of declining crop yields. Average cotton yields in the Central Asian republics declined from over 2,800 kilograms per hectare in the late 1970s to 2,300 kilograms in 1987 despite increased application of fertilizers.

Apart from relatively easily measurable economic costs, the ecological disaster is having a serious long-term impact on health. Drinking water is becoming increasingly contaminated by salts and pesticides, which have even been detected in mothers' milk. Typhoid, hepatitis, kidney disease, and chronic gastritis all increased markedly during the last thirty years of Soviet rule. Infant mortality rates were the highest in the USSR, and increasing. Mortality, morbidity, and gynecological ailments appear to have been worst in the Karakalpak autonomous republic, which is centered around the Amudarya delta, although reports tend to be anecdotal.

The full extent of the ecological disaster is impossible to appreciate. Gradual climatic change is taking place in Central Asia, although how much of this is due to the shrinking of the Aral Sea is disputed. What is accepted is that large water masses have a moderating impact on climate, and that as the Aral Sea has shrunk, the Central Asian climate has become more extreme with hotter summers, colder winters, and shorter growing seasons.

The existence of a disaster was already accepted in the 1980s, but dealing with the problem poses difficulties. One simple solution for the Central Asian republics was to divert economically useless water from a Siberian river system.[2] Environmentalists and Siberians protested, and Mikhail Gorbachev shelved the idea. In the post-Soviet world it is inconceivable. Thus, the only solution is to reduce the withdrawals from the two rivers' runoff; even to stabilize the Aral Sea at its current reduced size, the runoff must be increased from five to an average of thirty cubic kilometers a year. This, however, requires agreement among five republics about how much water each is entitled to use. The central planners in the USSR Ministry of Water Resources created a regional ecological disaster, but they at least avoided conflicts over the distribution of water rights.[3]

The Karakum Canal alone was diverting 14 cubic kilometers a year from the Amudarya River in 1987, up from 1 in 1956. This 1,300-kilometer canal runs from the Amudarya River close to where the borders of Uzbekistan, Afghanistan, and Turkmenistan meet and provides irrigation for almost all of the agriculture in southern Turkmenistan (where most of the country's population live). This engineering achievement was politically untouchable in the USSR, but it is an obviously inefficient use of scarce water; for the most part it is a simple cut across the desert, and therefore a large amount of water is lost to seepage before it reaches the areas to be irrigated. Now could be a time for a clear-eyed look, but the political obstacles to reducing the diversion to the Karakum Canal are immense. Since Turkmenistan is dependent upon the canal for its cotton crop, closing the canal would wipe out the country's second export activity, and would certainly be regarded by the Turkmen as an unfair distribution of the burden of restoring the Aral Sea.

Even if the five republics could reach an agreement about sharing the burden, implementing reductions in irrigation would be politically difficult domestically. Since all of the republics have experienced large output losses in the early 1990s and face the prospect of growing unemployment, the idea of deliberately closing down a segment of agriculture is highly unattractive.

OTHER ENVIRONMENTAL ISSUES

About 470 nuclear devices were detonated in the Semipalatinsk nuclear-testing range between 1949 and 1989, of which until 1963 some 115 were above ground.[4] The testing was secret and the nearly 2 million inhabitants of East Kazakhstan who were directly at risk were informed about potential hazards only in 1992. Epidemiological studies from as early as 1957 indicated high levels of cancer, but USSR authorities ascribed health problems to local nutritional status, and detailed results of studies were suppressed. Archival records now indicate exposure levels of one hundred times permissible levels. In 1992 the Kazakhstan government drafted a decree to declare the affected area an "ecological disaster area," but if accepted by the parliament, the financial outlays for compensation and relocation would be high. The antinuclear movement is strong in Kazakhstan (as in other Soviet republics, such as Ukraine and Belarus, since the Chenobyl disaster). One obstacle to improved relations with China has been the continued nuclear testing in Xinjiang; Kazakh complaints meet a deaf ear in Beijing.

The western areas of Kazakhstan and Turkmenistan have also suffered recently from a difficult-to-explain rise in the level of the Caspian Sea. The sea level fell from the 1920s until the 1970s, but in the 1980s and the early 1990s, it rose by over two meters. In 1993 severe floods in the littoral regions of Kazakhstan left many villages under water, and about twenty thousand square kilometers of arable land has vanished. In Turkmenistan the town of Cheleken, which stands on a peninsula, is about to become an island. Azerbaijan, Iran, and Russia are also affected, and the presence of many oil wells on low-lying land is a serious environmental hazard. Already the oil content of Baku harbor is twelve times the officially permitted level.[5] Clearly such pollution threatens the ecological balance (including the valuable sturgeon stocks) and affects all littoral areas.

Soviet central planning created a more general environmental disaster, on top of the specific catastrophes of Semipalatinsk and the Aral Sea.[6] Soviet central planning promoted the achievement of output targets with little concern for the amount of inputs or for negative externalities, such as pollution. Extensive recourse to subsidies ensured that enterprises did not have to worry about costs, and many inputs (fuel and energy in particular) were priced below cost. Obsolete technologies failed to incorporate environmentally friendly innovations. The public was not informed (or sometimes deliberately misled) about environmental problems, and, although environmental laws were introduced in the later part of the Soviet era, they were ineffectively enforced. The consequence is high levels of water and air pollution.[7]

Other major sources of air pollution are power stations and motor vehicles. The predominant fuel for power generation is coal, which has a high fly ash content in Kazakhstan. Scrubbers and electrostatic precipitators installed for particulate control operate at low levels of efficiency. Automotive pollution is exacerbated by the low octane of fuels (as low as 76 octane) and is particularly serious in Almaty because of the siting of the city.

The Soviet system also devoted few resources to waste disposal. Some cities have no wastewater treatment facilities (including seven medium-sized cities in Kazakhstan with a combined population of nearly a million), and in others the system is incomplete. There is no source separation or recycling before the huge quantities of solid waste are dumped in landfills, and no inventory of hazardous solid wastes exists.

Morbidity levels are high in Kazakhstan, especially in the industrial centers. In 1991, 48 percent of adults and 76 percent of children contracted various illnesses, with extended absences from work or school. In Semipalatinsk and other parts of East Kazakhstan, 100 percent of children were ill at least once during the year. The Karakalpak autonomous republic in Uzbekistan, around the southern shore of the Aral Sea, has also experienced terrible deterioration in health standards in recent decades.

STRUCTURE OF PRODUCTION

Before the Brezhnev era the Central Asian economies had been developed along the Soviet model of agricultural collectivization (despite violent opposition in the 1920s and 1930s) and emphasis on heavy industry. They had been incorporated into the Soviet/CMEA division of labor, with extreme specialization. Most notably many parts of Central Asia had been turned into monoculture economies based on cotton, which crowded out grain production. The main exception is northern Kazakhstan, where under Khrushchev grain farming was greatly expanded under the Virgin Lands scheme.

The industrial development was more limited in Central Asia than elsewhere in the USSR and often made sense only in the wider context of the Soviet economy (if then), as enterprises produced for captive markets or participated in a Sovietwide processing chain. This was most obvious with respect to intermediate goods (such as the aluminium ingots produced in the South Tajikistan complex or the output of the mining and smelter complexes in Kazakhstan), but even consumer goods production was highly specialized; Kyrgyzstan supplied washing machines throughout the USSR, but imported TVs and refrigerators. Only Tashkent had developed a diversified industrial base, which was built upon when industrial activities were moved there from the western part of the USSR during the 1941–1945 war.

One peculiarity of Central Asia and the Caucasus during the Brezhnev era was the emergence of a neofeudal system, in which whole republics became criminal networks led by the first party secretary.[8] When the leaders were local figures, they could enjoy strong popular support (as a source of nationalist pride and standing up to Moscow) even when proven

TABLE 3.1

Average Annual Growth in Net Material Product, 1971–1989 (percent)

	Growth in NMP		Growth in NMP per Capita	
	1971–1985	1986–1989	1971–1985	1986–1989
Kazakhstan	3.1	1.9	1.8	0.9
Kyrgyzstan	4.2	4.9	2.1	2.9
Tajikistan	4.4	3.2	1.4	0.0
Turkmenistan	3.1	4.9	0.4	2.2
Uzbekistan	5.1	2.9	2.2	0.3
USSR	4.4	2.7	3.5	1.7

Source: IMF et al. 1991, 1:215. Original sources: 1971–1985 *Osnovnye pakazateli* (1990), 29–30 and 33; 1986–1989 *Narkhoz 1989* (1990), 13.

Note: These official growth rates are universally considered to be upward biased (see discussion on p. 140 of the source) because the price deflators underestimated actual inflation. Thus, they are useful only to compare the republics' performance with one another or with the USSR average.

to have embezzled huge amounts from the public purse. The most publicized example was that of the Uzbekistan cotton magnates who were alleged to have stolen more than 4 billion rubles, of which they appropriated half for themselves.[9] In December 1986, when the corrupt Kazakh, Dinmukhamed Kunayev, was replaced by a Russian (Gennady Kolbin) as Kazakhstan's first secretary, thirty thousand people demonstrated in Alma Ata, and two people were killed when the police dispersed the protesters.[10]

Under Brezhnev the pace of development slowed in Central Asia as in the rest of the USSR. Table 3.1 presents the notoriously unreliable official statistics. The official growth rates overstate the real growth because Soviet techniques systematically understated the price deflator (see note to Table 3.1), but they are consistent enough for cross-sectional comparisons. All the CARs' per capita net material product grew at a rate substantially below the Soviet 1971–1985 average. Long-term stagnation is most apparent in the three largest CARs, whose output per head was growing by less than 1 percent per annum during the second half of the 1980s. Only Kyrgyzstan maintained reasonable economic growth, based on livestock production (see Chapter 8), and Turkmenistan's growth rate increased during the 1980s with exploitation of natural gas.

Agriculture remained the dominant economic activity in Central Asia. In Tajikistan, Turkmenistan, and Uzbekistan the share of the labor force working in agriculture was double the USSR average in 1987 (see Table 3.2). Even though the Virgin Lands program had established a large

TABLE 3.2
Sectoral Distribution of Employment, 1987

	Agriculture	Industry	Transportation	Trade	HSEA	Other
Kazakhstan	23	31	11	8	19	8
Kyrgyzstan	34	27	7	7	18	7
Tajikistan	42	21	7	6	17	7
Turkmenistan	41	21	8	6	17	7
Uzbekistan	38	24	7	6	19	6
USSR	19	38	9	8	18	8

Source: IMF et al. 1991, 1:219.

Notes: The sectors are agriculture and forestry, industry and construction, transport and communication, trade and catering, health, science, education, and art, and other.

TABLE 3.3
Major Agricultural Products, 1990–1992 Average (thousands of metric tons)

	Kazakhstan	Kyrgyzstan	Tajikistan	Turkmenistan	Uzbekistan
Cereals	23,218	1,432	300	571	1,985
Seed cotton	288	66	697	1,393	4,568
Fruits	270	141	318	222	1,120
Vegetables	1,220	424	775	386	3,650
Meat (slaughtered weight)	1,510	210	76	100	510
Milk (and milk products)	5,265	961	521	471	3,675
Wool (metric tons)	169,230	59,867	6,950	26,300	41,133

Source: Theunissen and Kimmo 1994.

grain-growing sector in northern Kazakhstan, the Kazakhstan economy was the most diversified in Central Asia, with half the work force employed in industry, construction, trade, or communications.

Table 3.3 presents data on the major agricultural products of the CARs. These countries accounted for four-fifths of cotton output in the USSR, with production most concentrated in Uzbekistan, Turkmenistan, and, to a lesser extent, Tajikistan.[11] The cotton monoculture, with its lack of crop rotation, led to falling soil productivity, which was compensated for by increased fertilizer use. Fertilizer application, however, could not reverse the long-term decline, and it also increased contamination of underground water.[12] Mechanization of cotton harvesting since the 1960s has added to ecological problems, because defoliants were sprayed from the air to ease the harvesting. Soviet planners' emphasis on quantity discouraged attention to quality, and a growing reputation for low quality had a negative impact on hard currency exports. Declining export competitiveness was exacerbated in the early 1980s when China entered world cotton markets on a significant scale after agricultural reforms had encouraged diversification into cotton in some provinces.

Kazakhstan is the only CAR that is a significant grain producer. Within the USSR, it was the third-largest producer, behind Russia and Ukraine, and together with Ukraine the only consistent net grain-exporting republic. Grain production is, however, very unstable in Kazakhstan because of the low rainfall and short growing season, and yields per hectare are low (less than a quarter of yields in Ukraine and about half those in Russia). Because the other four CARs rely heavily on grain imports, they were vulnerable to bad regional harvests. In 1991, for example, the poor harvest in Kazakhstan led to grain scarcity throughout the region, and the reduced availability of feed led to large-scale slaughtering of livestock in the other four CARs. In consequence, the governments encouraged transfer of land from cotton to grain production, and the area under grains increased by 20 percent in Kyrgyzstan, 38 percent in Uzbekistan, 46 percent in Tajikistan, and 65 percent in Turkmenistan between 1989 and 1992.

The CARs also have substantial livestock farming. Kazakhstan is the most important producer of meat and milk. Wool is an important export for both Kazakhstan and Kyrgyzstan

The CARs were significant energy producers within the USSR, but reserves are not spread evenly across the region (see Table 3.4). Kazakhstan accounts for over 85 percent of the CARs' oil reserves (its proved and probable reserves are roughly equal to the proved reserves in all of Western Europe), while Turkmenistan has 43 percent of the region's proved natural gas reserves.[13] Kazakhstan is the only net exporter of oil, and Turkmenistan and Uzbekistan the only net exporters of natural gas. Kazakhstan produced almost one-fifth of the coal mined in the USSR, and the Karaganda miners were a politically important group of workers during the final years of the USSR. Hydroelectricity is produced in the mountainous areas of Kyrgyzstan and Tajikistan.

The design of the energy sector was based on USSR-wide thinking. Much of the oil, coal, and gas produced in the region was exported to Russia for refining or use in power plants. Only three of the CARs have oil refineries, and these were not always designed to refine local oil; for example, the oil refineries in eastern Kazakhstan were designed to process oil from Siberia, while unrefined oil was being exported from western Kazakhstan. Uzbekistan has far larger refinery capacity than domestic crude oil production; in 1990 the refinery intake of crude came 25 percent from Uzbekistan, 7 percent from other CARs, and 68 percent from Russia. When Russian supplies of crude oil to Uzbekistan were reduced from 5.5 million tons in 1990 to less than 3 million tons in 1993 refined oil products

TABLE 3.4

Oil and Natural Gas in Central Asia, 1991

	Reserves[a]	Production[b]	Consumption
Oil			
Kazakhstan	2,140	530	430
Kyrgyzstan	25	5	55
Tajikistan	5	—	50
Turkmenistan	210	110	200
Uzbekistan	115	55	205
Natural Gas			
Kazakhstan	1,830	130	225
Kyrgyzstan	6	—	35
Tajikistan	7	—	30
Turkmenistan	2,720	1,395	135
Uzbekistan	1,820	695	565

Source: Petromin, September 1993, 40.

[a] Oil: proved and probable, in millions of tons. Natural gas: proved, in billions of cubic meters.

[b] Thousands of barrels per day, oil equivalent.

were soon in short supply in Uzbekistan, and even more so in the other CARs, which had earlier imported refined oil from Uzbekistan.

The greatest oil potential in the region lies around and under the Caspian Sea. Exploitation of contiguous reserves requires cooperation among the Caspian states (Kazakhstan, Turkmenistan, Russia, Azerbaijan, and Iran), and there is also a need to cooperate in designing pipeline routs.

The CARs also claim to have abundant mineral reserves, but it is difficult to know which of these are commercially viable. Certainly the gold mines of Uzbekistan will be exploited quickly, but there are greater question marks over the multimineral deposits in Kyrgyzstan and Tajikistan.

ECONOMIC INTEGRATION

The Soviet economy was characterized by a high degree of self-sufficiency combined with a high degree of regional specialization. The net effect was to make the Central Asian republics fairly open economies, but with highly distorted trade patterns. Thus, although the Central Asian republics traded approximately the same share of total output as did Canadian provinces (see Table 3.5), the proportion of their trade with other Soviet republics was double the corresponding proportion for Canadian provinces.[14]

TABLE 3.5

Comparison of Trade Flows of Central Asian Republics and Canadian Provinces

	Total Trade as % of GDP[a]	Intraregional Trade as Share of Total
CARs (1988)		
Kazakhstan	33.9	86.3
Kyrgyzstan	45.2	86.9
Tajikistan	41.6	86.3
Turkmenistan	39.3	89.1
Uzbekistan	39.5	85.8
Canadian Provinces (1984)		
Alberta	39.1	60.3
British Columbia	33.6	38.3
Manitoba	40.3	61.0
New Brunswick	61.5	51.5
Newfoundland	45.6	59.1
Nova Scotia	49.9	54.0
Ontario	49.5	33.9
Prince Edward Island	50.5	75.5
Quebec	42.2	48.0
Saskatchewan	51.4	52.2

Source: IMF, *Common Issues and Interrepublic Relations in the Former USSR* (Washington, D.C.: IMF, 1992), 37.

[a] $[(X+M)/2]/\text{GDP}$.

The Central Asian republics' place in the Soviet system was mainly as producers or processors of raw materials. The latter activities could be especially vulnerable as either input supply or access to markets breaks down, or the entire Soviet production chain could prove uneconomic at world prices.[15] Kyrgyzstan imported Cuban sugarcane (equal to 3 percent of GDP in the late 1980s) for refining and reexporting within the USSR. Tajikistan imported alumina, refined in Odessa from Guinean bauxite, to be smelted for sale within the USSR. Neither of these production chains makes sense in the absence of the Soviet Union. Primary product activities are likely to be more durable, but Soviet mines were developed without concern for production costs or ore quality, and some may be uneconomic at world prices. The irrigation- and chemical-intensive agriculture producing cotton and grain will survive, but must adjust to reduce the huge ecological and health costs imposed in the past.

During the final years of the USSR, interrepublic trade began to decline in line with the fall in overall economic activity, culminating in an estimated decline of 15 percent in 1991. Trade with countries outside the USSR declined even more drastically; all of the Central Asian republics experienced a drop in exports of 35–40 percent and in imports of 39–48

TABLE 3.6

Central Asian Republics' External Trade, 1991 (millions of U.S. dollars)

	Imports	Exports	
Kazakhstan	1,356	1,254	
Kyrgyzstan	555	23	
Tajikistan	200	219	
Turkmenistan	846	1,187	(of which gas = 1,052)
Uzbekistan	3,628	773	(of which cotton = 495)

Sources: IMF Economic Reviews (Washington, D.C., April 1992) of Kazakhstan (p. 24), Kyrgyzstan (p. 24), Tajikistan (p. 21), Turkmenistan (p. 87), and Uzbekistan (pp. 43–44).

Notes: Figures for Kazakhstan and Turkmenistan were constructed from volume and price data. Those for Kyrgyzstan, Tajikistan, and Uzbekistan are ruble amounts, converted at the commercial exchange rate of 1.75 rubles/$. In most cases the numbers are marked "estimate" in the source, and in all cases they should be treated as orders of magnitude. Export figure for Uzbekistan is exclusive of gold.

percent.[16] Table 3.6 gives estimates for the external trade of the CARs in 1991, which apart from Turkmenistan is very small on a per capita basis.

The collapse of interrepublic trade was exacerbated by the growth of export restrictions as republics tried to conserve their national resources and to prevent arbitrage trade due to "excessive" price increases or tax cuts in neighboring republics. A further problem by late 1991 was declining confidence in the ruble and in the payments mechanism, which led to doubts about when sales would be paid for, and what the currency would be worth when payment was received.

By the time the CIS was formed in December 1991, interrepublic trade was increasingly being done by government-to-government barter, with any shortfall in supply to be met in hard currency or ruble payments at a negotiated rate. The negotiations were often difficult and sometimes broke down; for example, trade between Turkmenistan and Ukraine came to a halt in March 1992 because of failure to agree on gas prices, and a compromise was not reached until September. Faced by critical shortages of food or oil, some republics turned to outside suppliers (for example, Ukraine turned to Iran for oil, and Kyrgyzstan to Canada and Australia for wheat). Such moves, however, encouraged the raw material–exporting republics to insist on an even faster move toward world prices and immediate payment in hard currency. Given the large external trade deficit of the USSR in its final years and the chronic shortage of hard currency, these moves toward greater insistence on hard currency payment could only accelerate the decline in interrepublic and extra-CIS trade.

Although the decline in trade was primarily a consequence of general economic decline, it also feeds back to contribute to further decline. The Central Asian republics in particular are poorly equipped for a rapid retreat into autarchy, since their modern economic development has involved a high degree of specialization. Thus, an immediate issue facing these countries is how to halt the disruption of trade, and this is closely related to the currency issue discussed in Chapter 11.

Moving toward an open economy incorporated into the global rather than the Soviet trading system will obviously be easier for Central Asian republics with readily exportable resources (Kazakhstan, Uzbekistan, and Turkmenistan) than for others (Kyrgyzstan and Tajikistan). For all of these countries, however, physical constraints have arisen from the past trading patterns. Thus, efficient export of oil or natural gas will require construction of pipelines from the producing areas to the markets or to ports; negotiations are under way, but even under the most optimistic projections, it will be the second half of the decade before pipelines to the Black Sea or the Mediterranean Sea are completed.

All of the Central Asian republics are landlocked economies, and improvements in transport links are desperately needed. Creating access to the nearest seaports in Iran or Pakistan will require cooperation with neighboring countries. Even intrarepublic transport will often require cooperation with neighbors as the Soviet planners built transport networks without regard to the USSR's internal borders. The railway between the two largest towns in Kyrgyzstan, Osh and Bishkek, runs from Osh through Uzbekistan, Tajikistan, Uzbekistan again, and then Kazakhstan, before reentering Kyrgyzstan just before Bishkek. The main road between the capitals of Uzbekistan and Kyrgyzstan runs almost entirely through Kazakhstan. Upgrading airports and communications systems are also high priorities, which require large funds.

OVERVIEW

Whether the Central Asian republics on balance benefited or suffered from being in the Soviet Union is not easy to say. Evaluation depends upon the counterfactual of what would have been their history had they remained outside the USSR, and upon which countries they are compared with. They remained poorer than other Soviet republics and other economic dependencies of the USSR in Eastern Europe, but better off than their southern neighbors in Afghanistan and their western neighbors in Xinjiang and better off than most of the inhabitants of the successor states to British India. In these latter comparisons, however, must be weighed the facts that Afghanistan retained its independence and India since 1947 has against some odds remained a functioning democracy in which citizens enjoy important civil rights, while the Central Asian republics were not independent and their citizens' human rights were circumscribed.

Even a strictly economic evaluation of the CARs' Soviet experience is difficult because the major costs and benefits are not comparable. Against the costs of economic inefficiency, extreme specialization, and ecological degradation must be weighed the benefits from the large net inflow of resources into the region from the rest of the USSR and the subsidized provision of some services. The record on basic needs, such as education, nutrition, health care, and housing, was generally good during the Soviet period, at least until the ecological disasters started to have a greater impact in the 1980s. Associated with the achievements in education (notably, almost universal literacy) came major social changes, including improved economic status for women as girls became educated and more females entered the work force. In 1960 the proportion of women in blue- and white-collar occupations varied from 36 percent in Turkmenia to 41 percent in Kirghizia, while by 1986 it had increased in every republic, reaching 45 percent in Kighizia and Kazakhstan, 43 percent in Uzbekistan, 41 percent in Turkmenia, and 38 percent in Tajikistan.[17]

Whether in recognition of the benefits of Soviet rule or because the communist leadership kept a tight rein, there was little pressure for leaving the Soviet Union. Even with the growing ethnic disputes and occasional anti-Soviet Union demonstration, as in Almaty in December 1986, the situation in Central Asia was in no way like that in the Baltic republics or in Azerbaijan after the January 1990 Baku massacre. Dire predictions that the Moslems of Central Asia would rise up and cast off the Russian yoke simply did not come true during the lifetime of the Soviet Union.[18]

The disintegration of the USSR was a result of events far away, upon which the Central Asian republics had little influence and whose outcome they did not particularly desire. Nevertheless, it profoundly affected the Central Asian republics, leading them to become independent nations in 1991 and creating the immediate political and economic background to their independence. The story is told in the next chapter.

CHAPTER 4

The Economic and Political Collapse
of the Soviet Union

THE DRAMA of the disintegration of the USSR was mainly played out in Moscow. While some Soviet republics participated in the political moves for decentralization and openness (glasnost), the CARs remained apart. The occasional demonstrations were against Mikhail Gorbachev's anti-corruption campaign or were inspired by old ethnic disputes, rather than being in favor of political and economic reform or national self-determination. The CARs were practically untouched by economic reform (perestroika) before 1991.

Nevertheless, the collapse of the USSR was an event of vital importance for the CARs, since it created them as independent nations. During 1991 and 1992 the CARs' economic performance was as much affected by Sovietwide factors as by local developments; inflation accelerated and output fell. The CARs also faced common problems of transition from the Soviet economic system to more market-oriented economies.

FROM USSR TO CIS

The Soviet economy was in serious trouble by the end of the 1970s. All commentators now agree that economic growth had stopped, although there is disagreement about real output measures.[1] Open discussion was stifled, and no reform steps were taken as the political leadership waited for Brezhnev to die. On the external front, signs of the paralysis were the bogged-down intervention in Afghanistan and the failure to intervene in Poland in December 1981.[2]

After Brezhnev's death in 1982, reform ideas began to be floated in the USSR. It is indicative of the unsustainability of the status quo that these first steps were taken under the leadership of Yuri Andropov, former KGB head and communist hardliner. The leadership, however, remained incapable of decisive action, and even when Andropov died in February 1984, a caretaker successor was appointed. Only after Konstantin Chernenko also died after a brief term in office was a younger, more dynamic leader chosen. After Mikhail Gorbachev took office in March 1985 he soon gained a positive reputation in the West, but he was a protégé of

Andropov, and any "reformist" statements he made were cautiously hedged.[3]

Economic reform in the second half of the 1980s proceeded on several fronts: changes to improve the existing system, geographically limited reform experiments, and systemic reform. Changes within the system were all ineffective in the long run, as had been the 1965 reforms in the USSR and the various pre-1989 reforms in Eastern Europe. A well-publicized case was the antialcohol campaign, with which Gorbachev personally identified himself. In the short run, alcohol consumption was reduced, perhaps with beneficial economic effects from reduced absenteeism and so forth, but after the first year of the campaign, the black market grew and alcohol consumption began to increase again. The long-run effect was to reduce government tax revenue and stimulate organized crime (as Prohibition had done in the United States sixty years earlier, and in tsarist Russia in 1914), with no effect on alcohol consumption. The acceleration program introduced by Gorbachev in 1985 to stimulate technical change through increased spending on investment was also unsuccessful, generating repressed inflation but not long-term growth.[4]

Reform via geographically limited experiments has been a hallmark of post-1978 China. Some reforms were introduced in the USSR in this way, but they were much more cautious than, say, the Chinese agricultural reforms, and they remained small-scale. Nevertheless, since some republics initiated many experiments (Georgia, Estonia, Lithuania, and Armenia), the cumulative impact was to move their economies in the direction of the Hungarian model. Other republics (Belarus, Latvia, and parts of Russia and Ukraine) used more limited experiments to improve the existing system within their jurisdiction, following a DDR approach. In a final group of republics (Moldova, Azerbaijan, and the Central Asian republics), there were no experiments with reforms.

The personal interest of many officials in the existing system (described in Chapter 3) helps to explain the absence of economic experiments in Central Asia. Also, the Soviet appointees in the Central Asian republics were disproportionately Russians, who must have been acutely aware that they were operating in an alien cultural environment, as violent outbreaks recurred during the 1980s.[5] In this setting they would have been cautious about initiating any change that might loosen governmental control.[6]

Slow progress along these two reform fronts, coupled with continuing economic decline, encouraged more radical reform. The Law of State Enterprises, which took effect at the start of 1988, aimed to turn over decisionmaking to enterprise managers, and is sometimes identified with the abolition of central planning. There was, however, a fundamental contradiction between the law's aim and allowing state orders to continue.[7] State orders still accounted for over 90 percent of industrial production in 1988 (IMF et al. 1991, 1: 26). Agencies at all levels of government continued to have the authority to buy at the fixed prices, and the scramble for goods meant that enterprises continued to sell almost all of their output as before—only now the central planners were playing less of a coordinating role.

The scramble for goods by public agencies came on top of declining government tax revenue from alcohol sales and falling world oil prices, and increased expenditure on the acceleration program, on social services, and on the military. As government spending increased, the budget deficit exceeded 10 percent of GDP, growth in the money supply accelerated, and the external account deteriorated. As shortages became more pronounced, open inflation rose to 10 percent in 1988, 12–14 percent in 1989, and over 19 percent in 1990, and falling real wages led to labor unrest.[8]

The failure of partial reform to solve the USSR's economic problems led to continued radicalization of the policy debate, but the leadership remained overcautious and extremely suspicious of market mechanisms. Only after 1987 was open discussion of market-determined pricing permitted. When any price changes were mooted, opposition was strong, and the leadership remained skeptical. The leaders' fundamental problem lay in the lack of any palatable alternative to the failed central-planning model. Gorbachev's role in economic policymaking is debated; whether he was unreceptive or constrained by opposition within the top leadership, he failed to embrace the more radical solutions proposed as economic conditions deteriorated.[9] The most notable example was the Shatalin Plan of August 1990, which was implemented by the Russian republic, but after several months' delay the USSR adopted the less drastic Pavlov Plan.

During the first half of 1991, disputes over the pace and extent of economic reform overlapped with conflicts over the decentralization of political power. In January the situation in the Baltic republics came to a head as Soviet military forces intervened; although the number killed was far less than in Baku a year earlier, events in Lithuania and Latvia drew more international response and statements of support for the Baltic leaders from political leaders in other republics (notably Boris Yeltsin in Russia). As the republics usurped Union taxes and disregarded macroeconomic policy, the Union deficit mushroomed and by April had reached its projected level for the whole year. A vaguely worded referendum in March received popular endorsement for renewal of the Union. Between April and August recognition of a crisis of governance led to attempts to draft a new political basis for the Union. The political initiative had now shifted to republican leaders, who wanted greater decentralization, and in Russia and the Baltic republics, these leaders wanted to pursue more rapid economic reform than the USSR leadership was willing to countenance. The direction of the negotiations over center-republic relations inspired the

August 1991 coup, aimed at preserving the centralized USSR under communist government. The failure of the coup and the role played by Boris Yeltsin (elected president of Russia in June) highlighted both disputes, and hastened the collapse of the USSR.

After a two-month hiatus, a new Russian government was announced in November 1991. Of its radical economic reform program, the first measure to be applied was a halt to the funding of seventy-three all-Union ministries and committees. By imposing dependence on Russian funds, the USSR institutions were effectively placed under Russian control. At a meeting in Minsk on December 8, Russia, Ukraine, and Belarus declared the USSR dissolved. The dissolution was finalized on December 25.

The replacement of the USSR by the looser Commonwealth of Independent States allowed for differing speeds of economic reform, although in practice the composition and direction of the CIS has been strongly influenced by relations with Russia. The more independent-minded Baltic countries and Georgia stayed outside the CIS, and Azerbaijan left the CIS when Russia appeared to be siding with Armenia.[10] At the January 1993 Minsk summit, Ukraine, Moldova, and Turkmenistan argued for a looser association, while Russia, Belarus, Armenia, Uzbekistan, Kazakhstan, Kyrgyzstan, and Tajikistan reaffirmed their desire for closer defense and economic cooperation (for example, by having an interstate bank operate a clearing mechanism). In practice, this desire to maintain the Russian connection meant that even after becoming independent, the Central Asian republics were pulled along by Russian economic reforms (for example, they mimicked to a greater or lesser extent the January 1992 price liberalization), even though some may have preferred to move more slowly.

Nevertheless, the replacement of the USSR by the CIS represented a decisive break in the CARs' political history.[11] They became internationally recognized sovereign states. In February 1992 they joined the United Nations, and subsequently acceded to other international institutions such as the IMF and World Bank. Embassies opened in the CARs' capitals, exposing them to the influence and aid of countries other than Russia.

THE IMMEDIATE POSTINDEPENDENCE PERIOD IN CENTRAL ASIA

Statistics on the Asian republics of the CIS are scarce and subject to serious questions about their reliability (see Appendix 1). The precise figures on output, inflation, and unemployment must be treated with caution. Nevertheless, the general picture they present is consistent and clear.

After the dissolution of the Soviet Union in December 1991, the Asian republics operated as independent economic entities for the first time in

1992. The break was, of course, less clear-cut in economic areas than in the political sphere, with many old links being retained. In particular, the ruble continued in use in all of the Asian republics, and they shared in the high inflation of the ruble zone. Because the Asian republics' economies had been tightly integrated into the Soviet system, there was considerable disruption of supplies and loss of markets, which translated into substantial drops in output throughout the region. Thus, the two dominant features of economic performance in 1992 were high rates of inflation and falling output levels.

In the unique situation of the post-USSR regime of 1992, national economic well-being did not depend only on output levels. First, within the Soviet Union there had been substantial net interrepublic flows, from which all of the Asian republics had benefited. Cessation of these subsidies would lead to a reduction in national expenditure. Second, the shift from trading at artificial prices to trading at world prices changed the former Soviet republics' terms of trade, with large improvements for Turkmenistan and Kazakhstan and deterioration for Tajikistan. Both the removal of subsidies and shift to world prices were phased in, so it is impossible to determine when their full impact was felt. Nevertheless, the magnitudes were sufficiently large that Turkmenistan may well have attained a higher national income (in terms of international purchasing power) in 1993 than in 1991 despite a drop in domestic output, while a country such as Kyrgyzstan may have suffered a much larger fall in living standards than is suggested by the output figures alone.

The underlying inflation rate throughout the ruble zone was almost certainly in the four-digit zone in 1992. Most estimates are of changes in consumer prices; all are approximations because there are no data on consumption patterns that can be used to determine appropriate weights. In practice, government offices were calculating inflation rates on the basis of a small number of items, so there is wide variation in the figures. The inflation rates in Table 4.1 are from PlanEcon, an independent research institution based in the United States, which has at least tried to make the estimates consistent (based on a Russian inflation rate of 1,750 percent).

The monthly rate of inflation was several hundred percent in January and February, when all of the Asian republics followed Russia in removing many price controls and raising the remaining fixed prices. In Russia the monthly inflation rate then dropped substantially for the next four months, before starting to accelerate during the last part of the year, when monetary policy became more accommodating.[12] Kyrgyzstan and Kazakhstan, which followed Russia in substantially liberalizing prices and enjoyed annual inflation rates practically identical to Russia's, undoubtedly followed the same time path. Turkmenistan and Uzbekistan, whose initial price reforms were more cautious and which then retained wide-

TABLE 4.1
Economic Performance Indicators, 1990–1992

	Per Capita GNP, 1990 (U.S. dollars)	Net Material Product (% change)		Inflation, 1992 (% change in CPI)	Budget Deficit, 1992 (% of GDP)
		1991	1992		
Kazakhstan	2,600	−10.3	−14.2	1,738	−6
Kyrgyzstan	1,570	−5.2	−26.0	1,760	−15
Tajikistan	1,130	−8.4	−31	1,450	—
Turkmenistan	1,690	−0.6	—	980	—
Uzbekistan	1,340	−0.9	−12.9	640	−12

Sources: "Measuring the Incomes of the Economies of the Former Soviet Union," World Bank Policy Research Working Paper, WPS 1057 (December 1992); UN Economic Commission for Europe, *Economic Survey of Europe in 1992–1993*, 73; PlanEcon Report no. 5–6 (1993), 2–3; IMF, *World Economic Outlook*, May 1993, 59.

spread price controls and subsidies, had significantly lower open inflation rates. The retention of controls in Turkmenistan and Uzbekistan was reflected in the smaller variety of available goods; shoppers in Almaty or Bishkek could buy higher-quality goods more easily than could shoppers in Tashkent or Ashgabat. The inflation rate in Tajikistan, whose government was cautious on price reform, was adversely affected by conditions of civil war.

By the end of 1992 the governments of the Asian republics viewed inflation as a serious problem, although there was no consensus over how to reduce it. In October 1992 at the Bishkek summit of the Commonwealth of Independent States, the presidents of the Central Asian Republics reaffirmed their commitment to remain in the ruble zone, but nothing was done to reform the monetary institutions in order to permit the pursuit of price stability (see Chapter 11). By early 1993 all of the Central Asian republics had had national banknotes printed, so that they would be prepared to introduce their own national currencies at short notice. Kyrgyzstan introduced its national currency, the som, in May 1993. Turkmenistan introduced the manat on November 1, 1993, and Kazakhstan and Uzbekistan followed with the tenge and the som coupon two weeks later. Thus, the monetary situation became more complex in 1993, but price stability remained elusive.

Output levels are even more difficult to measure than inflation rates. The disintegration of the USSR disrupted many supply chains and reduced output of many goods and services. In addition, some goods produced under the command system had no market after 1991. Even conceptually, it is impossible to value some of these changes; using pre-1992 relative prices will give too much weight to items whose output has fallen, while some previously produced items do not have post-1992 prices because they cannot be sold.[13] In addition, there is a reporting bias: under the old system managers had an incentive to overstate their production levels, while in the new system producers are wary of publicizing their sales because this might attract the tax collectors' attention. On top of all this, are the difficulties of reorienting national accounts from Soviet practices to international norms and of making international comparisons when the exchange rate is changing rapidly.

In conjunction with the national governments, the IMF and World Bank have been working to construct national accounts for the former Soviet republics.[14] To provide a benchmark for cross-country comparisons, the first column of Table 4.1 gives the current best estimates of per capita GNP in the Central Asian republics in 1990. These have been constructed by the World Bank staff to be consistent with the estimates for all countries given in the World Bank's annually published *Atlas*. All of the CARs fall into the World Bank's category of middle-income countries, although there is a wide range, from Tajikistan's $1,130 up to Kazakhstan's $2,600. Kazakhstan is clearly far richer than the other Asian republics. The other four Central Asian republics were, together with Azerbaijan, the poorest of the fifteen Soviet republics.[15]

In 1991 output fell slightly in Kyrgyzstan, Turkmenistan, and Uzbekistan, and more substantially in Kazakhstan and Tajikistan. At this stage, the first three republics did better than the USSR average, but largely because they had not embarked on any serious economic restructuring. In 1992, following the price reforms and introduction of other reform measures, as well as the more serious collapse of interrepublic trade, output fell more rapidly throughout the region. The decline was greatest in Tajikistan, where it was exacerbated by civil unrest. The cumulative decline in output over 1991–1992 was less in Turkmenistan and Uzbekistan, where reform was slower, and more in Kazakhstan and Kyrgyzstan, where reform proceeded faster. The different time profile in Kazakhstan reflects in part that republic's different economic base; the important grain sector experienced a poor harvest in 1991 and a good harvest in 1992.

Under normal circumstances, changes in output per head closely parallel changes in income per head. In the former Soviet Union, however, expenditure and income changes diverged from output changes because of the disruption in interrepublic transfers and because adoption of world prices substantially affected terms of trade. Both of these phenomena are difficult to quantify precisely, but the existing estimates reveal that they are likely to have been dominant in determining changes in economic well-being in some CARs between 1991 and 1993.

The magnitude of interrepublic transfers within the USSR is difficult to

TABLE 4.2

Gross National Expenditure of Kyrgyzstan as Share of GDP,
1990 and 1991 (percent)

	Consumption	Investment	Exports Minus Imports	Net Transfers from the Union
1990	83	34	−6	11
1991	66	34	12	12

Source: World Bank estimates.

establish. Many enterprises were run as all-Union enterprises, with centralized accounts irrespective of where actual production took place. Table 4.2 gives estimates of Kyrgyzstan's gross national expenditure (GNE), divided into consumption and investment, for the last two years of the USSR. In 1990 GNE exceeded domestic output by 17 percent, which is a very substantial aid package. In 1991 this gap had been eliminated, even though official net transfers were more or less constant. The most plausible explanation of this phenomenon is that all-Union enterprises (mainly based in Russia) were anticipating the breakup of the USSR and transferring resources from subsidiaries to headquarters. Whatever the explanation, GNE fell drastically in 1991 and the entire burden fell on consumption expenditure.

The magnitudes and time path undoubtedly varied from country to country, but all of the Central Asian republics had been net beneficiaries of interrepublic transfers in the USSR, and all suffered a substantial drop in GNE during 1991–1993. Given the dominant role of Russia within the USSR, a country's chances of moderating the speed with which the transfers were cut off depended upon retaining good relations with the Russian Federation in the post-Soviet world. Russia continued to run a surplus on intra-CIS trade in 1992, but official estimates of its magnitude vary widely (from 58 to 3,000 billion rubles, according to the UN Economic Commission for Europe (ECE), *Economic Survey of Europe in 1992–1993* [86]) and there is little information on the trade position of individual CIS members with Russia.

One reason why the Central Asian republics were the firmest adherents to the ruble zone was Russia's willingness to continue extending credit to them through the monetary system. This softened the blow, but was at best only a fraction of the aid they had received up to 1990. Kazakhstan was the most favored of the Central Asian republics; according to World Bank estimates, interrepublic flows to Kazakhstan still amounted to 11 percent of GDP in 1992. Kyrgyzstan was the least satisfied with Russian credit availability, and credit disputes were the catalyst for the decision to leave the ruble zone in spring 1993.

TABLE 4.3

Estimated Terms of Trade Impact of Moving from
Soviet Prices to World Prices

	% Change from 1990 Base
Kazakhstan	+19
Kyrgyzstan	+1
Tajikistan	−7
Turkmenistan	+50
Uzbekistan	−3

Source: Tarr 1994.

Prices within the USSR remained unrelated to world prices despite discussion of price reform in the final years.[16] With the replacement of the USSR by fifteen independent countries, there was a more or less rapid transformation to using world prices for interrepublic trade. A major exception was Russia's decision to change oil prices gradually, which was the second major incentive for oil-importing republics to remain within the ruble zone. In general, however, prices quickly converged toward world prices, and individual republics experienced major changes in their terms of trade. The impact depended crucially on the composition of imports and exports, with producers of manufactured goods losing and primary producers gaining.

Table 4.3 gives estimates of the net terms of trade effects of the move to world prices, based on an analysis of 1,990 trade flows using a 105-sector aggregation. The most striking point is the huge terms of trade gain accruing to Turkmenistan, whose exports are dominated by natural gas, which was underpriced in the USSR. Kazakhstan also enjoyed a fairly substantial terms of trade gain. The other Central Asian republics all suffered less from the shift to world prices than did the other nine non-Russian republics of the USSR, and for Kyrgyzstan and Uzbekistan the net effect was small. The author of the study from which these estimates are taken makes the comment that for Kyrgyzstan, Uzbekistan, and Tajikistan "the loss of interrepublic transfers is likely to be a more serious shock than the terms of trade shift" (15).

In sum, although GDP fell substantially in all of the Central Asian republics in 1992, the economic impact varied. In Turkmenistan the huge benefit of shifting to world prices sheltered the economy, placing less pressure on the government to undertake serious economic reforms, which in turn reduced the disruption of output. Given Turkmenistan's trade/GDP ratio of 43 percent, the shift to world prices represented a one-shot boost to GDP of over one-fifth. Kazakhstan also enjoyed a terms of trade gain, which probably offset the loss of interrepublic transfers (which was limited because Russia continued to favor Kazakhstan), but because the government proceeded with economic reforms, output was disrupted and average incomes fell.

Kyrgyzstan and Uzbekistan were not much affected by the shift to world prices, but as poor republics, they undoubtedly suffered from the loss of interrepublic transfers. The disruption of trade and the pursuit of economic reforms, particularly in Kyrgyzstan, led to a sharp decline in output, which exacerbated the decline in living standards. The situation was even worse in Tajikistan, where armed conflict added to the terms of trade loss and economic disruption. Since Kazakhstan and Turkmenistan had the highest income levels in 1990, the changes in 1992 widened the regional income gaps as the three poorest republics experienced the biggest drop in living standards.

Finally, and even more difficult to quantify, the distribution of income probably became more unequal with the collapse of central planning and the move to a more market-oriented economy. This was certainly the perception in all of the countries.[17] As the newly independent countries struggled to establish a social safety net, the incidence of poverty appeared to be growing. The sense of social disruption was augmented by increasing crime and outbreaks of disease.

Falling expenditures were accompanied by changes in the composition of consumption. Spending on nonfood items fell by more then spending on food. Expenditure on bakery products and vegetables changed little (in Tajikistan and Kyrgyzstan, potato and vegetable consumption increased in 1992), but meat and especially dairy product consumption fell; in Tajikistan and Turkmenistan, dairy product consumption in the first three quarters of 1992 was only about two-thirds that of the comparable 1991 period.[18] In sum, a significant change in diet occurred in 1992, with bakery products and potatoes coming to account for two-thirds of caloric intake, while the protein component declined sharply.

Other signs of economic distress were the growing unemployment and rising crime rate in 1992. Reported unemployment rates have long been difficult to interpret in the Soviet Union, and job shortages appear to have been a source of discontent in some of the Asian republics for several years despite low official unemployment. Even in 1992 reported unemployment remained low, although the number increased dramatically during 1992 (for example, by five times in Kazakhstan and by eleven times in Tajikistan). This was accompanied by the widespread and growing practice of granting workers additional "leave," partly paid or unpaid. Reported crime rates are also subject to problems of interpretation, but the numbers soared, especially in the republics showing the biggest drops in retail sales; in the first nine months of 1992, 50 percent more crimes were registered in Tajikistan and Kyrgyzstan than in the corresponding period of 1991.

In 1993 outbreaks of crime and disease became more striking. In Kazakhstan policing had broken down in many areas, while police officers concentrated on using their authority to extract "tolls" from motorists and similar money-making ventures. During the summer of 1993, cholera outbreaks in Uzbekistan, Kazakhstan, and Kyrgyzstan led to extreme but ineffectual responses.[19]

TRANSITION ISSUES

The Central Asian Republics face problems similar to those of other countries making the transition from a centrally planned to a market-based economic system. They need to establish a rational set of relative prices, which will actually determine resource allocation—an outcome for which macroeconomic stability and an appropriate incentive/property rights system are prerequisites. Without a reasonably stable aggregate price level, relative price changes are difficult to identify, and without economic agents' having some claim to the financial returns associated with their efforts, there will be little response of output or investment to relative price changes.

The CARs' situation is, however, further complicated by their history of being tightly integrated into the Soviet economy (see Chapter 3). Thus, although the Eastern European countries and Vietnam were negatively affected by the sudden collapse of the CMEA, the short-term disruption of trade patterns is likely to be even more pronounced for the CARs. Furthermore, unlike the nominally independent CMEA members, the CARs did not have their own currencies and were caught up in the hyperinflation and collapse of the ruble in 1992–1933. The most immediate problem in the two years following independence was dealing with the monetary chaos, and the next most pressing problem was to establish new trading patterns. Both of these issues caught the CARs unprepared in that they still participated in the Soviet economic system, and had little reason to expect the collapse of the USSR, until the second half of 1991.

After the USSR disintegrated, many observers recommended continued coordination among CIS members, in particular by forming a payments union.[20] A payments union would permit multilateral clearing of intra-CIS payments and allow some short-term trade credits. The immediate concern is felt by creditor republics, who are afraid of not being paid, although this worry could be alleviated if international agencies would provide financial assistance for the establishment of the payments union. A longer-term concern is that a payments union would perpetuate reliance on the "soft" internal markets, delaying the eventual move to full convertibility and exposure to international markets.

A second coordination issue is for price liberalization and tax reform to move more or less in line across CIS members in order to prevent the emergence of arbitrage trade.[21] Again, there is a conflict between the immediate goal of preventing erosion of interregional trade (because republics with high taxes or subsidized prices will impose barriers) and the long-term goals of transition to a market-based economy. Coordination of price liberalization and tax reform means either following the lead of the dominant economy (as happened in January 1992, when all ruble zone members had to follow Russia's price reforms), which may be an unacceptable challenge to national sovereignty and pride, or moving at the pace of the slowest reformer.

An alternative approach is for individual republics to move more quickly toward the ultimate goal of incorporation into the world trading system. All of the CARs are small economies, for whom the appropriate set of relative prices is world prices. Economists have tended to advocate a current-account-first approach to economic reform, although experience in Latin America and in Eastern Europe has pointed to the need for supporting reforms of macroeconomic policy and in the financial sector. Thus, in order to move to convertibility on the current account, it is desirable to have first of all established macroeconomic control with low inflation and a real exchange rate that makes exporting attractive, as well as a financial system that can arrange trade credit.

A Big Bang approach to trade reform will also involve large short-term adjustment costs, because existing output mixes based on intra-USSR specialization are very different from the output mix that would be appropriate at world prices. For countries that experienced large output losses in 1991–1992, the prospect of further decline in output and increase in unemployment may be politically unacceptable. The choice is not a pleasant one. The experience in Eastern Europe and in Ukraine is already showing that delaying the move to world prices in order to reduce adjustment costs perpetuates economic inefficiency and in the long run is likely to be even more harmful.

In practice, trade reform progressed slowly in the CARs during 1991–1993. Export controls remained common, surrender requirements for foreign exchange earnings tended to be high, and exchange rates paid to exporters tended to be low. The immediate reasons for these measures are understandable, but they are not conducive to long-run export promotion. Imports have, for the most part, been liberalized, but they are subject to varying import duties. One obvious transition danger is that governments facing fiscal deficits will turn to high import taxes as an easy revenue source, especially if they are predisposed to arguments about the benefits of import-substituting industrialization (ISI). Perhaps most fundamentally, isolation from world markets and from exposure to the experience of countries pursuing different development strategies may lead the newly independent CARs to repeat some of the policy mistakes made by the newly independent developing countries of the 1940s and 1950s.[22]

All of the CARs are officially committed to the ultimate goal of establishing a market-based economy. Their progress with economic reform was, however, among the slowest in the USSR, and in general these republics were among the most economically conservative. Kyrgyzstan has been the most progressive, in terms of both political and economic reform. Kazakhstan has moved more slowly, explicitly extolling the virtue of the Chinese approach of gradual economic reform and political stability. Uzbekistan and Turkmenistan have reform programs, but practical implementation is slow and extremely cautious. Tajikistan also appears to have politically conservative leadership, but the situation is complicated by the domestic unrest. The individual experiences will be described in greater detail in the next five chapters, but the ingredients of economic reform can be summarized first.

Price reform is central to the transition process. The artificial price structure inherited from the USSR distorts resource allocation and reduces welfare. Even if freeing prices had no impact on output, it would increase welfare by improving the utilization of existing output; for example, creating a housing market would allow a better allocation of the existing housing stock and would have indirect benefits, such as aiding labor mobility. Appropriate relative prices would also direct resources to the use that maximized the value of output, that is, enabled the CARs to maximize GNP at world prices. During the transition process, however, price changes and the accompanying change in the output mix will impose costs on some groups. Thus, governments face political pressure to postpone increases in the prices of basic consumer goods or inputs and yet to allow pensions, wages, and other sources of income to increase whether or not they are justified by the budget situation or by productivity. In sum, price liberalization is fundamental to the establishment of a market-based economy, but it is politically difficult to implement—especially by governments dependent for support on beneficiaries of the old system.

In January 1992 the CARs all followed Russia's price reforms, but in several cases out of necessity rather than conviction. Caps were placed on the price increases of sensitive items, and in some republics the price increases were quickly reversed.[23] Table 4.4 provides some indication of the variety of outcomes, and of the universally lower price increases in the CARs than in Russia. As Russia pressed ahead with reforms during the first half of 1992, the differences became more marked. Table 4.5 shows prices of sixteen consumer goods in Moscow and in four CAR capitals at the end of July. A simple indicator of the pace of price reform is calculated by ranking prices for the fifteen commodities with five observations and

TABLE 4.4

Selected Basic Food Prices after Price Liberalization by Republic, February 3, 1992 (rubles)

Commodity	Unit	Tajikistan		Turkmenistan		Kyrgyzstan	
		State	Market	State	Market	State	Market
Beef	kg	50.0	60.0	30.00	50	—	50.0
Sausage	kg	76.0	—	38.00	—	29.30	—
Butter	kg	30.0	—	46.26	—	104.96	120.0
Milk	l	1.5	—	1.50	—	2.10	—
Eggs	10	—	20.0	—	18	12.00	13.0
Sugar	kg	7.0	—	8.80	—	7.20	—
Bread	loaf	1.8	—	2.25	—	7.90	—
Vodka	0.5 l	44.0	—	40.00	—	80.00	—
Salt	kg	—	—	0.45	—	1.40	—
Potatoes	kg	—	7.5	4.50	8	3.93	8.0
Cabbage	kg	—	2.5	2.50	4	—	7.5
Onions	kg	—	5.0	3.50	7	5.13	5.5

		Uzbekistan		Kazakhstan		Russian Federation	
Commodity	Unit	State	Market	State	Market	State	Market
Beef	kg	30.0	50.0	46.00	65.0	36.0–87.0	172
Sausage	kg	—	—	71.50	—	52.0–110.0	—
Butter	kg	60.0	—	65.00	150.5	45.0–127.0	220
Milk	1	1.5	—	1.50	10.0	1.9–8.0	—
Eggs	10	5.0	18.0	18.64	—	16.0–22.0	29
Sugar	kg	8.0	—	7.70	—	7.8	—
Bread	loaf	1.2	—	2.25	—	5.4	—
Vodka	0.5 l	35.0	—	40.00	—	—	—
Salt	kg	—	—	0.80	—	—	—
Potatoes	kg	3.0	6.0	—	—	4.8–7.5	12
Cabbage	kg	—	3.5	—	—	6.3–10.0	13
Onions	kg	3.5	5.0	—	—	7.0–13.0	—

Source: IMF Economic Survey: Tajikistan, April 1992, 42.

Notes: Data for Russian Federation relate to Moscow, except for sugar data, which relate to Leningrad. Dash indicates that information is not available.

TABLE 4.5

Prices of Consumer Goods in State and Cooperative Trade,
End-July 1992 (rubles per kilogram)

	Moscow	Tashkent	Almaty	Bishkek	Dushanbe
Flour	12.00	6.00	6.10	17.0	5.0
Bread	12.82	5.33	3.15	9.0	3.3
Beef	77.85	60.00	92.50	—	60.0
Boiled sausage	128.91	80.00[a]	172.50	65.0[a]	87.0
Butter	184.95	119.00	232.50	182.0	145.5
Vegetable oil	38.35	10.00	80.55	64.0	8.4
Milk (liter)	9.00	4.00	15.00	2.4	3.0
Sour cream	67.00	50.00	78.50	37.0	32.0
Eggs (10)	20.73	25.00	27.43	18.0	19.0
Sugar	74.21	15.00	9.00	66.0[a]	65.0
Tea	214.34	80.00	172.00	250.0	148.0
Vodka (500 cl)	121.50	98.00	110.00	94.0	97.0
Potatoes	11.29	3.70	12.00	9.0[a]	6.5
Onions	23.08	3.50	11.00	6.0	3.5
Fresh cabbage	13.34	1.40	4.50	5.0[a]	3.0
Rice	35.85	15.00	10.70	11.0[a]	23.0
Sum of ranks[b]	26.00	56.50	36.00	47.0	59.5

Source: World Bank, *Uzbekistan: Agenda for Reform* (Washington, D.C.: World Bank, September 1993), table 8.2.

[a] End-August 1992.

[b] For each good except beef, rankings are 1 to 5, from the highest to the lowest price.

then summing the rankings for each capital; although crude,[24] this indicator presents a clear picture of the CARs' lagging Russia, but with Kazakhstan and then Kyrgyzstan ahead of Uzbekistan and Tajikistan.

Enterprise reform and privatization should ideally proceed apace with price liberalization. Without changes in property rights and incentive structures, the responsiveness to price changes will be muted. Moreover, if enterprise reform is delayed, there may be undesirable opportunities for rent-seeking by people with key positions in the economy. The extreme situation is when privatization from within occurs as employees or bureaucrats appropriate assets of state firms.[25] Such opportunities for private enrichment based on position rather than ability are socially disruptive, and could cast disrepute on the whole reform process.

By 1991–1992 all of the CARs had begun to enact property laws and to announce privatization programs. Actual progress in 1992–1993 was, however, slow, apart from small agricultural plots and some service activities. For the most part, "privatization" consisted of leasing state property rather than granting full ownership rights. Kyrgyzstan had the most advanced privatization program, including a voucher scheme for privatizing larger state enterprises. In the other CARs there was little (Kazakhstan) or no (the others) real movement toward privatizing large and medium-sized enterprises.

The CARs are also seeking foreign investment to promote technology transfer and help create exports. Apart from well-publicized Kazakhstan deals with foreign oil companies (including a 50 percent joint venture agreement signed in May 1992 under which Chevron will contribute $20 billion over forty years),[26] there was little response in 1992. Uzbekistan passed a law on direct foreign investment in June 1991, and appears to have the most joint ventures, but in 1992 and 1993 they were all small. Other CARs have since introduced similar legislation, which typically allows remission of import duties, tax holidays, and profit repatriation guarantees. As of 1993, the number of registered joint ventures was few and they were small-scale, with few actually operating yet.[27]

In sum, privatization from above is progressing slowly in Central Asia. There has undoubtedly been privatization from within. Privatization from below, that is, the creation of new private enterprises, has also occurred, especially in Kazakhstan and Kyrgyzstan, but primarily involves small trading activities (most obviously in the ubiquitous kiosks, which sprouted up in Almaty and Bishkek, and in the casinos of Almaty). Privatization from outside in the form of direct foreign investment has been limited. Thus, the overall position during the first two years of independence was of official commitment to systemic change, but slow progress in the crucial area of changing the ownership structure.

The most critical resource misallocation in centrally planned economies concerned the use of capital, and a fundamental component of the transition process must be establishment of capital markets.[28] Economists typically advocate leaving financial market reform until after price or enterprise reform, because with irrational prices it is impossible to determine socially desirable investment projects, and without enterprise reform, managers may expropriate scarce capital (or at least may misuse it because they are not subject to a hard budget constraint). In practice, financial reform is often long delayed because policymakers are reluctant to surrender control over capital allocation decisions, and reform occurs only when the evidence of the cost of undeveloped capital markets becomes glaring (as in China in the early 1990s).

All of the former Soviet republics have been forced to promote their branches of Gosbank as national banks, but otherwise the pace of financial reform has varied and generally been slow. The basic step of creating a two-tier banking system was taken by Kazakhstan in December 1990, by Uzbekistan and Tajikistan in February 1991, by Kyrgyzstan in June 1991, and lastly by Turkmenistan. The increase in the number of banks has been substantial in some of the CARs (for example, in Kazakhstan, where they increased from eight to seventy-three during 1991, and in Uzbekistan, which wound up with twenty-one), but loan issue remains dominated by the old specialized banks, which continue to deal with their traditional customers (that is, in agriculture, industry, construction, or trade). Interest rates have been partially liberalized in all of the CARs, although they remain far from freely market determined. As of 1993, none of the CARs had yet established a bond market or stock exchange.

A final element of reform deserving mention is fiscal reform. In some respects this is likely to be crucial. In the short term, controlling the budget deficit will be an essential component of successful resolution of the monetary problems described above. In the longer term, the nature of the tax system is an important determinant of how well a market economy can function; all taxes distort market prices. At the start of 1992 all of the CARs replaced the old enterprise and sales tax system by a value-added tax (VAT) and excise taxes, an enterprise profits tax, and a personal income tax. They will also need to establish a social security system which will contribute to achieving equity goals in a market economy.

All have started to issue government securities, which provides a revenue source and will help to permit more sophisticated monetary policy implementation once secondary markets develop. IMF estimates of budget outcomes for 1992 suggest that Kyrgyzstan and Kazakhstan had gone furthest in taking difficult expenditure reduction decisions. The more conservative regimes, which continue to subsidize energy, basic foodstuffs, and so on, will face difficulties in financing such programs.[29] On the other hand, republics with substantial royalties from oil and natural gas production will have a helpful cushion.[30]

In 1992 all of the CARs had fiscal deficits, and the dilemma facing tax reformers was whether to create the ultimately desirable tax system or to resort to ad hoc temporary measures during the transition period, when government budgets would be under exceptional pressure (Shome and Escolano 1993). The VAT introduced in January 1992 was initially set at the high rate of 28 percent, in order to sustain revenues at the levels yielded by the old turnover tax. The high rate, however, led to pressures to reduce the basic rate and to permit exceptions; the latter pressures found a response from policymakers still inclined to use tax policy as an instrument for economic restructuring and income redistribution.[31] By mid-1993 the basic VAT rate had been reduced to 25 percent in Uzbekistan and to 20 percent in Kazakhstan and Kyrgyzstan. Even more harmful for tax revenues was the proliferation of exemptions, which also made administration cumbersome and created distortions. The enterprise profits tax has also been widely used to promote industrial restructuring via preferential rates (favoring agriculture and some manufacturing industries, and penalizing service activities). The profits tax has been further complicated by measures to deal with "excess wage payments," even though these measures have been difficult to enforce in the private sector and appear to have little impact on state enterprises' behavior. In sum, tax reformers started with a new broom in January 1992, but then allowed the tax system to become complex and distortionary, losing the virtues of either high revenue generation or simple, nondiscriminatory taxes.

Focusing on the budget deficit as a simple indicator of macroeconomic progress runs the risk of distracting attention from the ultimate goal of a successful transition. The government's role is changing, and it is better that new functions be taken on explicitly even if they increase the budget deficit, rather than using off-budget mechanisms to hide the size of the "true" deficit. For example, the transfer of many social security functions from state enterprises to government agencies is a crucial component of transition, which should not be postponed for cosmetic reasons. Similarly, encouraging state enterprises to continue labor hoarding just because unemployment benefits will be paid from the state budget delays the emergence of profit-oriented companies, and giving subsidies to enterprises via soft bank loans rather than explicit government outlays hampers the creation of an entrepreneurial banking system. The pressure to pursue such counterproductive policies increased in 1993 as the CARs left the ruble zone and potential foreign aid donors, seeking simple guidelines to reassure them that macroeconomic stability would be achieved, paid particular attention to the budget deficit.[32]

CONCLUSIONS

The CARs were passive observers taken unawares by the rapidity with which the Soviet Union disintegrated in 1991. Within the USSR their economies had been affected by the limited perestroika undertaken during the Gorbachev years at the all-Union level, but few republic-level initiatives had been taken, and the CARs were among the least reformed Soviet republics. In 1992 the pace of economic reform accelerated, but since all of the CARs remained in the ruble zone, they were constrained to follow Russian price reforms to a large extent and their macroeconomic performance was mainly determined exogenously; inflation accelerated, as in the rest of the ruble zone, and output fell, as in all transition economies (with the added negative impact of the disruption of intra-USSR trade). By 1993 the five republics were set on differing economic trajectories, and the adoption of national currencies put future macroeconomic policy decisions more firmly in the individual governments' hands.

Turkmenistan and Uzbekistan entered 1993 with little commitment to economic or political reform. Turkmenistan's gas wealth permitted its government to buy popular support with such measures as free gas, oil, and water for households. Uzbekistan is in a far weaker economic position, and postponement of economic reform is likely to be unsustainable. The cost of subsidizing enterprises and consumers is reflected in the large and growing budget deficit (equal to 12 percent of GDP in 1992; see Table 4.1). In Tajikistan the civil war continued to smolder, and the government paid little attention to economic policy. The economic disruption was massive with huge refugee problems (commonly estimated to involve half a million people in 1992 and 1993), as well as physical destruction.

By the second half of 1993, only Kazakhstan and Kyrgyzstan remained committed to economic reform. The economic prospects are far brighter in Kazakhstan, which is the most diversified and richest of the Central Asian republics. The oil and mineral sectors have already been targets for substantial foreign investment, and Almaty is emerging as the regional financial center. Kazakhstan in 1992 was the only former Soviet republic outside the Baltics to reduce its budget deficit as a share of GDP. The model is Asian: gradual economic reform within a stable (authoritarian) political system.

Kyrgyzstan faces a more uncertain future. It was the Soviet republic least prepared economically to exist as an independent economy. In 1991 its hard currency exports were the lowest of any Soviet republic (estimated by the IMF to be a paltry $23 million), and its main potential exports (minerals, hydroelectricity, tourism) will take years to develop. It has, however, the most liberal government in Central Asia, has progressed farthest with economic reforms, and was the first Central Asian republic to adopt an independent currency. One reward has been that in 1993 Kyrgyzstan received by far the most substantial foreign assistance on a per capita basis.

Part Two

THE COUNTRIES

CHAPTER 5

Uzbekistan: Oriental Despotism

UZBEKISTAN IS the most populous of the newly independent Central Asian nations and occupies a central geographical position. Its territory is more or less defined as the area between the two great rivers, the Amudarya and Sirdarya, from the foothills of the mountains down to the Aral Sea. Most of the historically richest towns of Central Asia (Samarkand, Bukhara, Khiva, and Kokand) lie within Uzbekistan. Apart from the nonirrigated grain farming, orchards, viticulture, and pasturelands in the piedmont, settlement is concentrated along the rivers and in the areas irrigated from the rivers. About three-fifths of the territory is desert or semiarid land used for extensive grazing.

The key long-term economic issue in Uzbekistan is the balance between the fragile resource base and the rapidly growing population. Of the 21 million inhabitants in the early 1990s, about 60 percent were under age eighteen. Employment had been created in the previous thirty years by extending the area under irrigation, mainly to grow cotton, but the desiccation of the Aral Sea and salinization of large tracts of land created an environmental disaster, which is now widely recognized but economically and politically difficult to deal with.

Tashkent, with over 2 million people, is by far the largest city, and the only real industrial metropolis in Central Asia. The Uzbekistan government sees it as the natural capital of Central Asia, which is a source of rivalry with Almaty and with Kazakhstan. Kazakhstan is larger geographically and richer than Uzbekistan, as well as being the only nuclear power among the new Central Asian states.

The other Central Asian republics are nervous about Uzbekistan's assumption of hegemony. Kyrgyzstan and Tajikistan both have substantial Uzbek minorities in fairly well-defined locations near the Uzbekistan border (for example, in Osh and Khojand), fueling fears of irredentism.[1] Another potential, but as yet below the surface, conflict is over water rights (see Chapter 3). Finally, there are religious and political sources of conflict. The mufti in Tashkent was the leading Islamic clergyman in the USSR, and Islam is stronger in Uzbekistan than in more secular Kyrgyzstan and Kazakhstan. The current regime in Uzbekistan is secular and has taken a hard line against "fundamentalists," both domestically and in

TABLE 5.1
Demographic Profile of Uzbekistan

Population (thousands)	21,930
Population density (per sq km)	49
Annual growth rate (percent)	2.2%
Crude birth rate (per thousand)	33
Crude death rate (per thousand)	6
Infant mortality rate (per thousand)	38
Life expectancy at birth	
Females	72
Males	66
Percentage of population aged	
14 or less	41%
60 or more	7%
Ethnic composition	
Uzbeks	71%
Russians	8%
Tajiks	5%
Kazakhs	4%
Karakalpaks	2%
Population of main towns (thousands)	
Tashkent	2,094
Samarkand	370
Namangan	312
Andijan	297
Bukhara	228

Sources: ESCAP, *Population Data Sheet 1993* (Bangkok: United Nations, 1993); for urban populations, Economist Intelligence Unit, *Country Profile.*

Note: Ethnic composition is as of 1989; town populations are as of 1990; all other data are for 1993.

the Tajikistan civil war. Whether religious conflicts will expand is unclear; they are less likely to expand if Karimov remains president, but then Uzbekistan's authoritarian regime may run into conflict with Kyrgyzstan's liberal regime.

Uzbekistan itself is ethnically fairly homogeneous (Table 5.1). In 1989 Uzbeks accounted for 71 percent of the population and the biggest minority was Russians (8 percent), but large numbers of Russians have emigrated since the late 1980s.[2] There are about a million Tajiks and slightly fewer Kazakhs. The 411,878 Karakalpaks, a separately identified group with a close affinity to Kazakhs, are concentrated in an autonomous republic in the far west of Uzbekistan. The Tajiks are concentrated in the ancient cities of Bukhara and Samarkand, and concern over perceived discrimination against their conationals in these revered cities has fueled Tajikistan nationalists' anti-Uzbek feeling.

If ethnic tensions explode, the flashpoint is likely to be in the Fergana Valley, the most densely populated part of Central Asia, which Stalin subdivided among Uzbekistan, Tajikistan, and Kyrgyzstan in the mid-1920s. In June 1990 border crossings were sealed to prevent an armed mob of about fifteen thousand Uzbeks from crossing into Kyrgyzstan to liberate their conationals in Osh. The economic situation in the Fergana Valley has deteriorated since then, with as many as 35 percent of the work force in the Uzbekistan part of the valley believed to be unemployed by the end of 1992.[3] During 1993 Uzbekistan's border with Kyrgyzstan was closed on several occasions under various pretexts.[4]

HISTORY

The Uzbeks are descended from nomadic Mongol tribes, who mixed with sedentary inhabitants of Central Asia in the thirteenth century. Linguistically Uzbek is closer to the eastern Turkic group than to the western group (Turkmen, Azeri, and Turkish), but Kazakh, Karakalpak, and Kyrgyz are closer to one another than they are to Uzbek. The Uzbeks came to dominate the urban areas of Central Asia, and modern Uzbekistan views itself as the successor to the three emirates that ruled much of the region before their conquest by the Russians (Chapter 2). Formally, however, there had never been an Uzbek national state before the Soviet delimitation of Central Asia in 1924.

Soviet power was established in Tashkent in November 1918, but armed opposition to Soviet rule continued in Uzbekistan until the early 1920s. The old khanates of Khiva and Bukhara retained nominal independence in the early 1920s but were incorporated into Turkestan in 1924. In the delimitation of 1924–1925 the Uzbek Soviet Socialist Republic (SSR) included the Tajik Autonomous Soviet Socialist Republic (ASSR). In 1929 the Tajik republic was separated, and in 1936 the Karakalpak ASSR was added to the Uzbek SSR.

The republic borders established in Central Asia between 1924 and 1936 appear to have been driven by political considerations, especially a divide-and-rule approach to the region. They are, however, tremendously important because the borders were little changed after 1936 and became the countries' international borders when they became independent in 1991. In view of Uzbekistan's geographical focal position and the numerical superiority of Uzbeks, most of the contentious points involve Uzbekistan and raise fears of Uzbek irredentism. The most obvious area of dispute is the Fergana Valley, but there are others. When the Tajik SSR was created in 1929, Khojand was transferred to it from the Uzbek SSR, and the area still has a large Uzbek population. The Uzbek minority in Turkmenistan is geographically concentrated in the region around Tashauz, bordering Uzbekistan. The Chimkent oblast in Kazakhstan has historically been linked to Tashkent, just a few kilometers from its southern border, and with a large cotton-growing sector, it is more economically similar to Uzbekistan than to anywhere in Kazakhstan. Thus, in every direction there are potential border conflicts and claims for border adjustment.

Under Soviet rule a strict cap was maintained on ethnic tensions, and after 1936 border adjustments were firmly off the agenda. After that date the influence of the republican authorities over economic decisions was curtailed, and the main task of the Central Asian republics leaders appears to have been maintenance of internal control.

During the 1960s and 1970s Uzbekistan was the archetypical Brezhnevian Central Asian republic. The local leader, Sharaf Rashidov, ruled in a quasi-feudal fashion from 1959 to 1983. He kept Moscow happy by delivering the cotton and by maintaining internal peace. The latter was achieved by a mixture of patronage, corruption, and repression. When Mikhail Gorbachev began his anticorruption drive, its first target was Rashidov (although he died in 1986), who was found not to have delivered as much cotton as he had claimed; the overstatement of deliveries allowed Rashidov to siphon off about $2 billion during his rule. The posthumous disgracing of Rashidov and imprisonment of some 2,600 officials in 1987 for their part in the scam led to an upsurge of national feeling in Uzbekistan, where people were unworried about the corruption (which diverted funds into Uzbekistan) but incensed about the victimization of Uzbeks among the many thousands of corrupt officials in Brezhnev's USSR.

Glasnost led to more open media discussion of environmental and ethnic issues, but in the February 1990 elections the main opposition party was not allowed to stand, leaving many communist candidates elected unopposed. In the following month, Islam Karimov was selected for the newly created post of executive president. Karimov supported the new Union Treaty in spring 1991 and did not oppose the August 1991 coup in Moscow. Once the coup collapsed, however, Uzbekistan declared independence on August 31, 1991. Despite the declaration of independence, Karimov remained one of the strongest supporters of continuing cooperation among the Soviet republics. Uzbekistan joined the CIS in December 1991 and subscribed to the various declarations of closer economic cooperation made by a dwindling number of former Soviet republics in 1992 and 1993.

ECONOMIC STRUCTURE

At independence, the economy was dominated by cotton production. Uzbekistan hoped to benefit from this by selling the cotton on international markets, but the early 1990s were a time of depressed prices on world cotton markets. The episode included a dispute with Russia, which responded by seeking to purchase its raw cotton on world markets. Disruption of supply caused major problems for the Russian cotton textile industry and led to protests in the mill town of Ivanov. Eventually the two countries reached an agreement to barter raw cotton for petroleum.

Other important agricultural products include grain, fruit and vegetables, and silk cocoons. Grain production, however, covers only about a quarter of consumption. Despite Uzbek complaints that the USSR deliberately destroyed Uzbekistan's grain-growing capacity in order to create the cotton monoculture, it has proven technically difficult to reverse this development, and grain remains a major import. In 1993 Uzbekistan contracted to purchase 1.75 million tons of wheat from Turkey, financed by the Turkish export credit agency; this followed a 100,000-ton grant from Turkey in 1992.

Uzbekistan's other major primary product exports are gas and minerals. Uzbekistan has few energy resources besides the gas, although a major oil field was discovered in the Fergana Valley in 1992 and the country has unexploited hydro potential. Uzbekistan is by far the biggest oil importer among the CARs (Table 3.4).[5]

The most accessible mineral export is gold, of which Uzbekistan was the USSR's second-largest producer. Joint venture agreements are bringing foreign technology to exploit Uzbekistan's gold mines.[6] Other mineral deposits include silver, lead, copper, zinc, and tungsten, although many of the mines have low ore content, which suggests that they may not be profitable at world prices,[7] and small coal mines at Angren. Uranium mines west of Bukhara are reported to have been closed after independence.

The manufacturing sector dates from the first two Five-Year Plans (1928–1937), when substantial investment in industry led to rapid growth from a low base (Table 5.2). During the late 1930s, however, Soviet planners increasingly focused industrial investment in established industrial centers, and industrial growth slowed in Central Asia. After the outbreak of war in late 1941, many industrial enterprises were evacuated from the western USSR to more secure locations. This particularly benefited Tashkent, which became the dominant industrial complex in Central Asia. Between 1940 and 1950 Uzbekistan's steel production increased

TABLE 5.2

Growth Rate of Industrial Production in Uzbekistan,
1928–1985 (percent)

	Annual Growth Rate of Industrial Production
1928–1932 (1st Five-Year Plan)	9.4
1933–1937 (2d Five-Year Plan)	19.3
1938–1941 (3d Five-Year Plan)	9.4
1946–1950 (4th Five-Year Plan)	11.4
1951–1955 (5th Five-Year Plan)	10.0
1956–1958 (6th Five-Year Plan)	6.0
1959–1965 (7th Plan)	8.7
1966–1970 (8th Five-Year Plan)	6.3
1971–1975 (9th Five-Year Plan)	8.6
1976–1980 (10th Five-Year Plan)	4.9
1981–1985 (11th Five-Year Plan)	4.7

Source: Rumer 1989, 54.

from 11,000 to 119,000 tons, coal output from 3,000 to 1.5 million tons, and electricity output from 481 to 2,679 million kilowatt-hours, while machinery output increased by 653 percent (Rumer 1989, 54).

After the war, however, Soviet resources were concentrated on rebuilding industrial enterprises in European areas. With less investment, the growth rate of industrial output in Uzbekistan declined (Table 5.2). Temporary reversals of this trend occurred during the Khrushchev era, when some decentralization of the planning process was introduced, and in the aftermath of the 1966 Tashkent earthquake, when central funds went especially to support the local construction industry. Nevertheless, the long-term trend was of falling industrial growth rates.

Manufacturing industry in Uzbekistan was originally developed in close relation to its primary product base. Machinery for the cotton sector was a major output, and food-processing industries were also important. The wartime evacuations brought heavy industry to Uzbekistan, and this was built upon in the 1960s and 1970s, when local planners tried to diversify the industrial base. Some military and related industries were introduced (for example, the Chkalov aircraft factory moved from Russia to Tashkent during the war is the largest machine-building enterprise in Uzbekistan and the only aircraft factory in Central Asia), while other industries utilized the new raw material base of natural gas (for example, the gigantic Navoi plastics and synthetic fibers plant built in the 1970s).

The general problem is of technical obsolence and low standards of quality. The main approach to this problem, which is widely recognized within the government, is to encourage joint ventures. Many joint venture agreements were signed in 1992 and 1993, but there was little actual foreign investment. The most promising partners appeared to be South Korean firms, led by Daewoo, which invested in consumer electronics and announced plans to invest $100 million in a 180,000-capacity automobile factory, which would begin production in 1995.[8] The car project was approved by the South Korean government in March 1993, at which time it was the largest Korean project in the CIS. Daewoo's plans contrast to the Japanese wait-and-see approach to Central Asia: Toyota had earlier announced an expansion of capacity in Pakistan, which could be used to supply the Central Asian markets if demand warranted it.[9]

Communication systems are also backward by modern standards. In 1993 a joint venture was formed with the Turkish company Teletas (which is 39 percent owned by Alcatel of France) to install seventy thousand lines using Alcatel System-12 exchanges, and then in a second stage to produce System-12 in Uzbekistan.

Uzbekistan hopes to become the transport hub of Central Asia. When the Aeroflot fleet was shared out after the dismemberment of the USSR, Uzbekistan utilized its share of the planes most positively to earn hard currency. After initially leasing out planes (a strategy marred by a highly publicized crash in India), Uzbekistan created an international network in the spring and summer of 1993, with the goal of making Tashkent a hub for budget travel between Europe and Asia; flights were established to Karachi, Delhi, Kuala Lumpur, Bangkok, Beijing, Frankfurt, and London. Israel provided training assistance to Uzbekistan Airways, and the airline raised its credibility by acquiring several Airbuses, which featured in its publicity material.

ECONOMIC REFORM

Uzbekistan has been officially committed to economic reform since independence, but the government favored gradual change, and the pace became slower and slower through 1992 and the first eight months of 1993. In January 1992 Uzbekistan followed the Russian price reform, but less thoroughly than almost any other ruble zone member. Besides the conservative leadership, one force for caution was that Tashkent was the only Central Asian city to experience major riots after the price reforms were introduced, reflecting the large organized industrial labor force and recalling the 1917 tradition of Red Tashkent. Slow price liberalization was, however, difficult to maintain as long as Uzbekistan remained within the ruble zone, because arbitrageurs had an incentive to buy fixed-price goods in Uzbekistan and sell them to consumers elsewhere in the ruble zone.[10]

Labor market and enterprise reform have been limited, and indeed the major reason behind Uzbekistan's slow price liberalization has been the desire to maintain the value of real wages and subsidies. Thus, when controlled prices were doubled on June 1, 1993, wages and benefits were increased by 150 percent. The minimum wage in Uzbekistan was then 11,000 rubles a month (higher than the average wage in Tajikistan), in contrast to the almost irrelevant minimum wages in the more reformist countries (for example, compare the situation in Kazakhstan described in Chapter 6). The government promised to keep wages and benefits increases ahead of any future price rises. The state purchase prices of key agricultural products, such as cotton and milk, were increased in order to raise the state subsidy to farmers.

Privatization has also been glacially slow. One reason is that land privatization ahead of establishing a guaranteed water supply regime would be meaningless for the irrigation-based agricultural sector. In the rain-fed areas of the Fergana Valley some five hundred hectares had been privatized by spring 1992, but this also slowed. In industry, not only was progress in privatizing state enterprises slow, but there was also very little privatization from below (that is, the creation of new small-scale activities by entrepreneurs). Most visibly, fewer kiosks appeared on the streets of cosmopolitan Tashkent in 1993 than in Almaty or even backwoods Bishkek, and few private restaurants. The exception has been residential housing, which has been privatized, creating large inequities as occupiers obtained property of varying value.[11]

Slow reform meant less disruption, and in 1991–1992 Uzbekistan's output fell by less than in all its neighbors except Turkmenistan. This difference became even more pronounced in 1993, when Kyrgyzstan and Kazakhstan experienced the large output drops generally associated with economic transition, while the Uzbekistan government tightened its control and the pace of reform slowed to a standstill by late summer. Output may even have stabilized in 1993, thanks to a recovery in agricultural production. Despite this relatively good short-term performance, there are pressures for change. Loss of transfers from the USSR have shifted Uzbekistan's gross national expenditure down, and with an unreformed economy, there is little chance of offsetting this decline by growth in the medium term.

Continuing subsidies for enterprises and consumers led to a growing budget deficit (see Table 4.1). Perhaps even more harmful have been the pervasive implicit subsidies, which distort incentives and impede a successful transition to a market-oriented economy. It is impossible to trace all the implicit subsidies, but among the major mechanisms are low prices for agricultural inputs, low energy prices, subsidized credit, and import subsidies. Financing of these off-budget implicit subsidies comes from a variety of sources, including the agricultural sector (especially via the profits from hard currency cotton sales), Russia (via cheap energy and credit), the central bank, and gold sales.

The foreign trade regime in 1992–1993 discouraged hard currency exports, in contrast to the official strategy of export-led growth. Exports of cotton and some nonferrous metals and fertilizers were centralized; the Ministry of Economic Relations and Trade purchased the goods at domestic prices, and then exported them for higher world prices. Other exporters were required to deposit 35 percent of their earnings in the Republican Hard Currency Fund. The export tax was a significant revenue source in 1992 (Table 5.3), but raised far less revenue than expected in 1993, as many exporters were unwilling to export at the after-tax price (especially in the chemicals branch).[12] The government's hard currency revenue was used to finance its foreign currency spending (including loan servicing, embassy maintenance, and so on), and also to import a number of goods, which were sold at regulated domestic prices. Since the domestic prices were below world prices, these imports represented implicit subsidies, largely financed by the cotton growers.[13] They also meant that Uzbekistan had a multiple exchange rate system; the most extreme example concerned some pharmaceutical imports whose domestic price in rubles was 1.6 times the world price in dollars, when the market exchange rate was over 1,000 rubles per dollar. Interest groups (such as the health authorities) opposed change, but to economic policymakers it was obvious by late 1993 that the system was harmful to exports and encouraged gross misallocation of the foreign currency that the country did earn.[14]

Another stimulus for reactivating the reform process was the collapse in the final quarter of 1993 of Uzbekistan's strategy of reducing economic disruption by remaining in the ruble zone. The first sign of change was President Karimov's speech to the September session of the parliament, in which he emphasized market-related reforms. State prices of meat and sugar were doubled (although this still left them below market prices) and the prices of transport, telephone communications, and postal services were increased by similar amounts on October 16 (although they remained below costs). After struggling to maintain regulated prices since independence, the government finally gave up and announced that prices would be gradually liberalized by January 1994. It is unclear whether this decision was intended to keep Uzbekistan in the ruble zone with a Russia that was removing its final price regulations or was a prelude to leaving the ruble zone and adopting a more liberal economic policy stance.

In the same session, the parliament passed the Law on Securities and Stock Exchange, which provides a legal framework for trade in shares, government bonds, treasury notes, certificates of deposit, and bills of exchange.[15] Privatization, however, still appeared to be on a slow track.

Large enterprises can issue shares to raise cash, but there is no mechanism by which shareholders can enforce control. Most joint stock companies formed in 1992–1993 were "closed" companies, in which the state retained a controlling shareholding.

MACROECONOMIC CONDITIONS

Uzbekistan has the second-lowest per capita income among the CARs. The country is under especial pressure to maintain national income levels, because population is growing rapidly and in consequence dependency rates are high. The demographic pattern may have benefits in the medium term, but in the short-run it is a burden.

In common with most other Central Asian republics, Uzbekistan enjoyed a net subsidy from the rest of the USSR. The exact size of the subsidy is obscured by Soviet accounting, especially by the existence of all-Union enterprises, for which flows across republic borders were not identified. The best indicator of the net subsidy is the World Bank's estimates of total expenditure as a share of GDP: in 1990 private consumption was equal to 80 percent of GDP, government consumption to 11 percent, and investment to 23 percent, implying a net "capital inflow" equal to 14 percent of Uzbekistan's GDP. Some of this inflow was in the form of interenterprise debts, but most was effectively a grant with no repayment obligation. Uzbekistan was deemed liable for 3.3 percent of the USSR's external debt, but made no repayments and eventually ceded to Russia its share of Soviet international assets and debts.[16]

The republic's state budget was more or less balanced until 1990, thanks in part to the grants from the Union budget, which accounted for a quarter of Uzbekistan's state revenue. In 1991, as open inflation accelerated, a significant budget deficit began to emerge, mainly because of a drop in turnover tax receipts in real terms. Then in 1992, despite a tax reform replacing the turnover tax by a more efficient combination of VAT and excise taxes, a large budget deficit resulted from the cessation of the Union grant (Table 5.3).

During 1991 and 1992 output declined by about 15 percent, which was less than in almost all other former Soviet republics. Open inflation was also low relative to that in other ruble zone members, although still in three digits (Table 4.1). In 1993, as mentioned above, output stabilized. At the same time, however, exports to outside the CIS fell (by about 10 percent in the first eight months of 1993).

Through 1992 and 1993 Uzbekistan was one of the republics most committed to remaining in the ruble zone, despite the hyperinflation. President Karimov had political reasons for retaining close links with

TABLE 5.3
Actual Government Budget of Uzbekistan, 1992

	Billions of Rubles	*% of GNP*
Revenue		
VAT	38.5	9.2
Excise taxes	35.2	8.4
Export taxes	8.0	1.9
Enterprise profit tax	24.6	5.9
Personal income tax	10.8	2.6
Total revenue	142.7	34.2
Expenditure		
Education	45.0	10.8
Health	21.1	5.1
Culture, science, etc.	2.2	0.7
Social safety net (including subsidies on consumer goods)	49.4	11.9
National economy	15.5	3.7
Centralized capital investment	12.1	2.9
Administration, law, defense	42.2	10.1
Total expenditure	188.4	45.2
Deficit	45.7	11.0

Source: World Bank 1993c, table 4.3.

Moscow, but the budgetary problem also provided an economic incentive to remain in the ruble zone. Credit provided by the central bank of Russia in the form of banknotes and the ability of the central bank of Uzbekistan to create bank credit without bearing the full inflationary burden of its profligate monetary creation provided an attractive way of financing the budget deficit without taking tough economic decisions.[17] Moreover, for a government less than fully committed to economic reform, hyperinflation appeared less of a burden; if resources are to be allocated by command rather than in response to changes in relative prices, then the absolute price level is of little economic worry. Nevertheless, in the second half of 1993 this easy option became unsustainable for reasons discussed in Chapter 11, and Uzbekistan introduced its own currency on November 15. This step was followed by a large inflationary surge.

Despite its commitment to the ruble zone, an active program of promoting trade links beyond the CIS was pursued in the fall of 1993. The October visit of Iranian President Rafsanjani focused on trade, as did Karimov's earlier visit to Germany and his high-profile trip to France and the

United Kingdom in November. Nevertheless, actual reorientation of trade in 1993 was much less than in Kazakhstan, whose more market-oriented policies allowed largely unregulated trade with China to flourish; by contrast, small traders in Uzbekistan complained about the number of approvals required (often involving payment). Uzbekistan also mended local fences when presidents Karimov and Akayev met in Osh to sign an agreement on economic integration between Uzbekistan and Kyrgyzstan, which was followed in October by a regional agreement among all the CARs (see Chapter 12). Although monetary policy coordination between Uzbekistan and Kazakhstan was not maintained in November, their exit from the ruble zone on the same day was symbolic of a joint shift away from Russia's economic sphere.

CONCLUSIONS

Uzbekistan's hydraulic economy has produced political regimes with close affinity to those described as "Oriental Despotism" by Wittfogel.[18] The government has a crucial role to play in maintaining the irrigation system, without which much of agriculture (including the cotton sector) would collapse. The Ministry of Water Management is by far the largest government ministry in terms of employment.

The importance of government management and control appears to spread beyond water management. Policymakers remain suspicious of unregulated market mechanisms, despite official commitment to market-oriented reform. Prices were liberalized gradually and reluctantly, and enterprise reform is proceeding even more slowly. In the area of trade policy, a regime based on detailed quotas and taxes with multiple goals is likely to be replaced by a regime less openly harmful to exports, but far from simple. For example, the import tariff regime proposed at the end of 1993 envisioned tariffs varying not only across goods, but also by country of origin, with preferential tariffs for imports from the CIS and extra-low tariffs for imports from Central Asian partners.

As the Karimov regime becomes more repressive it may be able to control popular discontent, but that will be difficult to square with Karimov's desire to make Uzbekistan the core of Central Asia; closer contact with neighbors who start to be more economically dynamic will make it difficult to prevent the domestic population from questioning why they are being kept poor.

CHAPTER 6

Kazakhstan: Wild West in the East

KAZAKHSTAN, the other large economy of Central Asia, is more economically diversified than Uzbekistan. With 17 million people living on over 2.7 million square kilometers of territory, Kazakhstan was the second-largest republic of the Soviet Union and had the fourth-largest population and the third-largest economy (after Russia and Ukraine). The republic's delicate ethnic balance of roughly two-fifths Kazakhs and two-fifths Russians led Kazakhstan to play a key role in the final year of the Soviet Union as an intermediary between the Slavic and the Asian republics of the USSR, and the agreement replacing the Soviet Union by the Commonwealth of Independent States was signed in the Kazakhstan capital, Almaty, in December 1991.

Geographically, southern Kazakhstan shares many characteristics of the other Central Asian republics, but northern Kazakhstan is more akin to western Siberia. In the southeast, agriculture depends upon irrigation, using waters drawn from the Sirdarya River and the Ili River, which flows from the Tianshan Mountains in Xinjiang into Lake Balkhash. Central Kazakhstan is dominated by arid plains suitable only for extensive grazing. Northern Kazakhstan is less arid and supports rain-fed grain growing. The major oil fields and coal mines are in the north and far west of Kazakhstan.

Ethnically, Kazakhstan belongs in Central Asia, because the Kazakhs are closely related to the Kyrgyz and the Karakalpaks. Almaty's location, a ninety-minute flight from Tashkent and three hours' drive from Bishkek, reinforces the Central Asian focus, and the presidents of Kazakhstan, Kyrgyzstan, and Uzbekistan meet frequently, with Kazakhstan playing the pivotal role. President Nazarbayev also acts as an intermediary between the Central Asian countries and the Slavic republics of the former USSR. Although Kazakhstan is part of the region, its government looks beyond the region, while Uzbekistan seeks to make Tashkent the center of the region.[1]

Kazakhstan is the richest of the Central Asian republics, and has attracted by far the most foreign economic interest. The inflow of foreign money into the partially reformed economy has engendered a Wild West atmosphere of fortunes to be made within or outside the law. Almaty has the only casinos between Moscow and Macao, and they are doing good business; outside the Olympos Casino, the owner's stretch Cadillac is parked ostentatiously. In summer 1993, Mercedes opened its first Central Asian showroom in Almaty. Another side of the Wild West coin is the bulletholes in the windscreen of the truck arriving in the weekly service from Utrecht; in summer 1993 the Dutch drivers demanded that their company pay somebody to ride shotgun through Kazakhstan.

The Wild West feeling in Kazakhstan in 1993 was a double-edged consideration. It reduced the quality of life for many people and disrupted trade, but it was also a counterpart to the process of economic reform, which had unleashed entrepreneurship. Whether it is an essential ingredient of economic reform is uncertain (and Kazakhstan's leaders long for the combination of stability and growth that they perceive to characterize the Asian economic success stories), but the universal experience is that it is difficult to regulate economic reform closely. Too heavy a government hand will surely kill the reform process, as can be seen from the experience of neighboring Uzbekistan (see Chapter 5). The increased openness and feeling of lawlessness in Kazakhstan can (at least up to a certain point) be interpreted positively as concommitants to economic dynamism.

HISTORY

The Kazakhs emerged as an identifiable group among the Mongol and Turkic tribes of Central Asia when a confederation known as the Kazakh Orda was established in the late fifteenth century. The confederation dissolved in the early 1600s, and a century later, the successor khans sought Russian protection against invasion from the east by the Oirot Mongols. Although the Oirot threat disintegrated in the 1750s, the Russians retained control and deposed the khans. After the abolition of serfdom in the Russian Empire in 1861, large numbers of Russian and Ukrainian peasants immigrated into the region, leading to conflict with the nomadic Kazakhs. Pacification plus an optimistic survey of arable land in 1895 encouraged increased immigration, which accelerated after 1905. The Kazakhs intermittently rose up against Slav settlement; in 1916 a major rebellion against Russian rule was suppressed with some 150,000 killed.

After the 1917 revolution, civil war raged across Kazakhstan. Bolshevik forces were victorious, and in August 1920 the Kirghiz Autonomous Soviet Socialist Republic was created within the Russian Federation; until 1925 the Soviet authorities called the Kazakhs Kirghiz in order to distinguish them from the unrelated Cossacks. In 1924–1925 the republic was enlarged by the inclusion of Kazakh-occupied territories to the south and renamed the Kazakh ASSR. In 1932 the Karakalpak region was detached from the Kazakh ASSR. In 1936 the Karakalpak region became an autonomous republic within the Uzbek SSR, and the Kazakh SSR became a full Union republic. During the campaign to collectivize agriculture and settle nomadic peoples in the early 1930s, more than a million people are estimated to have died of starvation.[2]

Apart from the voluntary movement of peasants seeking land, Kazakhstan was also the destination of forced immigrants. Trotsky was the most notable among the political prisoners exiled to the republic in the 1920s. During World War II Stalin resettled large numbers of people belonging to groups whom he viewed as potential fifth columns. The largest groups were Germans, Koreans, Crimean Tatars, and Caucasian peoples. Many of these displaced people were farmers, and the German minority in particular became associated with the best farmland.

During the 1950s and 1960s Kazakhstan became the most diversified economy in Central Asia. Over 60 percent of the republic's arable land (about 25 million hectares) was brought under cultivation during the Virgin Lands campaign initiated by Khrushchev in the late 1950s, as a means of reducing the USSR's dependence upon cereal imports and of sedentarizing nomadic herders. The Virgin Lands campaign turned northern Kazakhstan into a major grain-growing area (the third-largest producer and second-largest net exporter among the Soviet republics), but the expansion of the area under crop led to serious ecological problems. Hi-tech activities included the Baikonur space center, from which Yuri Gagarin became the first person in space, and the USSR's major nuclear testing area.[3] Huge industrial sites, such as that centered on the Karaganda coal mines, were developed in the north and east of Kazakhstan. All of these activities attracted large numbers of Slavic immigrants, and the ethnic Russians' share of the population increased from less than a fifth in 1926 to 43 percent in 1959.

The agricultural developments together with the diversification of the republic's economy under Soviet rule had two important consequences. First, they destroyed the nomadic lifestyle and replaced it by a predominantly sedentary culture. Second, by reducing the number of Kazakhs and increasing the numbers of other ethnic groups, they made the Kazakhs a minority in the republic. During the 1960s, 1970s, and 1980s the Kazakhs continued to be outnumbered by Russians, although the higher Kazakh birth rate had reversed this situation by the end of the 1980s (Table 6.1).[4] The ethnic mix has obvious political implications, including the potential for tension and the closeness of ties to Russia.

When Gorbachev replaced the corrupt Kazakh Dinmukhamed Kunayev by a Russian, Gennady Kolbin, as first secretary of the Communist Party of Kazakhstan (CPKaz), some three thousand people demonstrated in Alma-Ata, and two were killed when police dispersed the pro-

TABLE 6.1
Demographic Profile of Kazakhstan

Population (thousands)	17,185
Population density (per sq km)	6
Annual growth rate (percent)	0.8%
Crude birth rate (per thousand)	23
Crude death rate (per thousand)	8
Infant mortality rate (per thousand)	35
Life expectancy at birth	
Females	74
Males	65
Percentage of population aged	
14 or less	32%
60 or more	11%
Ethnic composition	
Kazakhs	39.7%
Russians	37.8%
Germans	5.8%
Ukrainians	5.4%
Uzbeks	2.0%
Tatars	2.0%
Others	7.3%
Population of towns (thousands)	
Almaty (Alma-Ata)	1,147
Karaganda	613
Chimkent	410
Semipalatinsk	339
Pavlodar	337
Ust-Kamenogorsk	330

Sources: ESCAP, *Population Data Sheet 1993* (Bangkok: United Nations, 1993); for urban populations, Economist Intelligence Unit, *Country Profile.*

Note: Ethnic composition is as of 1991; town populations are as of 1990; all other data are for 1993.

testers.[5] Ethnic conflicts in Novy Uzen, in southwestern Kazakhstan, in June 1989 provided the occasion for Kolbin's transfer to Moscow and the appointment of a Kazakh, Nursultan Nazarbayev, as first secretary of the CPKaz.

With glasnost, linguistic and environmental issues became the main subjects of public debate. In September 1989 Kazakh was established as the official language, while Russian remained the language of interethnic communication; officials dealing with the public were expected to know both languages.[6] Many non-Kazakh residents opposed the introduction of Kazakh as the official language, and some campaigned for annexation of northern Kazakhstan to the Russian Federation. The publication in September 1990 of Alexander Solzhenitsyn's proposals for transfer of territory from the Kazakh SSR to Russia added fuel to this fire.

Many environmental groups were formed during the late 1980s by people concerned with environmental issues, especially the consequences of nuclear testing, industrial pollution, and agricultural land degradation. Kazakhstan not only shared in the systemic environmental problems of the USSR, but also suffered from two of the major catastrophes (the drying up of the Aral Sea and nuclear contamination), and the environmental movement was probably stronger there than anywhere else in the Soviet Union. An explosion in a factory making nuclear fuel in Ulba in eastern Kazakhstan in September 1990, which led to contamination of a large area, including the city of Ust-Kamenogorsk, sparked off large demonstrations, and Nazarbayev demanded that the USSR declare the area an ecological disaster zone. In 1991 Nazarbayev announced that nuclear testing would not continue after the year's end.

Through all this, internal politics remained remarkably stable. The March 1989 elections to the all-Union Congress of People's Deputies were conducted in traditional Soviet fashion. A September 1989 reform established a full-time Supreme Soviet to which elections would be on a multi-candidate basis, but when the elections were held in March 1990 many candidates were unopposed and the CPKaz wound up with an overwhelming majority of seats. When the Supreme Soviet convened in April, it elected Nazarbayev to the newly created post of President.

In October 1990 the Supreme Soviet adopted a declaration of sovereignty that asserted republican control over natural resources and the economy. Protests against the legislation took place in Slav-dominated areas, such as the city of Ust-Kamenogorsk, while Kazakh nationalist groups criticized the legislation as too weak. With 90 percent of the enterprises in Kazakhstan under all-Union control, republican economic sovereignty was limited. In March 1991 President Nazarbayev took advantage of a miners' strike in Karaganda to persuade the all-Union government to transfer control over enterprises within the republic to the jurisdiction of the Kazakhstan government.

Despite these moves toward economic sovereignty, Nazarbayev remained a supporter of retaining the Soviet Union. In the March 1991 referendum, with a turnout of 88 percent, over 94 percent voted in favor of preserving the USSR. In June the Supreme Soviet approved the draft Union Treaty, but signature of the treaty was forestalled by the August coup in Moscow.

After a brief hesitation, Nazarbayev issued a statement on August 20 denouncing the coup. He resigned from the Politburo and the Central Committee of the Communist Party of the Soviet Union (CPSU), and ordered the CPKaz to cease its activities within the government and state organs. He became acknowledged as the foremost non-Slavic leader in the USSR and played a prominent role in negotiations for a new Union. When these negotiations were nullified by the summit of the leaders of the three Slavic republics in early December, Nazarbayev was initially reluctant to respond, but then led the Central Asian republics in agreeing to join the CIS. Kazakhstan declared independence on December 16 (the penultimate Soviet republic to do so), and the Commonwealth of Independent States was formally constituted in Alma-Ata on December 21.

ECONOMIC STRUCTURE

Agriculture is an important sector of the Kazakhstan economy; in 1991 over 1.7 million people (18 percent of the labor force) were employed in agriculture, compared to 1.5 million employed in industry (including mining). The relative importance of agriculture and industry in Kazakhstan's total output is difficult to measure. In 1990 agricultural output was valued at double that of industry, but in the next year industrial output was valued higher than agricultural output (Table 6.2). The explanation for this reversal is twofold: relative prices were drastically changed (in particular, the artificially very low oil and mineral prices moved closer to world prices), and 1991 saw the worst harvest in over a decade.

With a bumper harvest in 1992, employment in agriculture increased, while employment in industry declined. Both sectors' share of output increased in 1992 at the expense of construction. The medium term will see a growing importance of industry as oil output is valued at world prices.

The structure of agriculture in Kazakhstan, differs significantly from that in the other CARs. Cereals (especially wheat) and livestock farming are the dominant activities; cotton is of lesser importance, although it is geographically concentrated in the Chimkent region (Table 6.3).[7] Nevertheless, in the south of Kazakhstan, the reliance on irrigation systems, which are overstraining the capacity of the feeder rivers, is typical of the rest of the region. The grain farming in the north is rain fed, but the low rainfall and short growing season make output highly variable (Figure 6.1). Although short-term variability makes it difficult to identify any long-term trend from recent years' harvests, the situation may be deteriorating if desiccation of the Aral Sea is creating more extreme climatic conditions.

Apart from suffering from the ecological consequences of the desiccation of the Aral Sea, Kazakhstan's agriculture is contributing to the environmental problems. Inefficient irrigation techniques are contributing to the desiccation of the Aral Sea and Lake Balkhash, although Kazakhstan

TABLE 6.2

Sectoral Distribution of Employment and Output in Kazakhstan, 1990 and 1991

	1990	*1991*
Employment (thousands)		
Total labor resources	9,262	9,331
Full-time employment	7,563	7,494
Employment in the state sector	6,775	6,712
Industry	1,539	1,533
Agriculture	1,713	1,740
Forestry	14	14
Transport and communication	510	508
Construction	908	771
Trade	561	554
Other material sphere	161	190
Nonmaterial sphere	1,370	1,405
Output (millions of rubles)		
Net material product	33,358	68,603
Industry	7,003	24,764
Agriculture	13,937	22,810
Forestry	25	52
Construction	5,338	9,022
Transport and communication	3,257	7,435
Trade	1,602	2,683
Other material sphere	2,198	1,837

Source: Kazakhstan State Economic Committee, reported in World Bank, *Kazakhstan: Country Economic Memorandum,* Report no. 10976-KK (Washington, D.C.: World Bank, November 1992), Vol. 2, statistical appendix.

Note: The output data correspond to the material sphere of employment.

is not the major culprit in the former case. Although Kazakhstan is, in most years, a net exporter of grain, this does not reflect at the margin the republic's comparative advantage: the Virgin Lands campaign expanded onto land that cannot support grain farming, and for ecological reasons, the grain sector should contract rather than expand.[8] The replacement of extensive livestock farming by intensive (dependent on fodder production) livestock production fails to best utilize natural endowments.

In addition to the environmental problems, three other serious problems inherited from the Soviet agricultural system are the state-administered rural credit system, the obsolete, fuel-inefficient machinery, and the inadequate and inefficiently utilized food-processing, storage, and distribution facilities. Despite the commercialization of Kazagroprombank, rural finance continues to be administered by the state and discriminates in favor of collectives and state farms. When Kazakhstan experimented in

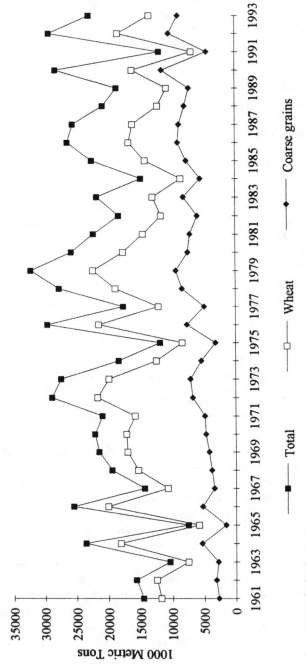

Cereal production in Kazakhstan, 1961–1993

Source: FAO/Goskomstat

Figure 6.1 Cereal Production in Kazakhstan, 1961–1993. *Source:* Constructed by Joop Theunissen from FAO/Goskomstat data.

TABLE 6.3

Agricultural Land Use in Kazakhstan, 1990 (millions of hectares)

Grazing, pastures, and rangeland	180
Arable	40
Cereals	23.4 (wheat 14.1)
Fodder crops	11.1
Fallow	4.4
Cotton	0.1
Sugar beet	0.1
Sunflowers	0.1
Vegetables	0.3
Total	220

Source: Government of Kazakhstan.

1991–1992 with offering cultivators fifty-year land leases that could be passed on, most of the leaseholders discovered that they could not effectively manage their farms because they could not afford inputs and lacked access to credit. This episode was used by conservatives in 1992–1993 as evidence of the infeasibility of land privatization.[9]

The crucial point is that the value of any land to be privatized depends upon the availability of complementary inputs. For traded inputs this is related in turn to the availability of credit and perhaps issues of monopoly pricing. For irrigated land, the land will be of much lower value if its privatization is not accompanied by guarantees of continuing availability of water at a reasonable price. Given, however, that the cultivated land area is greater than optimal, such guarantees should not be given to all landholders. Ideally the decisions should be based upon agronomically well-backed economic criteria, but in practice decisions about the future of the irrigation network are likely to be highly politicized.

The desirability of upgrading the stock of agricultural machinery is a strong argument for increasing the outward orientation of the economy so that equipment can be purchased on world markets from the most appropriate supplier. In the medium term, however, the large stock of Comecon-produced machinery will be a motive for maintaining trading links with the former communist countries, because spare parts will be obtainable only from those countries.

Agriculture is a foreign-exchange earner for Kazakhstan. The full potential is, however, being wasted by the lack of adequate processing, storage and distribution facilities. When Kazakhstan enjoyed a bumper 30 million-tonne wheat harvest in 1992, as much as a third was likely to be lost.[10] Almost all food-processing activities have experienced severe output declines in recent years (Table 6.4). Remedying these problems will re-

TABLE 6.4
Output of Selected Industrial Products in Kazakhstan, 1989–1992

	Unit[a]	Number of Units			
		1989	1990	1991	1992
Coal	2	138	131	130	127
Brown coal	2	3.1	3.4	3.9	4.5
Natural gas	3	6.7	7.1	7.9	8.1
Crude petroleum	2	22.0	21.7	22.0	21.7
Iron ore	2	23.8	23.8	22.0	17.7
Electricity	4	89,657	87,379	85,984	81,293
Cotton yarn	1	41.7	39.9	36.9	38.6
Cotton fabrics	5	150	151	134	135
Tires	6	2,450	2,633	3,029	2,904
Paper	7	2,909	1,510	1,029	700
Cement	1	8,650	8,301	7,575	6,436
Meat	1	946	899	846	519
Milk products	1	1,491	1,470	1,377	952
Butter	1	83	85	76	61
Oil	1	92	95	101	56
Wheat flour	1	1,968	1,962	2,014	1,932
Sugar	1	377	319	307	153

Source: State Committee on Statistics and Analysis of Republic of Kazakhstan, *Statistical Bulletin no. 2* (Alma-Ata, 1992), 23–9.

[a] 1 = thousands of metric tons, 2 = millions of metric tons, 3 = millions of cubic meters, 4 = millions of kilowatt-hours, 5 = millions of square meters, 6 = thousands, 7 = metric tons.

quire some investment, but perhaps more crucial in the short term is the need to change incentives. Privatizing agricultural marketing could help to ensure that a larger proportion of output actually reaches the market.

The most important industrial sectors are mining and energy. In 1989 Kazakhstan produced 19 percent of coal, 10 percent of iron ore, and 4 percent of oil in the USSR (IMF et al. 1991, 1: 216). Mineral resource data were secret in the USSR, but according to World Bank and IMF reports, Kazakhstan had 90 percent of the chrome reserves, perhaps three-quarters of the lead and zinc reserves, and half of the copper and wolfram reserves in the Soviet Union. Nearly 50 percent of Soviet lead-smelting and -refining capacity was located in Kazakhstan, including the USSR's two largest refineries (Chimkent and Leninogorsk), and the largest zinc refinery in the USSR was at Ust Kamenogorsk.

The importance of mining and energy, as a share of GDP, is growing rapidly as the move to world prices increases the relative prices of these items and the energy and mining subsectors include the only branches of industry in which employment has increased since independence. Uniquely, real output from some of these branches (for example, crude petroleum) remained stable, and for some (for example, natural gas and brown coal) it even increased (Table 6.4). Future prospects are extremely bright for petroleum and natural gas, but less so for coal because the existing mines are running into seam exhaustion and are using obsolete equipment. This has important regional implications, because the new oil fields are in the far west of Kazakhstan, while the established coal mines are in the northeast, in the Karaganda and Pavlodar areas.

The manufacturing sector is diverse, and has had mixed experiences during the transition period. For most products, Kazakhstan's share of Soviet output was less than the republic's share of population, but much bigger than any other CAR's share.[11] Some heavy industries, such as paper and cement, have experienced large output drops since the late 1980s, while others such as cotton spinning and weaving and tire-making have proven more stable. One consequence of the large industrial sector is that although Kazakhstan generates more electricity than any other CAR, it is a major net importer of electricity (mainly from Turkmenistan and the Russian Federation).

ECONOMIC PERFORMANCE SINCE INDEPENDENCE

From the 1970s on, Kazakhstan shared in the general economic stagnation of the USSR, and in the 1980s growth in output per head was close to zero. As in all of the former Soviet republics, the early 1990s were characterized by high inflation and falling output levels. Kazakhstan's inflation followed fairly closely that of Russia. The 1991 fall in output was larger in Kazakhstan than in the rest of Central Asia, but the 1992 percentage drop was smaller than in other Central Asian republics. The welfare implications of falling output were alleviated by improved terms of trade, due to moving from Soviet to world prices, and by continuing credit from Russia.

Inflation in 1992 was in the four-digit range. Official figures for the increase in consumer prices are 2,567 percent (compared to 2,323 percent in Russia), with a large increase in January followed by monthly rates of 9–15 percent over the next four months and higher rates for the rest of the year (Table 6.5). Wholesale prices increased by much more: 12,490 percent over 1992. The big difference arose primarily because the largest increases in wholesale prices affected exports.[12]

Net material product fell by 10.3 percent in 1991. In line with other Soviet republics, this reflected the disruption of trade within the USSR and the introduction of economic reforms that promoted a change in the output mix. The fall was less than in some of the more reformist republics in

TABLE 6.5
Monthly Percentage Changes
in Consumer Prices in
Kazakhstan, 1992

January	256.4
February	8.8
March	11.9
April	15.3
May	14.9
June	24.2
July	30.0
August	14.0
September	13.7
October	20.4
November	22.4
December	18.8

Source: IMF, *Economic Review 5: Kazakhstan*, June 1993, 63.

the western USSR, but higher than in any other Asian republic. In part, Kazakhstan's fall in output reflected a severe drought that led to a very poor grain harvest. The recovery in grain production, which was three times higher in 1992 than in 1991, alleviated the percentage decline in output in 1992, which was 14.2 percent. The cumulative loss of output in 1991–1992 was similar to that in neighboring Kyrgyzstan, which had also adopted substantial economic reforms, less than that in Tajikistan, which had been disrupted by civil war, and greater than that in Uzbekistan or Turkmenistan, which had adopted more conservative economic policies.

The impact of the fall in output was exacerbated by the reduction of interrepublic transfers. In this respect, however, Kazakhstan was less adversely affected than other Asian republics, because Russia chose for political reasons to maintain significant credit flows to Kazakhstan. Kazakhstan also enjoyed a substantial improvement in terms of trade as a result of the shift from Soviet to world prices. Estimates of the net terms of trade effects, based on an analysis of 1990 trade flows using a 105-sector aggregation, show Kazakhstan to be one of the three republics enjoying an improvement, with a gain of 19 percent.[13] The price changes were introduced gradually, so it is difficult to know when this benefit accrued, but given Kazakhstan's trade/GDP ratio of around one-third, the improved terms of trade will shift GDP up by about 6 percent. In sum, although Kazakhstan suffered from a fairly typical output loss during the first two years of its transition process, in comparison to other countries suffering from the disintegration of the Soviet economic system, the impact on economic welfare was alleviated by favorable terms of trade effects and by continuing privileged economic relations with Russia.

In 1992–1993 the social effects of economic disruption became more apparent. Income inequality was more blatant—luxury cars became more common, while poverty was on the rise. Crime was increasing, and there were complaints of private initiative by the police in collecting tolls and protection money. In general, corruption was perceived as a large and growing problem, although by its nature this is difficult to document. Diseases that had been absent for decades reappeared; on several occasions in 1993, the government closed the borders in response to outbreaks of cholera.

Despite all these problems, Kazakhstan has the brightest economic prospects of any of the Asian republics of the former Soviet Union. Kazakhstan's per capita income was substantially higher than that of the other Asian republics in the USSR, which reflects its abundant physical and human resources and also provides it with more of a cushion for surviving short-term economic hardship.

In the short run Kazakhstan's trade profile enabled the country to switch its exports to hard currency markets and to switch imports to intra-CIS (subsidized) sources. Exports to countries outside the former USSR dropped from $1,402 million in 1990 to $928 million in 1991, but then recovered to $1,489 million in 1992. Imports from outside the former USSR dropped sharply from $1,490 million in 1990 to $584 million in 1991 and $469 million in 1992.[14] Despite this improvement in the external trade balance, Kazakhstan ran an overall trade deficit in 1992 of $1,670 million, due to a large deficit on intra-CIS trade. Trade with former Soviet republics has become increasingly trade with Russia (at the expense of trade with the Baltic states and Central Asian republics), and is largely financed by correspondent account credits (overwhelmingly with Russia). According to IMF balance of payments estimates, Kazakhstan was able to run a current account deficit equal to 10 percent of GDP in 1992 and still increase foreign exchange reserves by $100 million.

In the medium term Kazakhstan will benefit from direct foreign investment (DFI). Actual DFI inflows so far have not been large, amounting to about $100 million in 1992, and have mostly involved small-scale joint ventures. Pledged DFI is, however, huge. Under a contract negotiated in the final years of the USSR and signed in May 1992, Chevron will invest $1.5 billion in developing the Tenghiz oil field northeast of the Caspian Sea; this is the biggest DFI project anywhere in the former USSR. British Gas and AGIP are involved in a potentially even larger project to exploit the Karachaganak oil and gas fields in the Urals of western Kazakhstan, and Elf Acquitaine has signed a contract to explore a large area in central Kazakhstan. Whatever oil and gas reserves are found, their full exploitation will await construction of new pipelines to the Black Sea or the Mediterranean Sea, which will require international cooperation (as well as large funds) and will not be completed before the late 1990s.[15] Kazakhstan is also seeking foreign investment to expand and upgrade its oil-refining capacity. Although Kazakhstan was a net exporter of crude oil in the USSR, it was a net importer of oil products. Current plans are to expand the three existing refineries at Guryev, Pavlodar, and Chimkent and to construct new refineries, for which bids were made in 1993 by Mitsui, Mitsubishi, and Foster Wheeler. Despite the time lags involved, confidence in Kazakhstan's economic future is high within the international community, and Almaty has already become the financial center of Central Asia.[16]

ECONOMIC POLICIES

Kazakhstan shared in the economic restructuring (perestroika) of the Gorbachev years, but was not among the republics that introduced local experiments in economic reform. Activities in Kazakhstan were largely designed at the Union level, and the reforms of the late 1980s did not introduce any substantial change in the workings of the economy. At the end of 1990 about 90 percent of the stock of fixed assets was state owned. In 1990 the Kazakhstan government, like those of other Soviet republics, was given responsibility for fiscal operations within its territory, and in 1991 price and enterprise reform began to move.

Price Reform

In January and April 1991 administered prices were increased in the USSR, and free or negotiated prices were introduced for a range of goods. A more substantial price reform was taken by the newly independent government of Kazakhstan in January 1992, coinciding with a similar step in Russia. Prices of about 80 percent of goods covered by the retail price index were decontrolled and other prices raised substantially. During the course of 1992, more prices were freed, and remaining controlled prices were increased several times.

By early 1993 the only retail prices still regulated were for transportation and communication services, bread and bakery products, baby food, some energy products, and imported medicines. These had all been increased substantially since the end of 1991 (Table 6.6). Local authorities still controlled rents and related charges (heating, water, electricity, etc.) and urban transportation fares, although these were also increased several times.

TABLE 6.6

Regulated Prices for Selected Items in Kazakhstan, 1991 and 1993 (rubles)

		Price	
	Unit	*December 1991*	*March 1993*
Crude oil	ton	70	15,000
Natural gas	thousand cubic meters	50	18,500
Gasoline	ton	260	68,500
Diesel fuel	ton	164	39,792
Electricity	kw	0.03	9
White bread	kg	0.80	12
Flour	kg	0.93	14
Baby food	kg	5	15

Source: IMF, *Economic Review 5: Kazakhstan*, June 1993, 62.

Local prices of deregulated traded goods were close to world prices, adjusted for transport costs. Despite the large increases, regulated prices remained well below world prices, especially for energy products. Thus, in 1993 fuel shortages became a serious problem.[17]

In sum, prices have been for the most part freed, and with a few exceptions relative prices are providing the signaling function that they play in a market economy. During 1992 and 1993, however, this signaling function was obscured by the continuing high rates of inflation. Inflation could be blamed on the administered increases in regulated prices and the monopoly power of enterprises in concentrated industries whose prices had been freed, but more fundamentally the continuing inflation was due to lack of control over the money supply.

After independence, Kazakhstan continued to use the ruble as the sole means of exchange until November 15, 1993. The country thus shared in the 1992–1993 inflation of the ruble zone, which was in large part due to forces beyond Kazakhstan's control (Chapter 11). Kazakhstan benefited from ruble zone membership because it continued to receive credit and raw materials priced below world prices from Russia. Nevertheless, the government took the precaution of having banknotes printed, and in 1993 there were frequent rumors of the imminent introduction of a national currency.[18] Hesitation in taking the final step of issuing a national currency added to economic disruption because of cash shortages (for example, in July 1993) and arbitrary decisions in response to ruble cash flows (for example, the freezing of bank accounts in early November 1993). With a national currency, Kazakhstan would finally have the opportunity to make price reform effective by controlling inflation, if the government were willing to make the tough political decisions associated with a tight monetary policy.

Enterprise Reform and Privatization

In January 1991 the Kazakh State Property Committee was set up and made responsible for the privatization of state enterprises and the creation of new private enterprises. Privatization began in August, although initial progress was slow. Of roughly 37,000 state enterprises, 380 were sold in 1991 and almost 6,000 in 1992, but these were mostly small-scale. In addition many new private enterprises were established, although they were also small-scale and were mostly engaged in trade. Some larger joint stock companies have been created from former state enterprises, but the state continues to hold a majority of the shares.

Table 6.7 provides estimates of the size structure of the state enterprise sector at the end of 1991. Clearly the approach to privatization in 1991 and 1992 by dealing only with small enterprises (and privatizing less than a quarter of these) was not transferring jobs from the state to the private sector on a large scale. The size of the private sector is difficult to assess, because many small businesses' activities are unrecorded. The State Property Committee estimated that at the end of 1992 about seven hundred thousand workers were employed by privatized enterprises.

In March 1993 the government adopted a three-pronged approach to accelerate privatization, with a target completion date of 1995. Small-scale enterprises (those employing up to about two hundred workers) would be sold by open auction for cash or housing vouchers, with special discounts for existing employees. Enterprises with two hundred to five thousand employees would be converted into joint stock companies, for which workers' collectives could receive up to 10 percent of the shares, and the remainder would be bid for by Investment Privatization Funds (IPFs). Each resident would receive vouchers which could be exchanged for shares in IPFs. Distribution of vouchers began on July 1, 1993. Each urban resident received 100 vouchers, and each rural resident received 120, irrespective of citizenship. The rural-urban differential biased the distribution in favor of kazakhs, who were disproportionately rural. The Czech-style IPFs were intended to prevent fragmentation of ownership. Emerging details suggest that as of 1993 the program was fairly conservative, with a small number of IPFs all under government control and about half of state property excluded from privatization.[19] Very large firms and enterprises requiring special regulatory provisions will be privatized on a case-by-case basis. Implementation of the privatization program was delayed for about half a year, but it was reactivated in the autumn of 1993.[20]

Land and other natural resources remain state property, but can be leased for up to ninety-nine years and leases are transferable and inherit-

TABLE 6.7
Size Structure of State Enterprises in Kazakhstan, End of 1991

	Number of Firms	Total Number of Employees
Small (fewer than 200 employees)	27,500	1,000,000
Medium and large (200–4,999 employees)	8,000	2,900,000
Very large (5,000 employees or more)	200	1,600,000
Special enterprises	1,300	500,000

Source: State Property Committee, Government of Kazakhstan.

Note: Special enterprises include natural monopolies, enterprises filling major noncommercial functions, and enterprises exploiting nonrenewable resources and processing of certain agricultural and forest products.

able. Many state farms have now been privatized, and the significance of private sector production of agricultural products is rising (Table 6.8). More than 30 percent of the cattle, horses, and poultry were on private farms in 1992.

About half of all dwellings had been privatized by mid-1993. Housing is primarily the responsibility of local authorities (oblasts), and the methods and extent of privatization vary

In conjunction with the price and enterprise reforms the Soviet system of state orders has been practically abandoned. In 1991, despite the Gorbachev reforms, some 70–80 percent of Kazakhstan's output was covered by state orders. The 1992 plan tried to retain the essential features of this system, with enterprises required to trade with state organizations at prices fixed by the latter and to meet delivery dates irrespective of whether they had received payment. In practice, many delivery commitments were not met, in part because enterprises preferred to sell on the free market, but also because disruption of inputs prevented production of some items; given the difficulty of establishing fault, enforcement of penalties for nondelivery was rare. In 1993 the state orders system was replaced by a "State Needs" system under which state procurement (for schools, hospitals, etc.) and goods for export under interstate trade agreements are purchased from voluntary suppliers at negotiated prices.

Following the April 1991 price liberalization, an antimonopoly law was introduced in the USSR and an Antimonopoly Committee established in Kazakhstan, as in other republics. Since the law dealt with Unionwide monopolies it was soon irrelevant and it was never enforced. In September 1992, Kazakhstan introduced antimonopoly legislation, which listed about three hundred items produced by "monopolists" and required the Antimonopoly Committee to verify that prices charged for these items were not excessive.

TABLE 6.8

Private Sector Share of Production of
Selected Agricultural Goods in
Kazakhstan, 1991 and 1992 (percent)

	1991	1992
Meat	34.6	43.6
Milk	48.3	54.3
Eggs	32.0	36.9
Wool	30.0	35.6
Potatoes	61.0	67.0
Melons	43.0	51.0

Source: IMF, *Economic Review 5: Kazakh-stan*, June 1993, 72.

Financial Sector Reform

The monobank system of the USSR had begun to change in form during the late 1980s, although there was little fundamental change in deposit or credit policies. Specialized banks took over the commercial banking functions of the State Bank, but remained dependent on the State Bank for the bulk of their liquidity. Enterprises and cooperatives were allowed to establish their own banks, and the total number of banks in Kazakhstan increased from five in 1988, to thirty-two by the end of 1990 and seventy-two by the end of 1991. The Savings Bank, a department of the State Bank, continued to hold virtually all deposits, given interest regulations that prevented competition via interest rates and government deposit guarantees that applied only to the Savings Bank.

Following independence the State Bank was renamed the National Bank of Kazakhstan. The number of commercial banks increased rapidly, reaching 158 by the end of 1992, of which 48 were private banks. Most of the banks were small, and the three largest specialized banks plus the Savings Bank accounted for over three-quarters of assets. The Savings Bank had 4,477 branches and Agroprombank had 231, out of a total of 5,035.

Despite a government commitment to increase the allocative role of interest rates, they remain largely administered. The National Bank of Kazakhstan raised its refinance rate to 65 percent per annum in July 1992 (when the monthly inflation rate was 18 percent), but even this did not apply to over half of the credit, which was supplied at preferential rates of between zero and 25 percent.[21] In sum, real interest rates were negative and there was a big incentive to obtain credit at these rates. Most of the new banks had a small number of customers (often a single enterprise) and operated simply as a channel for subsidized credit from the central bank.

Labor Market Reform

As with financial reform, there has been some change in labor markets but without fundamentally altering their operation. The government places a high priority on alleviating the impact of the transition process upon workers; continued use of subsidized credit and unwillingness to increase unemployment are two facets of the same intention.

By the end of 1992, 18,153 people were receiving unemployment benefits, and 33,666 were officially classified as unemployed, about 4 percent of the work force. Even allowing for the 25,000 people on compulsory leave and 32,000 on compulsory part-time, employment had clearly not been allowed to adjust with the over 20 percent drop in output over 1991–1992. There were significant shifts in the sectoral employment structure as declines in employment in construction and in industry were offset by increased employment in state agriculture.[22] This shift implies some increase in labor market flexibility, assisted by the special condition of an exceptional grain harvest.

The major change in 1992 was the introduction of greater wage flexibility. Previously the minimum wage had served as a guideline for the general wage level, and had affected practically all wages directly or indirectly. The minimum wage was increased from 342 rubles at the end of 1991 to 900 rubles at the end of 1992, which implied more than a 90 percent reduction in purchasing power. Meanwhile, the average wage increased from 452 to 13,359 rubles, a 10 percent increase in real terms. Clearly, the connection between minimum and average wage had been severed, and by the end of 1992 the minimum wage was relevant only as a base for calculating civil servants' salaries, pensions, and other state benefits.

In order to limit widening income differentials, a tax-based wage policy was introduced in mid-1992. An enterprise's wage bill in excess of four times the minimum wage multiplied by the number of employees would not be tax deductible. This was easily evaded by increasing payments in kind as supplements to wages. In 1993 the government had no effective incomes policy, and growing income inequality (accompanied by conspicuous consumption of imported luxury goods) was an emerging social problem.

Macroeconomic Policy

Between 1985 and 1989 Kazakhstan's state budget deficits increased from 3 percent of GDP to almost 10 percent, covered by Union transfers. In 1990 republics were given greater responsibility for fiscal policy within their territory, subject to Union laws and obligations. In 1991 the republics' budgets were prepared independently, and with greater autonomy. Meanwhile, accompanying this decentralization, Union transfers fell to less than 5 percent of Kazakhstan's GDP.

After independence, Kazakhstan had complete freedom in conducting fiscal policy, subject only to the restraints imposed by membership in the CIS and in the ruble zone. Although the fiscal status of the CIS remains unclearly defined, members are committed to free internal trade and to the avoidance of double taxation. It appears that the CIS will operate as a free trade area with each member pursuing its own external trade policies, but in 1992 Kazakhstan's lack of a fully fledged customs administration made collection of trade taxes difficult. The CIS coordinated introduction in January 1992 of a value-added tax at a standard rate of 28 percent, which could be levied on the origin principle, but later exemptions and introduction of differential rates by Kazakhstan (and other CIS members) complicated VAT collection.

The government maintained a fairly tight fiscal policy, reducing the budget deficit as a percentage of GDP from 8 percent in 1991 to 5.6 percent in 1992.[23] Expenditures were cut from 33 percent to 24 percent of GDP, but revenues fell from 25 percent to 19 percent of GDP. Apart from failure to collect customs duties, the main taxes (VAT, excise taxes, and income taxes) all yielded less than expected, leading to several ad hoc tax measures during the year. A tax on export earnings with an average rate of 40 percent was introduced in April. This yielded revenue equal to nearly 2 percent of GDP, but was inimical to economic reform and to the goal of promoting export-led growth as it encouraged barter and unreported trade as well as discouraging some export activities. Among the other ad hoc measures were company-specific royalties levied on natural resource companies.

Selective tax impositions increased the incentive for negotiations to reduce the tax burden. The most striking example was the granting to four of the wealthiest oblasts of Free Economic Zone status, which permits them to modify the tax system within their territories and to retain all tax revenues collected. This move toward fiscal federalism within Kazakhstan will increase the autonomy of the regions and weaken central macroeconomic control.

In the later part of 1992 the government became increasingly concerned about the social effects of its fiscal policy, and drafted a 1993 budget with more targeted social provisions and proposals to increase revenue. Specifically, the government aimed to remove the many exemptions to the standard VAT and corporate income tax rates which had been introduced in 1992, but these proposals encountered strong resistance within the parliament.

During its first two years of independence the Kazakhstan government pursued reasonable fiscal stringency, avoiding the temptation to finance expenditure by excessive credit creation. Membership in the ruble zone reinforced this stance, both by placing limits on the National Bank of Kazakhstan's capacity to issue credit[24] and by continuing to provide cheap credit from the Central Bank of Russia. Once Kazakhstan had exited from the ruble zone, even stricter budget deficit reduction would be necessary in order to control inflation.[25]

CONCLUSIONS

The economic situation in Kazakhstan is among the most promising in the former Soviet republics. The economic reforms are progressing, not as quickly as in the Baltic republics, Kyrgyzstan, or even Russia, but faster than in the other nine former Soviet republics. Kazakhstan's advantage lies in the resource endowment that promises medium-term relief from the short-term economic problems of transition from central planning to a market-oriented economy.

President Nazarbayev has received far more favorable international press coverage than has President Karimov of Uzbekistan, but he is no liberal, and political opposition is kept on a tight rein in Kazakhstan. Nevertheless, the economic atmosphere in Tashkent and that in Almaty were in sharp contrast by the autumn of 1993. Tashkent appeared to be closing off again after a brief economic spring, while Almaty was a freewheeling city where deals could be brokered and fortunes made.

The immediate prosperity in Almaty is fueled by foreign money. Large oil and mineral contracts that require official approval and participation have surely contributed to the rampant corruption, but people in authority tend to use their position to let things happen (and then take a cut) rather than to obstruct and delay.[26] Also, small Chinese traders are much more evident in Almaty than in Tashkent. They are surely attracted by the greater wealth, but geography helps, too. The China trade is responsible for many of the cheap consumer goods that are more readily available in

Almaty, and a good part of the Chinese traders' profits appears to be channeled back into the Kazakhstan economy through the casino.[27]

The optimistic assessment is not to deny the severity of the immediate problems or the necessity to make difficult policy choices. Average income levels have declined sharply since 1990, and the bottom of the trough has not yet been reached. This decline has been accompanied by widening income inequality, repressed unemployment, which will surely become open unemployment in the near future, and increased poverty. Social services are deteriorating, leading especially to concern about the provision of health care.[28] President Nazarbayev maintains tight political control, but unless the majority perceives some improvement in its living standards in the near future, popular discontent could emerge.[29]

Despite the emphasis in official propaganda given to the stability of the Nazarbayev regime, the Wild West strategy carries high political risks. The nouveaux riches in their Cadillacs, Lincolns, Mercedes, BMWs, and Volvos are ostentatiously displaying their wealth, while the majority of the population feels itself worse off with high prices, declining public services and increasing health dangers. Whether the new class will be a target for popular discontent or a role model to be emulated will determine on whether Kazakhstan goes the way of Iran (to populist revolution and economic ruin) or of Hong Kong (to economic success). It is difficult to envisage a more moderate path being found in the near future.

The major policy decision in the short term will concern fiscal and monetary policy. If the government is tempted to increase spending on social services, poverty alleviation, or simply cushioning enterprises and workers against the adverse effects of economic reform, then it will almost certainly increase the budget deficit. In the underdeveloped financial system of Kazakhstan, a fiscal deficit can be financed only by outside assistance or by money creation. In 1993 Kazakhstan received aid from international institutions as well as the credits from Russia, but these will be insufficient to finance any major expenditure increases.[30]

The key monetary policy decision in 1992 and 1993 was whether to exit from the ruble zone. This step, finally taken in November 1993, could provide the opportunity to reduce inflation by adopting a tight monetary policy (as the Baltic states have done), but that would involve further reduction in the budget deficit. Alternatively, introduction of a national currency could be used to finance an increasing budget deficit, which would lead to higher inflation (as in Ukraine) and would undermine the economic reform process.

In sum, Kazakhstan's long-term economic prospects are bright. Policies adopted in the first two years after independence have set the country on the right path for economic success. The sweeping victory by supporters of

President Nazarbayev in the March 1994 parliamentary elections was widely interpreted as providing a mandate (despite election irregularities) and strengthening his ability to accelerate the reform process.[31] Nevertheless, politically difficult macroeconomic policy decisions will still have to be taken in the near future, and they will determine whether the economy will move from its present situation to the potentially positive future outcome.

CHAPTER 7

Tajikistan: Civil War

TUCKED IN the southeast corner of the USSR, Tajikistan was the poorest Soviet republic. The territory is mostly mountainous, with the two highest peaks in the Soviet Union, and settlement is concentrated in the valleys of the north and southwest. With the fastest-growing population in the USSR (see Table 7.1), Tajikistan suffered from population pressure and high unemployment even in the Soviet era.

The Tajiks are distinct from the other major ethnic groups of Central Asia. Their language is Persian rather than Turkic. Their history is sedentary, and large Tajik populations still exist in the historic cities of Bukhara and Samarkand in Uzbekistan. The Pamiri people in the autonomous oblast of Gorno-Badakhshan in the eastern part of the country were officially classified as Tajik in Soviet censuses, but have distinct traditions.[1] Badakhshan is the poorest part of the country, the most inaccessible, and the area where Islam has the strongest hold.

Since independence, Tajikistan has been racked by civil war. The battle lines are extremely confused. While it is often portrayed as a battle pitting old-style communists against a strange alliance of democrats and Islamic fundamentalists, in large part it is a revival of old clan loyalties and conflicts.[2] Overlying this is a strong ethnic component born of fear of Turkic domination of Central Asia, and especially reflecting Uzbek-Tajik conflicts. Several of these elements threaten to spill over to other parts of Central Asia, reducing areas (most immediately the Fergana Valley) to new Bosnias.

HISTORY

The Tajiks have been a distinct ethnic group for over a millennium, but never formed a political unit. In the nineteenth century the northern part of present-day Tajikistan came under Russian rule, while the southern part was annexed by the emir of Bukhara.

After the Bolshevik revolution, the area was slowly brought under Soviet rule in the face of guerilla opposition. The Bolsheviks controlled the north in 1918, Dushanbe and the south in 1921, and the east by 1925. In 1929 the Tajik Soviet Socialist Republic was enlarged by the transfer of

TABLE 7.1

Demographic Profile of Tajikistan

Population (thousands)	5,728
Population density (per sq km)	40
Annual growth rate (percent)	2.6%
Crude birth rate (per thousand)	38
Crude death rate (per thousand)	7
Infant mortality rate (per thousand)	41
Life expectancy at birth	
Females	71
Males	66
Percentage of population aged	
14 or less	44%
60 or more	6%
Ethnic composition (1989 census)	
Tajiks (including Pamiri people)	62.3%
Uzbeks	23.5%
Russians	7.6%
Tatars	1.4%
Population of main towns (thousands)	
Dushanbe (Stalinabad, 1929–1961)	602
Khojand (Leninabad)	163

Sources: ESCAP, *Population Data Sheet 1993* (Bangkok: United Nations, 1993); for urban populations, Economist Intelligence Unit, *Country Profile* (Tajikistan).

Note: Ethnic composition is as of 1989; town populations are as of 1990; all other data are for 1993.

Khojand from the Uzbek SSR, and declared a full Union republic. During the 1930s the livestock sector was severely disrupted by collectivization, and Stalin reacted to local opposition by replacing almost all Tajiks in the government by Russians.

Opposition to Russian control continued to simmer, with reports of large anti-Russian riots in the 1970s. The 1970s appear to have been characterized by rising Islamic influence. Activists opposing Soviet intervention in Afghanistan were arrested after 1979. The Soviet regime severely restricted any contact with Iran after the 1978 Islamic revolution there, but could not stop the growth of cultural contacts with Afghanistan, where many Tajiks acted as official interpreters during the war.

The Gorbachev campaign against corruption led to the dismissal in 1985 of the local leader, Rakhmon Nabiyev, who had been first secretary since 1982. His successor, Kakhar Makhkamov, emphasized the need to improve the republic's economy and also allowed more open discussion. The new openness mainly led to expression of popular concern over perceived injustices, such as the treatment of Tajiks in Uzbekistan and the fairness of the boundary between the Uzbek and Tajik republics. In 1989 Tajik was declared the state language, and teaching of the Arabic script was revived in the schools.

Outbreaks of ethnic violence had been reported during the 1980s, mainly involving villagers in border areas. In February 1990 more serious riots broke out in the capital, Dushanbe. Economic discontent, focusing on shortage of housing and of employment, appears to have underlain the rioting, although the immediate catalyst was a rumor that Armenian refugees were to be settled in the Tajik republic. Some demonstrators demanded democratic reforms and more radical economic change. Violence and looting broke out, Soviet troops were called in, and over twenty people died and hundreds were injured.[3]

After February 1990, the leadership became less flexible. The state of emergency imposed during the riots remained in place, and the opposition parties (Rastokhez, the Democratic party, and the Islamic Renaissance party) were not allowed to participate in the March elections to the Supreme Soviet. In November, Makhkamov defeated Nabiyev in a vote within the Supreme Soviet for the president of the Republic. Despite the political continuity, national and religious awareness were on the rise, and Slavs and better-educated Tajiks began to emigrate from the republic in 1990. In the March 1991 referendum, an overwhelming majority voted to remain in the Union.

The internal political situation became more confused after the Moscow coup in August 1991. President Makhkamov had not opposed the coup, and in the face of mass demonstrations he resigned as president on August 31. The Tajik Supreme Soviet voted to proclaim Tajikistan an independent state on September 9 (following Uzbekistan). The chairman of the Supreme Soviet and acting president, Kadriddin Aslonov, further acceded to the demonstrators' demands by banning the Communist party. In response, the Communist majority in the Supreme Soviet demanded Aslonov's resignation, rescinded the ban on the Communist party, and declared Nabiyev president. In the November 1991 presidential election, Nabiyev received 57 percent of the vote, and although the main opposition candidate complained of irregularities, the opposition parties were temporarily silenced. In December Tajikistan became a founder member of the Commonwealth of Independent States.

In January 1992 the ruling party, which had renamed itself the Socialist Party of Tajikistan in September, reinstated its original name, giving itself the distinction of being the only Communist party governing a former Soviet republic. In March mass antigovernment demonstrations resumed, and in early May President Nabiyev reached an agreement that gave the opposition parties a third of the seats in the government. The agreement was, however, rejected in Nabiyev's home town of Khojand and in the Kulyab region in the south, both areas with large Uzbek populations. The situation degenerated into violence, fueled by the availability of weapons smuggled from Afghanistan or privatized from the Soviet army. On September 7, President Nabiyev was forced to resign at gunpoint. The opposition parties established a new government in Dushanbe under President Akbarasho Iskandarov, but communists continued to control the regional governments of Khojand and Kulyab. In October pro-Nabiyev forces reconquered Dushanbe, but were driven out within two days. By then the year's fighting had, by government estimates, led to 18,500 deaths and the creation of over 300,000 refugees.

In November a special session of parliament was convened in Khojand. The presidency was abolished, and Imamali Rakhmonov, a former state farm manager linked to the communists, was appointed speaker and effective head of state. Abdumalik Abdullajanov, prime minister of the post-September anticommunist government, kept his position. The outcome was not accepted by hardline Islamic groups and some secular democrats, and forces loyal to Rakhmonov had to fight their way into Dushanbe in December in order to allow the government access to the capital.[4] The opposition forces continued to control many rural areas, while the main population centers were in the hands of local procommunist warlords.

During 1993 government forces pushed the armed resistance onto the defensive. The military operations were organized as a CIS peacekeeping exercise under Russian command and also involving troops from Uzbekistan, Kyrgyzstan, and Kazakhstan, with the official goal of sealing the external border of the CIS against smuggling of arms and drugs. As control was reinforced over the western part of the country, Islamic supporters fled east and south. The Gorno-Badakhshan region, in which Islam has a stronger hold than in the rest of Tajikistan, was largely left to itself, in an implicit deal that the local authorities would remain nominally loyal to the Dushanbe government. Opposition attacks mainly took the form of cross-border raids from bases in Afghanistan.[5]

The broader implications of the Tajikistan civil war for Central Asia became clearer during 1993. This was the arena for the reassertion of Russian strategic interests in the region, which had been largely subdued in the first post-USSR year. The Russians referred to the invitation of the Tajikistan government for CIS military involvement and the need to protect the integrity of the southeastern border of the CIS, as well as (more ominously for Central Asia) their legitimate interest in protecting the safety of ethnic Russians living in Tajikistan.[6] Whatever the motive, Moscow was keeping its government of choice in power by force of arms. The active involvement of Uzbekistan highlighted President Karimov's desire to play gendarme of Central Asia, as well as his intolerance of Islamic opposition to secular governments.[7] Kyrgyzstan and Kazakhstan supplied troops for the CIS operations to show solidarity and because they were afraid that uncontrolled fighting could spill over into ethnic conflict elsewhere in Central Asia. China was also discreetly encouraged to warn Pakistan not to interfere, an intervention that reflected Chinese nervousness about potential Islamic unrest in Xinjiang Province.

Internally the war has been a major tragedy. At least fifty thousand people had been killed by the end of 1993, and over half a million people made refugees. The few fortunate ones with relatives abroad have fled to Russia, Germany, and other richer countries.[8] The less fortunate are homeless or in UN refugee camps high in the mountains across the Afghan and Kyrgyz borders. Economic activity, other than the trading of military hardware and opium, has collapsed.

ECONOMIC STRUCTURE

Tajikistan's economy is primarily agricultural. In 1990 agriculture accounted for 38 percent of net material product and 43 percent of employment.[9] Agriculture is concentrated in the valleys leading to the Amudarya River (which forms the border between Tajikistan and Afghanistan) and, to a lesser extent, in the north, using water diverted from the Syrdarya River. The main crop is cotton, of which Tajikistan supplied 11 percent of Soviet production. Cattle raising and horticulture are also important, and dried apricots, nuts, and grapes are exported.

Industry accounted for 29 percent of NMP and 13 percent of employment in 1990. The most important activity is mining, including gold, coal, silver, zinc, lead, antimony, mercury, and tin. Otherwise there is little heavy industry, apart from the South Tajik Territorial Production Complex described below. Major hydroelectricity projects, completed in the 1970s and 1980s, supply about three-quarters of the country's power demand.[10] The Nurek Dam on the Vakhsh River is the largest hydropower station in Central Asia, with an installed capacity of three thousand megawatts. Its output is mainly used by the Tursunzade aluminium plant, which consumes about half of the country's electricity output. The aluminium smelter, with a capacity of five hundred tonnes a year of aluminium metal, is the most modern aluminium smelter in the former USSR and it accounted for 15 percent of the USSR's aluminium capacity. Textiles, carpet-making, and food processing are the other main industrial activities.

Gold production in 1991 was around 2.5–3 tonnes, worth some $30 million at current world prices.[11] All of the gold was shipped as concentrates to Chimkent in Kazakhstan. In 1992 the first domestic gold refinery was opened in Khujand, with an annual capacity of 2.1 tonnes. The plan is to increase gold output and self-sufficiency in all aspects of gold production.

The largest mining complex is the silver-lead-zinc polymetallic mine at Andrasman, eighty-five kilometers north of Khujand. The prospects of this mine are uncertain. The Tajikistan government publicizes it as one of the biggest ore bodies in the former Soviet Union, but the ore grade is very low (0.6 percent combined lead/zinc with sixty grams per tonne of silver). The concentrates are shipped to Chimkent in Kazakhstan, and at world prices the metals in the 1991 shipments were worth no more than $6 million, which is far too small a cash flow to support a mining operation on the scale of Andrasman. Thus, western mining experts have low expectations for the economic feasibility of the mine, although selective exploitation could be feasible.

The Andrasman deposit is the prime example of a common clash of mining cultures. In the USSR geologists were expected to identify exploitable minerals in the required quantities; cost of production did not matter. In market economies, mining companies are only interested in deposits that can be exploited profitably. Claims that the Central Asian republics are rich in minerals are therefore taken with a grain of salt by foreign experts, who want to know whether the minerals can be mined economically.

Since 1991 Tajikistan has been exporting marble on a small scale. The Carrara-style marble mined at Tillogul is of high quality, and the quarry has good road connections to the railway at Samarkand, 105 kilometers away. Modern marble-cutting equipment was provided by Italian companies. Other niche exports are precious and semiprecious stones from the Pamir Mountains in eastern Tajikistan.[12]

The South Tajik Territorial Production Complex (STTPC) is by far the largest "greenfield" industrial complex in the four southern CARs. The project was conceived in the mid-1960s, with a first phase consisting of the Nurek hydroelectricity plant, the Tursunzade aluminium smelter, and an electrochemical plant at Iavan, plus infrastructure, such as a railway line from Termez (Uzbekistan) to Iavan. The first phase was completed in the mid-1980s and heralded as a triumph of Soviet engineering and technology. In practice, however, the STTPC turned out to be an "utter fiasco" (Rumer 1989, 51). The bottoms of the aluminium plant's pot liners started to disintegrate immediately, and the absence of any treatment of the effluent going into the atmosphere or water led to obvious health hazards.[13] The Iavan electrochemical plant was no better, operating at 40 percent of capacity, and plans for reconstruction were being formulated from the day it opened.

The Tursunzade aluminium plant was lauded in the Soviet press as the embodiment of "the aluminium industry of tomorrow" (Rumer 1989, 52), but now that tomorrow has come it is looking like a white elephant. Apart from its technical and environmental shortcomings, the plant was part of an economically implausible production chain. In the Soviet era bauxite was shipped from Guinea to Odessa in the Ukraine, where it was transformed into alumina before being sent by rail to Tursunzade. The aluminium ingots produced in Tursunzade were then sent by train to European Russia for processing. In the new market-oriented environment, it is doubtful whether Tursunzade can ever be a competitive producer of aluminium.[14]

ECONOMIC REFORMS

After the collapse of the USSR, Tajikistan followed Russia in introducing a price reform in January 1992. In the following spring a series of laws was passed to lay the basis for the transition to a market-oriented economy. High priority was placed on creating conditions favorable to the attraction of foreign investment. Since then, however, the civil war has disrupted the reform program. Potential foreign investors, never numerous, were further discouraged when a prominent Pakistani businessman was shot dead in September 1992 while eating dinner. The government of the Badakhstan autonomous oblast made an agreement in April 1993 with the Taxkorgan district of Xinjiang Province to establish trade joint ventures, but there is no information on the practical results of this accord (negotiated with a political eye to showing the region's independence from Dushanbe).

In 1993 economic reform and economic policy in general were characterized by paralysis. Tajikistan continued to use the pre-1993 ruble banknotes, which during the year ceased to be legal tender anywhere else. There was a certain appropriateness that the only explicitly communist regime in the former Soviet Union retained banknotes with Lenin's picture on them as legal tender, but their increasing lack of acceptability elsewhere limited exchange even with CIS partners.[15] On November 26, Russia announced a $100 million loan (presumably in the form of new ruble banknotes and credits) to assist in the conversion from old to new rubles, which would keep Tajikistan in the ruble zone—and more firmly in the Russian sphere of influence.

ECONOMIC PERFORMANCE

The economy was already in decline before the outbreak of violence in 1990 and the disintegration of the USSR in 1991. Net material product fell by 9 percent in 1989, 3 percent in 1990, and 11 percent in 1991. With the heightening of the civil war in 1992, there was an even bigger decline than in other Central Asian republics. The situation was exacerbated by poor cotton crops in 1992 and 1993.

Tajikistan has come to rely heavily on credits from Russia, and has also been promised financial assistance from Kazakhstan and Uzbekistan. Aid from outside the former USSR has been limited. A Saudi Arabian promise of $750 million made in 1991 had still not materialized two years later, ostensibly for lack of suitable projects. Turkey, anxious not to be seen as excluding Tajikistan from its Central Asian aid, has sent humanitarian aid and opened a $50 million credit line. China and India have each granted $5 million credit. Iran supplied three hundred thousand tons of fuel oil in 1992, but I have no information as to whether this was on commercial or concessionary terms; oil shortages in 1992–1993 arose as much from physical difficulties of using the old Soviet supply system as from shortage of means of payment. The multilateral agencies have had a low profile, and Tajikistan was the last of the former Soviet republics to join the IMF (in April 1993).

CHAPTER 8

Kyrgyzstan: The Switzerland of Asia

KYRGYZSTAN IS a small, mountainous republic with a population of over 4 million. During the Soviet era, the local leadership was considered a byword for conservatism, and the economy was relatively backward. In the 1990s, however, Kyrgyzstan has become the most politically open of the Central Asian republics, and is progressing fastest with economic reforms. After a brief survey of the country's history, this chapter analyzes economic developments, particularly in the postindependence period, deals with macroeconomic performance in the early 1990s, describes the economic reforms undertaken since 1991, focusing on the privatization program, and analyzes structural aspects of the economy and the future prospects.

HISTORY

The Kyrgyz had never had a formal state structure before the twentieth century. They were a collection of clans, nominally under the suzerainty of successive overlords; the last khanate, the khanate of Kokand, was incorporated into the Russian Empire in 1876. After the 1917 revolution Kirghizia was included in various jurisdictions of the USSR, gaining gradual autonomy during the mid-1920s and full Union republic status in 1936.[1] The republic's borders, especially in the densely populated Fergana Valley, reflected political considerations and did not follow precise ethnic divisions.

During the 1920s rapid progress was made on cultural, educational, and economic fronts. A standard literary language was introduced, and literacy rates quickly raised. Land reforms in 1920–1921 and 1927–1928 promoted a more settled agriculture in place of the traditional nomadic pastoralism. Collectivization of agriculture in the early 1930s was, however, strongly resisted.[2] During the 1930s many of the local communist leaders were exiled or imprisoned for espousing "national communism," and the subsequent leadership was docile towards Moscow.

From the late 1920s through the 1950s large numbers of Slavs migrated to Kyrgyzstan. They joined Russian communities who had been

TABLE 8.1
Demographic Profile of Kyrgyzstan

Population (thousands)	4,576
Population density (per sq km)	23
Annual growth rate (percent)	1.3%
Crude birth rate (per thousand)	29
Crude death rate (per thousand)	7
Infant mortality rate (per thousand)	30
Life expectancy at birth	
Females	73
Males	65
Percentage of population aged	
14 or less	38%
60 or more	8%
Ethnic composition	
Kyrgyz	52.4%
Russians	21.5%
Uzbeks	12.9%
Ukrainians	2.5%
Germans	2.4%
Tatars	1.6%
Others	6.7%
Population of main towns (thousands)	
Bishkek (Frunze, 1926–1991)	625
Osh	218

Sources: ESCAP, *Population Data Sheet 1993* (Bangkok: United Nations, 1993); for urban populations, Economist Intelligence Unit, *Country Profile.*

Note: Ethnic composition is as of 1989; town populations are as of 1990; all other data are for 1993.

living in the northern river valleys since the late nineteenth century, but the newcomers also became the backbone of the administrative and technical staff of government and industry in the republic. During the 1941–1945 war other national groups, especially Germans, were shipped away from the front line by Stalin, and although most went to Kazakhstan, some ended up in Kirghizia. At the 1989 census, out of a population of 4.3 million, 52 percent were Kyrgyz, 22 percent Russian, 13 percent Uzbek, 3 percent Ukrainian, and 2 percent German (Table 8.1). The proportion of Kyrgyz has increased slightly in the early 1990s as Slavs and Germans have left.[3] Now the most important ethnic problem involves the Uzbek minority, which is concentrated in the Fergana Valley, around the country's second town, Osh.

During the postwar period some industrial development was brought to the republic, but the economy remained predominantly rural. The industrial activities introduced were mainly processing primary products or military-related.

Despite the suppression of nationalism, tensions appeared to be beneath the surface. The 1980 murder of Sultan Ibraimov, chairman of the Kirghizia Council of Ministers, was widely believed to be a result of his support for greater autonomy. Shortly after Mikhail Gorbachev came to power, the first secretary of the Kighizia Communist party was replaced. The new leader, Absamat Masaliyev, showed little commitment to glasnost or perestroika, but in 1988 and 1989 the local press began to be more openly critical.

The key event in Kyrgyzstan's recent political history was the clash between Uzbeks and Kyrgyz in Osh during the summer of 1990. The dispute was over land and housing, but the significance lay in the difficulty the Masaliyev regime had in restoring order; in official reports 230 people died in the fighting, but unofficial figures range up to over 1,000. Meanwhile, Masaliyev had set in motion elections for the newly created post of executive president, but by the time the elections were held in October, he had been seriously discredited by his mishandling of the Osh riots. The Supreme Soviet refused to elect Masaliyev as president, and instead elected the president of the Kirghiz Academy of Sciences, Askar Akayev.

Akayev proved to be an astute politician and he withstood all attempts by the old guard to unseat him in 1991–1992. He identified with the democrats and nationalists, symbolically renaming the capital Bishkek instead of its Soviet name of Frunze (after the Red Army general who won most of the region for Bolshevism during the post-1917 civil war). In March 1991, however, Kirghizia voted overwhelmingly in favour of a renewed federation of the Soviet republics, reflecting economic realities of its close integration into the Soviet system. During the August coup in Moscow, the local communist leaders declared their support for the plotters and attempted to depose Akayev. Akayev moved quickly, dismissing potential coup leaders, such as the chairman of the local KGB, ordering troops to remain in their barracks (in defiance of the commander in chief of Soviet military forces in Central Asia based in Tashkent), and establishing contact with Boris Yeltsin. After the collapse of the coup and dissolution of the Communist party, the Supreme Soviet voted Kyrgyzstan independent on August 31. In October Akayev was elected president of the Republic of Kyrgyzstan with 95 percent of the votes cast; no other candidate was nominated. In December, Kyrgyzstan, together with the other Central Asian republics, became a member of the Commonwealth of Independent States.

Akayev is seen as the most democratic of the Central Asian leaders. This is despite his being elected president unopposed, despite the legislature's still being the Supreme Soviet (renamed the Zhogorku Keneshom) consisting mainly of appointed communist deputies, and despite a tendency of Akayev to rule by decree. What does distinguish Kyrgyzstan is a fairly active media, and the willingness of the president to tolerate open debate with his opponents. Kyrgyzstan has also a constitutional amendment requiring separation of state and religion, and is progressing fastest in Central Asia on economic reform.

As an independent country, however, Kyrgyzstan faces some harsh political realities. It is landlocked and thus dependent on a series of other countries for any outlet to the sea. Its non-CIS border is with China, and trade with China is increasing rapidly, but there is suspicion of Chinese political motives (China was a former suzerain) and popular opposition fueled by reports of Chinese buying apartments in Bishkek. Relations with neighboring Uzbekistan remain tense since 1990, and are influenced by the situation in Tajikistan. Kyrgyz troops are part of the CIS contingent fighting in Tajikistan, ostensibly to maintain the integrity of the CIS's external frontiers, but in practice to ensure that the regime favored by Russia and Uzbekistan prevails in the civil war. Kyrgyzstan has a powerful motivation to do everything possible to prevent Tajik-Uzbek ethnic tensions from erupting, because they would almost certainly spread to Kyrgyzstan's part of the Fergana Valley, with the potential of turning the country into an Asian Bosnia. The bottom line is likely to be that Kyrgyzstan will play as high a profile as possible in the United Nations, and seek to involve such powers as Turkey and the United States in a limited way, but rely ultimately on Russia for protection.

ECONOMIC STRUCTURE

During the second half of the 1980s agriculture accounted for about one-third of GDP and about the same share of employment, with the livestock sector accounting for about two-thirds of the value of agricultural output. State production of grains declined sharply in 1991, and that of livestock products declined in 1992, although some of these losses were offset by increased private production. Livestock productivity is about half of Western European levels, and much of the pastureland has been degraded. Thus, productivity gains (in terms of yield per animal) should be possible, but the size of the herds will have to be reduced to ecologically sustainable levels. Food processing and distribution facilities are technically backward, leading to much wastage and few goods available out of season.

The main positive impact of reform has been to increase the diversity of agricultural produce available to citizens of Kyrgyzstan. In the longer run,

Kyrgyzstan should have agricultural export potential in wool, tobacco, and fur. Probably the most important case of diversification and perhaps Kyrgyzstan's main export by 1993 was opium, although data are unavailable and the ramifications go beyond agriculture. If agricultural incomes rise, then the sector could play a role in generating consumer demand and savings (as in post-1978 China, although the size of the agriculture sector is much smaller in Kyrgyzstan).

Industry (that is, manufacturing, mining, and energy) accounted for about 38 percent of GDP in 1991 and employed 20 percent of the labor force. Data on the manufacturing sector are subject to uncertainty because over two-thirds of output came from Union enterprises, many of them defense related. Since independence there has been some shifting of assets within conglomerates, including some asset stripping by workers and managers, and some privatization, which has been followed by underreporting of sales. In the Soviet system machine building and electrotechnical activities were overemphasized, and light industry neglected. Government officials in Bishkek believe there is scope for developing a textile industry to add value to the wool, cotton, and silk produced in the country, but it is not often true that comparative advantage in spinning and weaving is in the raw material–producing regions. Electronics may have potential based on the skills developed in the defense-related industries, but it is unclear just how fungible those skills are (and how many of the technicians have emigrated). A more appropriate concentration is likely to be on light, not-very-skill-intensive industries, an area where the market is a better arbiter of comparative advantage than government officials.

The energy sector is important for Kyrgyzstan's immediate future because the republic is an inefficient energy user: it imports almost all of its oil and natural gas (and has a small deficit on coal and other solid fuels), and exports hydroelectricity. The World Bank has estimated that if the 1991 trade volumes had been valued at world prices, then the energy trade deficit would have been around $400 million. Energy consumption levels are high for the country's income level (they are about the same per capita as Spain's), and a priority should be rational reduction of demand; in the meantime, energy savings are made by crude measures, such as virtually eliminating air traffic (which accounted for about one-seventh of oil consumption in 1991).

Hydroelectricity is one of the country's greatest potentials. Kyrgyzstan is linked to a grid with the other Central Asian countries and exported over 5 billion kilowatt hours in 1991. In 1992 Kyrgyzstan also began to export electricity to China. Current capacity is estimated to be less than one-tenth of the amount that could be generated, and costs seem comparable to the lowest international levels. Two schemes initiated under the USSR were not envisaged to be completed before the next century, but General Electric of the United States is engaged in discussions for speeding construction of electricity generation for export.

Kyrgyzstan has a specialized mining industry, whose potential is difficult to evaluate because data were classified and mines operated without concern for commercial considerations. The main commodities by value (at world prices) in 1991 were uranium oxide, gold, antimony, molybdenum, and mercury. The uranium may not be viable under current market conditions (that is, substantial stocks and worries about nuclear power), but the gold deposits have attracted foreign mining companies.[4] Cameco of Canada has agreed to fund a $10 million study of the Kumtar goldfield in return for a 33 percent share in the joint project, with expected annual output of sixteen tons. The Bush Creek–Morrison Knudsen joint venture has made a similar agreement for a smaller deposit with expected output of four tons of gold a year.

Outside the Soviet system, Kyrgyzstan may be able to establish new activities. In the long term, the country has tourism potential due to its outstanding natural beauty and possible winter sports development, but to realize this potential will require a large effort of upgrading transport services, building hotels, and creating the other infrastructure needed for international tourism.[5]

Infrastructure improvement is an essential prerequisite for future economic growth, especially if that is to be led by exports. The rail and road network are adequate, but were constructed as part of the USSR system, so Kyrgyzstan is dependent on continued good relations with its neighbors, as well as effective transit agreements with more distant countries in order to ensure access to the sea.[6] Although Bishkek has a good airport and Kyrgyzstan received its share of the Aeroflot fleet, air services were effectively suspended in 1993 for lack of aviation fuel. This problem should be surmountable, but as long as foreign businesspeople have to fly to Almaty before taking a three-hour drive to Bishkek it will dampen the growth of international business contacts. Telecommunications pose a more serious problem as the outdated equipment is operating at high capacity, causing frequent bad connections and overloading.

ECONOMIC PERFORMANCE

Kirghizia was one of the fastest-growing Soviet republics during the final years of the USSR, with net material product increasing by 4.5 percent per year during 1985–1990 (compared to 1.2 percent in the Russian republic). The growth largely came from livestock products. Within industry the fastest-growing sectors (but from low bases) were non-ferrous metals and hydroelectricity.

Nevertheless, Kirghizia remained one of the poorest republics and benefited from substantial transfers. Official transfers from the Union to the republic were equal to over 10 percent of GDP during the last years of the USSR. Many industrial enterprises were all-Union enterprises whose local accounts are impossible to disentangle, but which benefited from net inflows. Financed from these two sources, Kirghizia ran a trade deficit equal to about 20 percent of GDP in the second half of the 1980s. The republic's trade was almost entirely intra-USSR, with external exports accounting for less than 2 percent of total exports (imports from outside the USSR amounted to about ten times more than exports, but the total was still small).[7] The republic was self-sufficient in most foods, but imported grains, oil and gas (although it had begun to export hydroelectricity), and all of its pharmaceuticals. Its main exports were wool, tobacco, and nonferrous metals.

Output began to fall in 1991, and then dropped more severely in 1992. The World Bank estimates that real GDP fell by 3.6 percent in 1991, mainly because of lower agricultural output. These estimates are subject to all the caveats applicable to USSR national accounts data in 1991, when economic reforms and inflation were starting to change relative and absolute prices. Reported agricultural production may have been particularly understated in Kyrgyzstan, because there was already a relatively large private sector and farmers may have been reluctant to let government officials know how they were adjusting their output.[8]

Even if real output fell by little in 1991, consumption levels dropped sharply. Although official transfers from the Union remained more or less constant, expenditure within Kirghizia was curtailed by a dramatic turnaround in the trade balance from the normal deficit to a large surplus (Table 4.2). One explanation for this reversal was that growing pressure to require hard currency payments hurt Kirghizia's ability to obtain imports. Probably disintegrating all-Union enterprises tried to transfer as many resources as they could from subsidiaries to headquarters (which were mostly in Russia), and they did this by reducing supplies to the Kyrgyz facilities and increasing exports from Kirghizia. Whatever the explanation, total expenditure dropped from 17 percent above domestic output in 1990 to a level almost equal to GDP in 1991. With investment holding steady at 34 percent of GDP, the entire burden fell on consumption.[9]

After the final collapse of the USSR in December 1991, independent Kyrgyzstan suffered further economic disruption and GDP fell by about a quarter in 1992 despite a good harvest.[10] There are no reliable estimates of the breakdown of expenditure in 1992, but the cumulative drop in consumption over 1991 and 1992 must have been on the order of 40 percent.

Income inequality increased during these years, so the position of the poorer members of society deteriorated considerably.

Kyrgyzstan shared in the inflation of the ruble zone, which began in 1991 and turned into hyperinflation in 1992. According to the Ministry of Economics and Finance, inflation in Kyrgyzstan was 1,259 percent in 1992 and 155 percent in the first quarter of 1993. At this point monetary policy became dominated by the question of adopting a national currency, which happened in May 1993.

ECONOMIC REFORMS

Kyrgyzstan has the most dynamic privatization program among the newly independent states of Central Asia. The Fund of State Property, a nongovernmental organization established by special decree, has been endowed with strong powers, including the right to reject other decrees that contradict its mandate. The president himself issued a ukase setting out the privatization program for 1992–1993, with a target of privatizing 35 percent of state property during these first two postindependence years. By the end of March 1993, 13.7 percent of state property had been privatized.

During the first stages of the program, priority was given to employees of the enterprise. This approach has now been rejected. Experience elsewhere, advice from the World Bank, IMF, and other international organizations, and the country's own experience have indicated that replacing state enterprises by collective property does little to increase economic efficiency.

The administrators of the Fund of State Property are aware of the contradiction between efficiency and equity criteria and are pursuing several different privatization strategies: creating joint stock companies, leasing state property, auctioning or inviting tenders for purchase, or simply selling state property. The present approach emphasizes the attraction of private funds, including foreign investors, as well as a free distribution scheme.

Kyrgyzstan has introduced a mechanism for free distribution of some property to citizens. This voucher scheme has basic similarities to schemes in Eastern Europe, Mongolia, Russia, and other former Soviet republics, but also possesses some distinctive features. Every Kyrgyz citizen receives a voucher, whose value depends upon how long the holder has worked and upon his or her salary (as proxies for each person's contribution to the state).[11] The average allocation is 4,500 rubles, with children receiving 1,000 rubles and adults up to about 20,000; an average family of four will receive a voucher valued at 16,000 rubles, consisting of 8,000 for the husband, 6,000 for the wife, and 1,000 each for the two children. The vouchers can be exchanged for shares in state enterprises, which have been valued at 1984 prices. Employees of an enterprise have first option on 35 percent of the shares, and people not employed by enterprises that are to be privatized are allowed to give their vouchers to one of eight investment funds, which have first option on 25 percent of the shares of any company. By the end of March 1993 some 60 percent of the vouchers had been distributed. It is intended to eventually privatize about half of state property in this way.

The aim of the voucher scheme is to limit the concentration of wealth, which the authorities feel would be the consequence of selling all state assets. The vouchers are nontransferable to prevent exploitation of uninformed voucher holders, although the shares are transferable (at present, however, Kyrgyzstan has no stock exchange). The allotment system is less egalitarian than other voucher schemes, and in practice may reward the old elite rather than people who have worked hardest for the country.

The shareholding system is primarily being applied to enterprises in the industrial, transportation, and construction sectors. Trade companies are being sold on the basis of bids, and most service enterprises and housing can be purchased by existing operators or occupants. Agricultural land is either "privatized" as collective property (and the farmers can decide for themselves what to do with it) or leased to the user; use rights can be inherited, but there is no private ownership of land.[12]

The eventual target is to have a mixed economy: 70 percent private and 30 percent state-owned. Railways, electricity generation, and some other activities (especially where there is a natural monopoly) would remain in the state sector. Current progress is impressive among the formerly centrally planned economies, because Kyrgyzstan is relatively poor and unattractive to foreign investment so there has been little injection of private capital. Also, the Kyrgyz privatization program has moved beyond the small service enterprises, which are everywhere the easiest to privatize. Several larger enterprises (with eight thousand to ten thousand employees) have already been privatized, and a cotton-textile enterprise with fifteen thousand workers will soon become a joint-stock company.

Despite the progress in privatization, the efficiency benefits have so far been limited. The privatized enterprises have been unwilling to dismiss employees, in part because they still face a soft budget constraint. In April 1993 a bankruptcy law was presented to the parliament and its enactment would force overstaffed enterprises to cut their labor forces or face extinction.

A major problem is the absence of many institutions needed to support a flourishing private sector. In particular, the financial sector remains at a very rudimentary stage. In December 1992 a two-tier banking system was created, with a central bank independent of the government and sixteen commercial banks. The latter, however, had no freedom of action and distributed tied credits allocated by the government. A fund for local entrepreneurship provides loans for small private enterprises; in early 1993 the fund charged annual interest rates of 15 percent when the monthly inflation rate was above that, so that the fund was effectively subsidizing enterprises, and there is no evidence that the credit was being efficiently allocated. For the larger joint stock companies, there is also a problem of unfamiliarity with management practices in private companies; general managers are used to requesting resources directly, paying little attention to cost and being unaware of the need to gain the approval of a board of directors for major decisions.

Economists tend to emphasize the benefits of privatization in increasing economic efficiency, and on this basis the Kyrgyz program is a promising one because it is moving much faster and more purposively than other Central Asian republics' programs. The Kyrgyz authorities are aware of the potential inequities that may arise from rapid privatization, but their program may not be addressing this problem adequately. The voucher scheme is regressive, in that more affluent citizens will gain a greater ownership share than poorer citizens.

An even more blatant source of inequity has been the selling off of housing to existing occupants. In a hyperinflationary situation differences in assessed value have become small by the time actual payment is made, but some citizens have acquired far better housing than others. At the top, members of the old leadership are already renting their apartments to expatriates for monthly rents of $800 or more (in March 1993 this gave a monthly rental income of over half a million rubles, when average monthly salaries were below 10,000 rubles).

The privatization program still appears to enjoy popular support in Kyrgyzstan. The main opposition comes from ministries who try to delay the privatization of property under their jurisdiction for fear that loss of property will mean loss of power. Nevertheless, if wide income gaps emerge in a situation of slow (or negative) economic growth, popular discontent could fester. On the other hand, rapid privatization, even if inequitable, avoids the phenomenon of the alienation of state assets by managers and officials, which has reached huge proportions in Albania (sometimes described as a kleptocracy since 1991), Russia, and other former Soviet republics; such privatization from within is not only inequitable, but also leads to loss of respect for the rule of law and makes the transition to a private economy more perilous in the long-run.[13]

Price reform is a necessary concomitant of successful privatization. Kyrgyzstan followed Russia's price reforms of January 1992, apparently more thoroughly than other Central Asian republics. Nevertheless, some prices remain regulated. One of Akayev's autocratic rulings followed the February 1993 increase in the price of bread. In the face of popular protest, Akayev claimed he knew nothing about the decision, and both the chairman of the bread board and the minister of agriculture were dismissed by the president. Reduction of bread subsidies was, however, essential if the budget deficit were to be controlled (and if IMF financial support were to be granted). Akayev himself announced an even larger price increase on May 11, the day after the introduction of the national currency, when people had other things on their minds, and the ruble increase had to be converted into new currency units.[14] The outcome suggests that the government remained committed to reducing subsidies and liberalizing prices, even if the method was underhand.

Potentially the most important step was the withdrawal from the ruble zone. A national currency gives Kyrgyzstan control over its own monetary policy, offering an opportunity to end the hyperinflation undermining the economic reform process; high inflation both obscures the signaling function of relative price changes and alters the distribution of wealth as savings and entitlements lose value and some forms of human capital become more valuable and others less valuable. An independent currency also offers an opportunity to abuse the power of money creation, leading to even higher inflation than in the ruble zone. The first option is illustrated by the Baltic republics, the second by Ukraine. The third option of retaining strict physical controls is incompatible with commitment to economic reforms, and probably unenforceable by Kyrgyzstan's infant government given the country's porous borders.

All of the Central Asian countries made preparations for issuing their own currencies early in 1993, but Kyrgyzstan was the first to take the definite step. The immediate cause was a chain of events with some chance elements and misperceptions about Russia's behavior (described in Chapter 11), but fundamentally the decision reflected Kyrgyzstan's greater commitment to economic reform and hence greater unwillingness to continue accepting high inflation. The introduction of Kyrgyzstan's national currency on May 10, 1993, is described in Chapter 11. The decision stimulated international financial support and permitted the pursuit of more reform-oriented financial policies.

Kyrgyzstan received immediate support from the multilateral institutions. On May 12, the IMF's Executive Board approved a SDR 16.125 million ($23 million) loan under the Systemic Transformation Facility, which had been set up less than three weeks earlier, and a SDR 27.09 million ($39 million) stand-by credit. The first tranche of IMF assistance, released immediately, was bigger than Kyrgyzstan's last reported annual hard currency earnings.[15] The next day the World Bank announced its first credit to Kyrgyzstan of $60 million through its soft loan arm, the IDA.

Cofinancing of $60 million was provided from Japan's Overseas Economic Cooperation Fund. Grants and loans also came from the United States, the Netherlands, and Switzerland. In September the IMF released a second tranche of SDR 16.125 million.

An independent currency allowed the central bank to control monetary policy. The bank doubled its refinance rate and raised commercial banks' reserve requirements to a uniform 20 percent. Interest rates were allowed to be determined by auctions for treasury bills, at which simple annual rates reached 340 percent (equivalent to an effective annual yield of over 1,000 percent because interest is compounded quarterly) by mid-October. Inflation fell from 40 percent per month in the early months of 1993 to less than 20 percent per month by the late summer. The substantial drop in inflation was less than had been targeted for, apparently because of the continued availability of overdrafts with the central bank for the specialized banks, who used the overdraft facility to extend credit to enterprises in their sectors.[16]

The more difficult parts of the reform program are still at an early stage. Apart from financial reform, the government still has to make changes in the legal code and social security system if it is to provide a suitable framework for a market economy. In the short run, however, the critical issue is whether the government seizes the opportunity provided by the introduction of the som to achieve macroeconomic stability.

CONCLUSIONS

Kyrgyzstan has undertaken the most ambitious economic reforms among the Central Asian republics (although still lagging well behind the Baltic republics). At the same time living standards have declined substantially and inequality has increased; continuation of these trends could undermine the reformers' political position. Kyrgyzstan's economic potential lies for the most part in areas that will take years to build up, such as electricity, nonferrous minerals, and tourism. In the absence of any quick route to economic growth, the temptation to ease the pain by loose monetary policies will be great, and there was already evidence of this happening in the third quarter of 1993.

The moves by multilateral institutions and bilateral donors to provide financial assistance should help to ease the short-term pain, but to the extent that they are loans they increase the costs of failing to reach a long-term growth path. The introduction of a national currency in May 1993 also significantly raised the stakes; Kyrgyzstan now had the opportunity to shed the hyperinflation of the ruble zone and emulate Estonian and Latvian success in bringing inflation under control, but there was also the temptation to follow the Ukrainian route of using monetary independence to avoid hard economic decisions. If Kyrgyzstan yields to the "Ukrainian" temptation, then that short-term solution will undermine the prospects for longer-term growth because refueling hyperinflation will encourage speculative rather than productive investments and make markets less efficient. In that setting a sound transition to a market-based economy will be impossible, living standards will stagnate, and external debts will be unserviceable.

CHAPTER 9

Turkmenistan: The Kuwait of Asia

TURKMENISTAN IS geographically part of Central Asia, but it is difficult not to think of it as an appendage.[1] Even in the nineteenth century the Turkmen clanspeople were outside the three emirates that nominally ruled the rest of the area south of the Russian Empire. The Turkmen language is more closely related to Azeri and Turkish than to the mutually close Uzbek, Kazakh, and Kyrgyz languages. Turkmenistan is the most ethnically homogeneous of the Central Asian republics (Table 9.1), and few Turkmen live outside the republic (Table 1.2).[2]

Turkmenistan is the second-largest of the Central Asian countries by area, but has the smallest population. The Karakum Desert occupies four-fifths of the territory, and some 15 percent of the country is mountainous (along the border with Iran and Afghanistan). Population is concentrated in the oases of the south (such as Ashgabat and Mary), which are linked by the railway and by the Karakum Canal, and along the Amudarya River, bordering Uzbekistan.

Construction of the Karakum Canal (begun in 1954 and completed in 1962) enabled Turkmenistan to become the second-largest cotton-producing republic of the USSR and ostensibly similar to Uzbekistan. The total sown area increased from 368,000 hectares in 1950 to over 1.3 million hectares in the early 1990s. Over half of the arable land is occupied by cotton.

Turkmenistan's cotton sector has experienced the general problems of declining yields described in Chapter 3. Salinization is a major problem, affecting at least a third of the irrigated land. Faced by rapid population growth, the government first responded by continuing to increase the area under irrigation. The Karakum Canal is being extended west, so it will be 1,500 kilometers long, imposing further claims on the water flow into the Aral Sea. More recently the government has tried to diversify crop patterns, and the area under grain increased by about two-thirds between 1989 and 1992.

In the final years of the Soviet Union, agriculture's share of the republic's output fell as natural gas came to dominate Turkmenistan's exports. After independence Turkmenistan was the only Central Asian economy with a strong balance of payments. The natural gas had been underpriced in the Soviet economic system, so Turkmenistan benefited from an imme-

TABLE 9.1
Demographic Profile of Turkmenistan

Population (thousands)	3,962
Population density (per sq km)	8
Annual growth rate (percent)	2.6%
Crude birth rate (per thousand)	35
Crude death rate (per thousand)	8
Infant mortality rate (per thousand)	55
Life expectancy at birth	
Females	68
Males	62
Percentage of population aged	
14 or less	41%
60 or more	6%
Ethnic composition	
Turkmen	72%
Russians	10%
Uzbeks	9%
Others	9%
Population of main towns (thousands)	
Ashgabat (Ashkhabad)	407
Chardzhou	164
Tashauz	114

Sources: ESCAP, *Population Data Sheet 1993* (Bangkok: United Nations, 1993); for urban populations, Economist Intelligence Unit, *Country Profile*.

Note: Ethnic composition is as of 1989; town populations are as of 1990; all other data are for 1993.

diate improvement in its terms of trade (increasing GNP by over 20 percent), as well as having the luxury of a product that could be exported for hard currency. Confident in their gas wealth, Turkmenistan policymakers often refer to their country as the Kuwait of Asia.[3]

HISTORY

The ancestors of the Turkmen migrated to the region in the tenth century, and the Turkmen emerged as a distinct ethnic group around the fifteenth century. The Turkmen tribes were under the suzerainty of Persia in the south and the Uzbek khanates of Khiva and Bukhara in the north. During the eighteenth century, the Turkmen were on the boundary of Persian and Uzbek influence, and occasionally suffered from ethnic cleansing (for example, when the khanate of Bukhara captured Merv (Mary) in the eighteenth century and deported the entire population). In 1877–1881 the

Russians waged a bloody campaign, which successfully brought the Turkmen tribes under their control. Construction of the Caspian Sea port of Krasnovodsk and the Trans-Caspian railway from there to Tashkent reduced Turkmenistan's physical isolation.

In 1917 an anti-Bolshevik government was formed in Ashgabat, which was overthrown by Soviet troops in early 1918. In July 1918, however, the Bolshevik government was overthrown by nationalists, supported by British forces. The independent government was initially protected by a British garrison, but when the British forces withdrew two years later the Red Army under General Frunze quickly reconquered the city. The Turkmen Soviet Socialist Republic was established in 1924.

In 1928 a campaign against religion led to the closing of almost all Muslim institutions. Together with the collectivization program initiated in 1929, this provoked armed resistance, which lasted until the mid-1930s. During the 1930s many Turkmen leaders, initially intellectuals but later government and party officials, were purged. Russian immigration into the urban centers was accompanied by growing Russian preponderance in leading positions. When the first secretary of the Communist party of Turkmenistan, Babayev, suggested in 1958 that Turkmen should occupy more leading positions he was dismissed.

Public expression of nationalist feeling revived during the late 1980s with the formation of Agzybirlik, which was concerned with the status of the Turkmen culture and language as well as environmental and economic issues. The new party was soon banned, and the Communist party continued to dominate the political institutions, but some concessions were made; Turkmen was made the official language in May 1990, and in August the Supreme Soviet adopted a declaration of sovereignty. In the direct elections for the newly created post of president in October 1990, Saparmuryad Niyazov was unopposed and received 98.3 percent of the votes cast.

In the March 1991 referendum Turkmenistan voted overwhelmingly to preserve a renewed federation, and President Niyazov remained silent through the August coup in Moscow. After that, however, Turkmenistan moved quickly to hold a referendum, in which independence received overwhelming support, and to declare independence on October 27. Simultaneously President Niyazov moved to establish links with the country's two key neighbors outside the USSR, making an official visit to Turkey and announcing the establishment of an Iranian consulate in Ashgabat. Despite these independence moves, which were the most purposeful among the Central Asian republics in the autumn of 1991, Turkmenistan remained a strong supporter of retaining Soviet ties, and became a founder member of the CIS in December.

Following the disintegration of the USSR, Turkmenistan retained close ties with Russia, remaining a committed CIS member even though luke-warm on economic integration. The government, however, kept its dis-tance from the other Central Asian republics, most explicitly in avoiding involvement in Tajikistan.[4] The political stance was reinforced by post-independence economic links, which were strongest with Russia and Ukraine and which looked to future ties with Turkey and Iran, but had little to do with the CARs apart from importing food from Kazakhstan.

In trying to establish new friends outside the CIS Turkmenistan ap-peared to be taking a lesson from China's panda diplomacy. Important visiting statesmen were given presents of Turkmenistan's prized Akhal Tekke horses. Equine diplomacy, however, had its pitfalls. John Major politely accepted his present, but when Turkmenistan later learned that the horse could not be imported into the UK for quarantine reasons it was viewed as a diplomatic rebuff (later resolved by a British cavalry regiment being given special permission to accept the horse). Ali Rafsanjani took his gift horse in a more positive spirit by leaping on the horse's back to show his equestrian skills, but unfortunately the horse had not been bro-ken and the rider had to be dragged unceremoniously off the horse before relations with Iran (not to mention Rafsanjani's person) suffered disrup-tion. Gifts to Boris Yeltsin, Turgut Ozal, Helmut Kohl, and Bill Clinton were handled more smoothly.

Domestically, the leadership remained conservative. Niyazov an-nounced that the Communist party would remain the ruling party, al-though its official name was changed to the Democrat Party of Turkmeni-stan in December 1991. The two small opposition parties are subject to constant harassment. During the visit of the U.S. secretary of state, James Baker, in February 1992 the leaders of these parties were placed under house arrest. A year later when a delegation monitoring the Helsinki agreement visited Ashgabat, they were informed that there were no dissi-dents for them to meet.

Under the Soviet regime social conditions improved substantially. Less than 3 percent of the population was literate in the early 1920s; the liter-acy rate had been increased to over 90 percent by the 1950s. Health ser-vices had also been dramatically improved from a primitive base, al-though on such measures as infant mortality Turkmenistan continued to hold the worst record in the USSR.

ECONOMIC STRUCTURE

Turkmenistan was integrated into the Soviet economic system with even more extreme specialization than that of the other Central Asian republics. Turkmenistan's role was to produce raw materials, and secondary indus-try remained undeveloped. Before the 1980s the main product was cotton,

TABLE 9.2
Turkmenistan's Agricultural Trade, 1992 (millions of rubles)

Imports		
Grain	7,035	(Kaz. 6,138)
Flour	1,551	(Kaz. 738, Ukr. 549)
Semolina and other flour products	1,203	(Kaz. 1,011)
All grain products	9,789	
Meat and meat products	6,410	(Kaz. 1,686, non-CIS 2,503)
Tea	3,748	(Georgia 3,717)
Milk and milk products	3,584	(Russia 1,790)
Sugar	2,386	(non-CIS 1,800)
Total	28,307	(CIS 22,153, non-CIS 6,154)
Exports		
Cotton and cotton products	49,007	(non-CIS 17,926)
Vegetable oil	1,492	
Wool	583	
Total	51,768	

Source: Turkmenistan Ministry of Agriculture.

with irrigation provided by the Karakum Canal, at great ecological cost. During the last years of the USSR, however, the Turkmenistan economy enjoyed relative prosperity, based on the rapid expansion of natural gas production.

The agricultural sector employed over 40 percent of the labor force at the end of 1991. This sector is highly dependent on irrigation and heavily concentrated in cotton. Since 1990 the government has encouraged the expansion of food crops, but Turkmenistan remains a heavy food importer (Table 9.2). The country also exports karakul (Persian lamb) skins.

The industrial sector employed about a tenth of the labor force, and the only industries that developed were related to the primary products. The biggest branch is light industry, producing two-fifths of industrial output in 1991, of which 85 percent came from sixty-one textile enterprises.[5] In some of the smaller branches, production was extremely specialized (for example, a petrol pump factory in Mary or a gas oven producer in Ashgabat), serving the entire Soviet Union; such enterprises are in deep trouble now that the captive market has gone, especially as some factories date from the prewar industrialization drive and have obsolete equipment. Other significant branches are the oil refineries, food processing, production of construction materials, and a chemicals industry concentrated in Chardzhou, in eastern Turkmenistan.[6]

Today the economy is dominated by natural gas, and to a lesser extent oil and energy production. Natural gas is believed to account for 70 percent of GNP, and forms most of the country's exports (see Tables 3.4 and 3.6). It is used for almost all of the electricity generated in Turkmenistan, of which about a third is exported (mostly to Kazakhstan). Officials are optimistic about future prospects. So far only a quarter of the territory has been thoroughly surveyed, but it is thought that as much as 85 percent of Turkmenistan may lie over gas or oil deposits.

During the late 1970s Turkmenistan was producing 15 million tonnes of petrol a year, but this declined drastically during the 1980s—a phenomenon blamed on the diversion of Soviet investment to the oil fields of Siberia. The two oil refineries at Krasnovodsk and Chardzhou each have a theoretical annual capacity of 8 million tonnes, but because of technical inefficiency are only running at about 60 percent of capacity; even this level is beyond local supplies, so one refinery refines Russian oil and the other refines oil from Kazakhstan and Turkmenistan.

ECONOMIC POLICIES

The flourishing gas exports ensure that the fiscal constraint is less severe than in other former Soviet republics. The danger is that it permits short-run profligacy, which stores up future problems. Basic foodstuffs (flour, rice, sugar, etc.) remain heavily subsidized. Electricity, water, and gas are provided free for household use. Little urgency is being shown to introduce realistic pricing of irrigation water, despite the ecological disaster of the Aral Sea (of which water diverted by the Karakum Canal is a major cause).

Turkmenistan also has industrialization plans reminiscent of 1950s import substitution policies; for example, construction of iron and steel mills is being discussed, under the optimistic assumption that new technology allows them to be economic even in a country of some 4 million people. Local officials see the lack of self-sufficiency and the dependence on inputs from and processing facilities in other former Soviet republics as major economic problems. For example, most of the cotton is exported to textile mills elsewhere. Since independence, fifteen mills have been commissioned in cooperation with foreign companies, with the goal of having 30 percent of Turkmenistan's cotton locally processed by 1995.

In the short term the problem is a Dutch disease one. Especially after the introduction of the national currency in November 1993, the gas exports are likely to ensure that few other traded-goods activities will be profitable. There may be some argument then for subsidizing diversification, but there is also a danger that activities will be promoted that make little economic sense. The existence of a populist and highly personalized presidency, in which economic power is centralized in the Council of Ministers, rather than diffused among individual ministries, increases the likelihood of the gas rents' being spent on high-profile but economically unsound projects; for example, investigation of the feasibility of iron and steel mills was ordered directly by the president. While Turkmenistan's immediate future is bright, policymakers run the risk of contracting a long-term Australian (or Argentinian) ailment.[7]

The government is committed to economic reform and to the eventual goal of creating a market economy, but it is reluctant to relax its control over the economy. Turkmenistan followed Russia's January 1992 price reform, but within a week some of the price increases were rolled back and some liberalized prices were brought back under control. Since then, although some liberalization has occurred, Turkmenistan has not followed through by liberalizing prices by as much as the other CARs. Consequently goods in Turkmenistan's shops are cheaper than in neighboring Kazakhstan or Azerbaijan, but the selection is little better than in the Soviet era. Thus, while in 1992–1993 the government feared that bargain seeking by residents of other ruble zone members would empty Turkmenistan's shops, it was Turkmenistan residents who were making shopping excursions, packing the Baku-Krasnovodsk ferry with their bundles of goods purchased in Azerbaijan.

In other reform areas, there have been some radical steps on paper, but the actuality is of an economy that remains under strict state control.[8] On privatization, the Turkmenistan government early took the radical step of permitting private ownership of land, but actual privatization was minimal.[9] In the financial sector, there is a gap between legislation removing limits on interest rates and the absence of any competitive banks. Even before the introduction of the manat, the government enforced strict foreign exchange controls.

By 1993 economic reform had ground to a halt as official ideology proclaimed the success of the reform program. President Niyazov received honorary doctorates in political science and in economics, and he was elected to Turkmenistan's Academy of Sciences for his contribution to economic reform. He was also elected to membership in the recently renamed Niyazov Academy of Agricultural Sciences.

A degree of xenophobic paranoia was creeping into Turkmenistan's policies in 1993. To protect itself from anticipated floods of ruble-dumping shoppers in the wake of other countries' currency reforms, Turkmenistan imposed high taxes on practically all exports (exceptions were made for goods bought in hard currency stores) and banned export of valuables (antiques, furs, caviar, snake venom, etc.), construction materials, and electronic goods. The decision to introduce an independent currency in

November 1993 appears to have been both an assertion of economic independence and a defensive measure triggered by the Russian central bank's July 1993 announcement that it would no longer accept pre-1993 rubles (see Chapter 11), and not at all related to motives of macroeconomic stabilization as a prerequisite for successful transition.

ECONOMIC PERFORMANCE

Turkmenistan shared in the general decline of output and rapid inflation during the early 1990s, but both were more moderate in Turkmenistan than elsewhere in the former USSR. The lack of thoroughgoing economic reforms limited the pressures for economic restructuring and the ongoing price controls repressed inflation. Moreover, Turkmenistan enjoyed a sharp improvement in its terms of trade in 1992–1993 as a result of the shift from Soviet to world prices (Table 4.3), so national income increased even though the volume of output was falling.

The terms of trade gain required hard bargaining, because the physical infrastructure constrained Turkmenistan's choice of export markets. Negotiations with Ukraine over the price of natural gas lasted from March until September 1992 before a compromise was reached. Ukraine needed Turkmenistan's gas, but the pipeline route meant that Turkmenistan had either to sell to Ukraine or to negotiate transit rights, where Ukraine could be expected to levy heavy tolls or simply divert some of the gas passing through (as Russia alleged was being done with Russian gas exports to Western Europe).

Barter deals with Ukraine and Georgia in 1993 again tied a large portion of Turkmenistan's natural gas exports to non–hard currency markets (and in both cases, to countries whose economies might well be unable to produce the goods promised in the barter deal).[10] Turkmenistan is trapped by existing infrastructure into supplying gas to markets that will only pay a fraction of the world price, or leaving its main natural resource untapped. The long-term solution to realizing the maximum benefit from Turkmenistan's natural gas (and oil) endowment is obviously to construct new pipelines, but these are expensive, take time, and require delicate political assessment of alternative routes.

CONCLUSIONS

The otherness of Turkmenistan within Central Asia has been emphasized since independence by the extreme personalization of the government. Approaching Ashgabat on a Turkmenistan Airlines flight, passengers hear a recorded message extolling the prosperity of the country under the far-sighted and benevolent leadership of President Niyazov. A street in the capital and the Karakum canal have already been renamed after the president, government offices all have posters featuring him in benevolent and statesmanlike poses, and children wear T-shirts with his picture.

Politically, the regime is a repressive throwback based on strict control and propaganda. A referendum on January 15, 1994 posed the question of whether Niyazov's presidential term should be extended to 2002. With 99.9 percent of the electorate voting, 1,959,408 said yes to the extension, 212 voted against it, and there were 17 spoilt ballots.

Economically, the strategy is to use the rents from natural gas to keep the population content with an essentially unchanged economic system. Gas, water, and oil are free to households, and other essentials have subsidized prices. In the Ten Years of Welfare program, the president has promised everybody a house, car, and telephone within a decade of independence. The necessary condition for this to be achieved is that the natural gas and oil continue to flow and fetch good prices.

National aspirations and the desire for economic independence will be best served by broadening Turkmenistan's potential trade partners, so that the country does not feel threatened by economic blackmail from a dominant purchaser of its exports or by a dominant supplier of crucial inputs. This should not be difficult to achieve over the medium term. In particular, completion of the rail link to Iran by 1995 will provide an alternative outlet to the Russian rail network and the Caspian Sea port through which most of Turkmenistan's trade now passes.[11] Construction of new gas and oil pipelines and electricity networks to a variety of foreign countries will also contribute to greater economic independence. These links, integrating Turkmenistan into the international, rather than the Soviet, division of labor, offer an economically sounder solution to the fear of economic dependence than the ill-advised attempt to pursue an import-substituting industrialization strategy.

The reality may be grimmer if the Ten Years of Welfare program empties the treasury and encourages inflationary financing of budget deficits. The present government seems likely to be tempted along this route, and to try to hide symptoms of failure by imposing exchange and price controls. Turkmenistan is fortunate to be located over a gas field, but even that may be insufficient to avoid the bad consequences of poor economic policies.

Part Three

COMMON PROBLEMS AND
FUTURE PROSPECTS

CHAPTER 10

The Choice of Development Strategy

THE PROBLEMS and challenges facing the Central Asian governments after independence fall into three categories. This chapter analyzes development issues, focusing on the gap between aspirations to emulate the East Asian newly industrializing economies (NIEs) and policymakers' instincts to repeat the mistakes of import-substituting industrialization. The next chapter considers the more immediate problems of transition, and especially the crucial question of macroeconomic policy and its relationship to the decision of whether to adopt a national currency. Chapter 12 deals with economic aspects of the countries' international relations. In practice these three categories are likely to be intertwined; in 1992–1993, for example, a desire to maintain close political ties with Russia made it more probable that a country would try to remain in the ruble zone, losing macroeconomic policy independence and, in the short run at least, having serious difficulty initiating export-led growth.

AVOIDING THE MISTAKES OF THE 1950S AND 1960S

The newly independent Central Asian republics are in a situation that is in many ways similar to that of the newly independent countries of Asia and Africa in the 1950s. At that time, following the breakup of the colonial empires, policymakers were faced with a clean slate. Of course, there was a specific historical background, but these governments could make a fairly free choice on crucial issues, such as trade policy, the balance between public and private control of economic activity, whether to encourage or discourage particular sectors of the economy, and so forth. Once these initial decisions had been taken, subsequent policy change was made more difficult because vested interests favoring the status quo had been created. Following the disintegration of the last great European empire in 1989–1991, the former colonies of Russia also have a once-in-a-lifetime chance to make fundamental economic policy decisions.

The encouraging news from the 1950s and 1960s is that the newly independent countries as a group enjoyed historically rapid growth. Of course, this was aided by favorable conditions in the world economy, and some countries did much better than others. Nevertheless, there does appear to be some evidence that independence and the accession of a modernizing regime committed to economic development can itself have a beneficial impact on economic growth.

The bad news is that for most of the developing countries of the 1950s and 1960s, the growth performance started to flag after the initial burst. Even worse, many countries fell into patterns of stagnation, which seemed to be direct consequences of the policy decisions made shortly after independence. Thus, the general assessment of those policy choices is now negative. This is especially so, given that some developing countries adopted different policies and were successful in generating self-sustaining economic growth.

The core of the economic strategy adopted by countries across the developing world in the 1950s had three components—inward-oriented policies, distrust of market mechanisms, and favoring of industry at the expense of agriculture. The overall strategy is usually referred to as import-substituting industrialization (ISI). The reasons behind the dominance of this strategy are manifold, but it reflected distrust of markets (especially international markets) after the experience of colonialism and of the post-1928 depression and a conviction that a modern economy was an industrial economy.

The theoretical arguments against an ISI strategy are now well known; in fundamental respects, they are the content of international trade theory. Moreover, the practical shortcomings of ISI and the advantages of a more outward-oriented strategy are now widely recognized after the success of the Asian newly industrializing economies. Nevertheless, the temptation to use a little protectionism remains strong. In the CARs this temptation is supported by pressure from the state enterprises to grant them protection in order to alleviate the inevitable adjustment costs of moving to a market-oriented economy and by government budget needs which can be met by trade taxes.

Rejection of the ISI strategy should also allow us to reject the size fallacy. Projections of growth in developing countries from the early 1960s all overestimated the potential of large countries, such as India, Pakistan, and Egypt, while underestimating the potential of the smaller countries that later became known as the NIEs.[1] This is a natural consequence of assuming that ISI is the best development strategy, because then the countries with the largest domestic markets have the best prospects for prolonged import substitution. This belief also lay behind the many failed attempts to establish regional trading arrangements in Latin America; the goal of LAFTA, LAIA, the CACM, and similar structures was to create a larger protected market for the participating countries' industrial goods. The integration schemes all failed because although members wanted a bigger market for their own inefficient industries, they were not prepared to support the high-cost producers of their partners.

The size fallacy is incredibly resilient to casual observation. In Europe as well as in developing countries the argument that a larger market is essential for economic health is a recurring one, despite the counterexample of Switzerland. In fact, a scatter diagram plotting size against per capita income reveals no relationship (Nordhaus, Peck, and Richardson 1991, 323). The NIEs as a group are fairly small economies, and they, like Switzerland, prove the point that if you pursue an outward-oriented strategy, then your effective market is the world market.

Thus, the first and biggest lesson to be learned from past development experience is that neither an ISI strategy nor a large internal market is a necessary condition for economic growth.

OUTWARD-ORIENTED DEVELOPMENT STRATEGIES

The key components of an outward-oriented strategy are threefold. First, establish a realistic real exchange rate and a trade policy that is neutral between producing exports or import substitutes. Second, remove obstacles to obtaining inputs (including imported inputs) and capital, as well as to tapping export marketing expertise. Third, create a stable domestic economic background. The third point is vague and reflects an ongoing debate over the role of the government in the successful NIEs. These governments did provide public goods (infrastructure) and macroeconomic stability, although there is debate over whether they went further in supporting export activities.

The process of export-led growth varied quite considerably among the NIEs. It is often believed that once the favorable conditions described in the previous paragraph had been established, then the rest was simply a matter of tapping a huge unskilled labor pool. This may have been true of Taiwan and South Korea and to a lesser extent Hong Kong during the 1960s, but it is much less appropriate as a description of Singapore, where the unskilled labor supply soon dried up. Indeed all of the NIEs had by the late 1970s and early 1980s started to move up the quality ladder, away from unskilled labor–intensive goods to goods involving more skills; even within the archetypical labor-intensive good, clothing, "Made in Hong Kong" changed from being a sign of low price to being a sign of high quality.

This is encouraging for the CARs because their starting point is one where they have higher living standards (and human capital) than most developing countries. Indeed, they could not compete on low wage costs with the large transition economies of China and Vietnam. The international evidence, however, is that low wages are not the only basis for export-led growth. The point of outward-oriented growth is to maximize economic well-being by pursuing comparative advantage. Economists may be poor predictors of where detailed comparative advantage lies for most countries, but that does not matter because the market will give the answer if it is allowed to.

THE ROLE OF THE GOVERNMENT

Other lessons are less clear-cut, but may be important because they involve complements to the adoption of an outward-oriented policy. The choice between market and intervention remains controversial. No economy is pure laissez-faire, but if government intervention goes beyond a certain point then it will frustrate the adoption of an export-led growth strategy. In particular, policymakers often pay insufficient attention to the general equilibrium consequences of policy choices. Favoring industry, for example, invariably discriminates against agriculture by changing relative prices, increasing the cost of agricultural inputs, and generally drawing resources away from the agricultural sector. If policymakers respond too readily to requests for special treatment then the output mix is distorted and fails to match the welfare-maximizing output mix. This was, of course, a basic failure of Soviet-style planning and much of the adjustment cost associated with the transition to a market-oriented economy is nothing other than the need to change the output mix from the highly distorted pre-1992 pattern.

Providing infrastructure is a valid and important government function, although just how important it is remains unclear. The original NIEs had good infrastructure, but China has grown rapidly since 1978 despite inadequate electricity and internal transport networks. The CARs have a reasonably good infrastructure in many respects, as a legacy of the USSR's emphasis on electrification and education, but terrible transport networks for promoting exports outside the CIS—all roads, railways, and air routes led to Moscow. The CARs desperately need road, rail, and pipeline links to seaports, but given the geography, these will be expensive projects.

Thus, good government will matter, but it will be important to recognize the limits of government. To many observers, the biggest problem facing the former Soviet republics is that everybody has only known the Soviet system, where getting things done depended on the government and on connections. The hardest thing will be for the new governments to sit on their hands, especially when facing difficult problems of regionally concentrated unemployment as a result of the closing of unviable state enterprises.

The Soviet mind-set may also make it difficult to overcome the presumption that industry is inherently good. The symbol of ISI was the steel mill—which almost everywhere turned into an expensive white elephant with negative impact throughout the industrial sector as producers were forced to use expensive, poor-quality domestic steel. Ignoring the charm of smokestack industries will be easier in the resource-rich republics. Turkmenistan has the brightest short-term economic prospects because of its abundant natural gas. Kazakhstan, Uzbekistan, Tajikistan, and Kyrgyzstan are also pinning their hopes on abundant mineral and energy sources, although their economic value is still questionable. The danger here is that the rents will be squandered. Ironically, most of the economic success stories of recent decades have been resource-poor countries, while richly endowed countries such as Zaire and Zambia have performed well below expectations. The recipe for long-term economic success for a resource-rich country is not well known, but it must involve some form of reinvestment of the rents in developing human and physical capital.[2]

In sum, the first and clearest lesson is to avoid the temptation of ISI. The other and less clear lessons are to provide good government, but to also recognize the limits of government policy.

LESSONS FROM CHINA

China holds a fascination for many Central Asian policymakers, especially in Kazakhstan and Kyrgyzstan, which border China and have seen economic links expand rapidly since 1991. The combination of economic growth and political stability, as in the NIEs, has a strong attraction for those in power in Central Asia, even though there is some distrust of China's political intentions and a continuing superiority complex suggesting that little can be learned from such a poor country. Even accepting that the CARs can learn from China's experience, what are the lessons? Some observers have viewed China as a successful example of gradual transition, which can be used to refute the necessity for a Big Bang approach. I have included China in this chapter on development issues because the lessons are about development rather than transition, although clearly in China's case the two are intertwined.

The crucial difference between China and all other economies in transition is the large share of the labor force employed in Chinese agriculture on the eve of economic reform. In the late 1970s over three-quarters of the economically active population worked in agriculture, while in Eastern

Europe the comparable figure in 1989 was everywhere below one-quarter; in the USSR it was 14 percent.[3] Thus, the key components of post-1979 growth in China were to raise agricultural productivity and to transfer labor from agriculture to higher-productivity jobs in other sectors: a standard development track (Pomfret 1992). Eastern European and former Soviet Union countries faced the more quintessentially transition problem of relocating labor from inefficient activities promoted by the central planners (disproportionately in manufacturing and public administration) to more productive activities. Chinese agricultural workers had almost nothing to lose from reforms, while in the former USSR much of the labor force fears that it will suffer during the reform process.

The key elements of China's reforms, introduced in 1978–1979, were agrarian reform and the open door policy. Characterizing China's reform strategy as gradualist is simplistic. The agrarian reforms were supposed to be gradual, but once the government introduced the household responsibility system, under which farmers could choose what they produced after a certain amount of state orders had been met, the old collective farming system collapsed quickly. The open door policy, by contrast, appeared dramatic but had a gradual impact; the 1979 joint venture law allowed foreign investment for the first time in the People's Republic, but investors responded slowly until various restrictions were relaxed during the 1980s (Pomfret 1991). Similarly, foreign trade was decentralized only gradually and remains fairly controlled in the 1990s.[4]

After the introduction of the household responsibility system, agricultural output grew rapidly between 1979 and 1983 as farmers responded to the changed incentives. Higher rural incomes led to increased demand for consumer goods, and the rural sector released the labor and provided the capital to finance investment in consumer goods production. Because of restrictions on labor mobility and an underdeveloped financial system, the new activities were largely located in rural areas. The township and village enterprises expanded even more after 1983–1984, when they found foreign partners to help them produce labor-intensive manufactures for export. Export-led growth was assisted by the proximity of Hong Kong, which was being priced out of its original export markets by rising wages and land rents, and whose entrepreneurs were seeking alternative locations for exploiting physical and human capital, which was becoming obsolete in Hong Kong; the main location for secondhand machinery to make labor-intensive goods and for exploiting expertise in marketing exports of such goods was China. The most dynamic parts of China in the 1980s and 1990s have been those regions in which this process went furthest, that is, the coastal provinces of Guangdong, Fujian, Zhejiang, Jiangsu, and Shandong.

The rapid growth of agriculture in the early 1980s and then of the related township and village enterprises has been essentially market driven, with producers responding to market signals even if ownership is not well defined. Even if similar agricultural reforms were undertaken by the CARs, they would have less impact on the national economy. Not only is the agricultural sector far larger in China, but also collectivization was poorly suited to conditions in much of China (for example, there are few economies of scale in rice production). Decollectivization will be more difficult on the wheat farms of Kazakhstan, where economies of scale do exist, and in the cotton plantations, which depend upon coordinated irrigation

The manufacturing sector presents a mixed picture in China's reform period. The large state enterprises are the slowest-growing part of the economy, and many would be loss-making at market-determined prices. Some studies have shown a positive productivity response to reforms introduced in the 1980s, but the response was limited, and there is no doubt that the more market-oriented township and village enterprises have been the dynamic part of the manufacturing sector.[5]

China's state enterprises have been sustained by a dual-pricing system, which sets prices for a proportion of their inputs and output, allowing many uneconomic state enterprises to register financial profits. The dual pricing is at the heart of Chinese gradualism in enterprise reform, but it has a huge cost, due to the potential profits from arbitrage, which are partially prevented by draconian punishments but increasingly lead to corruption among those with good connections.[6] Since the beginning of the 1990s, Chinese policy has been to convert state enterprises into joint-stock companies, whose shares will be listed on the two stock exchanges opened in December 1990, but so far the government has been unwilling to cede control and has maintained majority state ownership.[7]

Financial sector reform has also moved slowly, and this sector is emerging as a serious obstacle to future growth and as the prime target for further reform in the 1990s. The lack of financial intermediaries reduces the efficiency of capital mobilization and allocation. It also makes monetary policy rather crude. The Chinese central bank has maintained price stability much better than has the Russian central bank, but each time inflation has accelerated in China, the credit restrictions adopted to curb it have appeared more arbitrary as the economy has become more diversified (Chinese inflation accelerated in 1985–1986, 1988–1989, and 1993–1994).

In sum, the Chinese model has important lessons about economic development in a labor-abundant economy. There is also a general lesson about the benefits of increased openness and specialization according to comparative advantage. China has far less to teach about the transition from central planning, because the difficult areas of reforming state enterprise and the financial sector have not been resolved, even in the favorable conditions of rapid growth. "Privatization" is an ambiguous word in the Chinese context, where property rights are unclear, but entrepreneurial behaviour has emerged from below; new enterprises have been far more important than reformed state enterprises in China, just as in East European transition economies. A similar process will be harder in the former USSR than in China, because the old state enterprises account for a much larger share of industrial activity; bypassing them still permitted high aggregate growth in China, but that is improbable in the CARs.

Whether it is a development or a transition issue, describing Chinese reforms as gradual is not helpful. A better distinction is between letting go and holding on. Chinese authorities let go of agriculture in 1978–1979 and to some extent let go of industry in the 1980s by allowing entry by nonstate enterprises. Without the former, the growth miracle would never have started, and without the latter, it would have stalled in the mid-1980s. Another aspect of letting go is the remarkable degree to which the central government has ceded decisionmaking power in economic (but not political) areas to provincial and local governments. This has permitted more market-friendly government policies in the coastal provinces, but at the cost of a serious squeeze on the national government's tax revenues. The authorities have held on to the state enterprises and to the financial sector, and these represent major unfinished business in the reform process.

Central Asian governments that try to hold on completely in the name of stability and gradualism are not following the Chinese model. Governments that let go are likely to stimulate entrepreneurial behavior, even if there is not a well-structured legal framework; economic activity can, and does, flourish in the gray area beyond the reach of tax collectors and regulators.[8] Stultifying stability produced stagnation in Turkmenistan and Uzbekistan in 1992–1993, while a more freewheeling government attitude in Kazakhstan encouraged greater economic dynamism. Too much instability, as in Tajikistan, is of course discouraging to business. Instability and lack of government control are like wine or whisky; a little is good for the economy's health, but too much can be fatal.

CONCLUSIONS

Leaders of all of the CARs have expressed admiration of East Asian development models. The presidents are especially attracted by the combination of rapid economic growth and minimal political change. They recognize that the models are based on export-led growth, but have limited understanding of how this has been achieved.

The most difficult lesson to learn is that small deviations from ideal policies can quickly add up to a different development strategy. The ease with which this can happen is illustrated by the rapid evolution of the CARs' tax systems from the simple, potentially growth-promoting systems introduced after independence in January 1992, to the myriad of special exemptions (each one having its own, possibly socially desirable, justification) that produced intrusive and distortionary tax systems in all of the CARs by the summer of 1993. The delay in introducing national currencies, due to an understandable desire to stretch out the impact period of the economic shocks of 1991–1992, was also harmful to long-term economic development—especially when staying in the ruble zone encouraged ad hoc restrictions on the financial system in order to counter distortions induced by the zone's operation (see Chapter 11).

Monetary issues are crucial in the short term because they encompass the key temptation to deviate from an effective development strategy. The temptation is to subsidize directly or indirectly groups suffering from transition (for example, by raising pensions or holding down bread prices) and to subsidize certain economic activities (whether because they are believed to have long-term potential or because the short-term social impact of closure is unacceptable). Whatever the motive, such measures involve increased government expenditures, which under current circumstances (that is, inadequate government revenues and limited opportunities to issue government debt) can only be financed by increasing the money supply. In the years following the collapse of the USSR the key question for all of the former Soviet republics was whether they would use monetary policy to control inflation or to keep providing subsidies. The choice and the CARs' response, which were complicated by membership in the ruble zone, will be analyzed in the next chapter.

CHAPTER 11

Macroeconomic Problems:
The Hyperinflationary Ruble Zone

THINKING ON both transition and development has come to emphasize the role of macroeconomic stability as a precondition for success. Thus, even if the government adopts an appropriate development strategy and deregulates prices and reforms the enterprise structure, the economy will perform poorly if the government loses macroeconomic control. The prime symptom of lost macroeconomic control is high inflation, which invariably reflects a government budget deficit financed by money creation.

All transition economies have faced problems of inflation, because changes in tax sources have been associated with declining government revenue while new demands have emerged for government expenditure. Some inflation was not undesirable, as it removed the monetary overhang that emerged in the Eastern European and Soviet economies during the 1980s, but the difficulty was to prevent short-term price increases from degenerating into hyperinflation. These problems were exacerbated in the Soviet Union by the institutional arrangements for conduct of monetary policy that emerged during the creation of the CIS. For the CARs a critical issue in 1992–1993 was whether to remain in the ruble zone or create their own national currencies.

Inflation has obvious effects on the distribution of income, which make it a political issue and easy for policymakers to decry. Even more serious for transition economies is that high inflation prevents the price mechanism from functioning effectively, because the relative price changes that should guide resource allocation are obscured by changes in the overall price level. Nevertheless, there is only limited understanding among CAR policymakers of the crucial importance of macroeconomics. They view the key economic issues as microeconomic (for example, industrial restructuring), reflecting the continuing hold of their experience with physical planning. Even when the importance of macroeconomics is recognized, there is little understanding of the interrelationships among, say, fiscal policy, monetary expansion, and the exchange rate.[1]

LIFE IN THE RUBLE ZONE

When the USSR was dissolved, all of the newly independent countries forming the CIS expressed the desire to maintain existing economic relations. Already in 1991 there had been some disruption of interrepublic trade as republics bargained for better prices for their exports and sought to prevent the outflow of subsidized goods. The drift to barter accelerated in 1992, but there was little desire to reinforce the decline in intra-CIS trade by breaking up the common currency area.[2]

The fundamental problem for the ruble zone in 1992–1993 was the failure to design an appropriate institutional framework. Russia assumed jurisdiction over the Soviet central bank (Gosbank) and, since the printing presses were physically on Russian territory, controlled the currency supply. Each republic, however, determined credit creation within its territory. Since there was no balancing mechanism for interrepublic trade, no institution within the ruble zone could exert effective monetary control. The result was an explosive increase in the money supply (100 billion rubles issued in the first quarter of 1992, 258 billion in the second quarter, and over 600 billion in the third quarter[3]), and rapid inflation.

Each country's central bank faced incentives to act as a free rider; by creating credit it could command more goods and services for its country, while the impact on inflation would be spread over the whole ruble zone. The only country big enough to exert control was Russia, and during the first half of 1992 the Gaidar government pursued a reform program supported by fairly tight monetary policy. Among the consequences of asymmetric monetary policies were increased sales from Russian enterprises to other republics, draining rubles away from the importing republics, which led to cash shortages in the latter and the proliferation of parallel currencies. Inflation accelerated after June 1992, when the Russian parliament forced abandonment of Gaidar's reform program. The new governor of the Russian central bank, Gerashchenko, favored providing loss-making state enterprises with credit.

By mid-1992 the ruble zone had become extremely complicated. Not only were various parallel currencies in circulation, but also credit rubles from different republics were being treated as having different values. While ostensibly at par with the ruble, the parallel currencies would often be accepted only at a discount (most notably in Ukraine). The market for deposit rubles was even less transparent, until late in the year when the Latvian central bank started to publish rates; at the end of 1992 the number of deposit rubles per Russian ruble was 1.50 for Tajikistan, 1.64 for Kyrgyzstan and Turkmenistan, 1.71 for Uzbekistan, and 1.80 for Kazakhstan (the CARs' deposit rubles traded at the lowest value of any CIS member apart from Ukraine). In the absence of well-functioning exchange markets, both the parallel currencies and deposit rubles encountered problems of acceptability outside their country of issue. The only universally accepted means of exchange was ruble banknotes, and even they traded in imperfect foreign exchange markets (that is, the ruble-dollar exchange rate could vary substantially across CIS countries).

The Baltic countries exited from the ruble zone during the summer and autumn of 1992 in order to regain macroeconomic control; Estonia created the kroon in June, and Latvia and Lithuania declared their temporary currencies to be sole legal tender in July and October, respectively.[4] Estonia had a fixed exchange rate, and Latvia and Lithuania had market-determined rates, but, more important, they all implemented tighter monetary policies than those of the Russian central bank. All three currencies appreciated against the ruble, and in the last part of 1992, the Latvian currency even appreciated against the U.S. dollar. By summer 1993 all three Baltic states had much lower inflation than did the ruble zone; in Latvia, the country with the most restrictive monetary policy, the monthly inflation rate was even negative. The cost of tight monetary policies was that without access to cheap credit, enterprises closed down, output fell, and unemployment increased.

In November 1992 Ukraine became the fourth republic to leave the ruble zone, when the "coupons," which had gradually taken on all characteristics of money since their first issue in 1991, were declared sole legal tender.[5] Unlike the governments of the Baltic countries, the Ukrainian government did not leave the ruble zone in order to achieve macroeconomic stability; it had no monetary targets and no plans to reduce government spending, but rather wished to gain monetary independence in order to pursue a *more* expansionary monetary policy than the Russian one. The consequence of providing limitless credit to state enterprises was accelerating inflation, which was reaching over 100 percent per month by the second half of 1993, and a fast-depreciating currency. In November the exchange rate and other prices were fixed by presidential decree, while the state order system and strict exchange controls were reintroduced. These desperate measures, trying to recapture past stability, can under present circumstances only hasten the country's economic collapse.

Thus, in the second half of 1992, membership in the ruble zone was clearly a policy choice. If a government wished to bring inflation under control, the only route in 1992–1993 was to introduce a national currency and to pursue a tight monetary policy, as the Baltic countries had done, although that route implied the closing of many state enterprises that could not survive without government credit. If a government wished to keep all state enterprises operating by meeting all their credit needs, then the falling value of the country's parallel currency would force it de facto to leave the ruble zone, as Ukraine did when faced by a rapidly rising discount on the coupon vis-à-vis the ruble.

The CARs kept a fairly low profile during the ruble zone upheavals of 1992. Parallel currencies were not introduced at the national level in the CARs.[6] Officially the countries remained committed to the ruble zone. At the October Bishkek summit of the CIS, Kazakhstan, Kyrgyzstan, Tajikistan, and Uzbekistan, together with Armenia, Belarus, and Russia, agreed to establish a single monetary system and to coordinate macroeconomic policies. Turkmenistan did not sign the agreement but continued to use the ruble. Nevertheless, the CARs were keeping all their options open. Over the winter they all contracted foreign companies to print national banknotes, so that by spring 1993 the notes would be in their central bank vaults and an independent currency could be introduced in a week if they decided to do so.[7]

During 1993 there was growing recognition that an effective ruble zone could be realized only by other countries' ceding monetary policy control to the Russian central bank. Initial plans by the newly created central banks of the CIS to create a banking union, modeled on the U.S. Federal Reserve System, had foundered on a dispute over the distribution of voting rights. Subsequent coordination efforts had also failed, and highlighted the difficulty of setting up a federal institutional system for monetary policy.[8]

Why did the CARs remain in the hyperinflationary ruble zone, when its only future appeared to be as a Russian-dominated economic sphere? Despite the drawbacks, remaining in the ruble zone had two advantages. First, ruble zone prices had not yet completely adjusted to world prices, so Russia still subsidized its ruble zone trading partners by supplying goods below world prices. Second, Russia subsidized ruble zone members by providing cheap credit, both by running trade deficits paid for by other republics' ruble credit creation and by supplying banknotes.[9]

From spring 1993 onwards, rumors of the impending issue of a national currency became common in all of the CARs; the banknotes were printed, and only a catalyst was needed. There was also considerable nervousness about Russia's intentions, especially after the appearance in March of new banknotes upon which Lenin's head had been replaced by the Russian flag. Would Russia leave the (old) ruble zone, and declare the pre-1993 banknotes worthless? This scenario threatened to come true in July when the chairman of the Russian central bank ordered the immediate withdrawal of old rubles, although that order subsequently was partly rescinded by President Yeltsin (see "Twilight of the Ruble Zone" section).

Meanwhile, it was increasingly apparent that Russia was becoming more assertive within the former USSR (see Chapter 12) and might use its creditor status for political leverage. After March the Russian central bank ceased granting credits to Azerbaijan, and this pushed the Azeris' parallel currency into being effectively the sole currency by June (given the war situation and correspondingly loose monetary policy in Azerbaijan, the manat depreciated against the ruble).[10] A similar process unfolded in Georgia during the summer of 1993.[11]

Physical problems of delivering banknotes added to uncertainty, as a delayed shipment might reflect a Russian political decision or a bottleneck in the rail network. After a lengthy period of nondelivery, Kyrgyzstan received a shipment of 21 billion rubles at the beginning of April 1993. When the banknotes were released over the next five weeks, they roughly doubled the currency supply in the republic. The Russian central bank argued that the notes should have been issued more slowly, and began to press for settlement of interenterprise debts between Kyrgyzstan and Russia, on which Kyrgyzstan was a net debtor. The bank threatened not to provide any more credit until the interenterprise debt issue had been resolved. This was the catalyst for Kyrgyzstan's becoming the first CAR to issue its own currency.

LIFE OUTSIDE THE RUBLE ZONE

The som was introduced in Kyrgyzstan during the week beginning May 10, and became the sole legal tender on May 15. Rubles were accepted in exchange for the new currency at the rate of 200 rubles per som.[12] The som was fully convertible and its exchange rate market determined, although the foreign exchange market was thin and segmented (that is, different rates appeared to be being offered at the same time in Bishkek).[13]

Despite being implemented at apparently short notice, the internal process of moving from the ruble to the som went smoothly. On Monday and Tuesday, there were reports of the som's not being accepted by traders, but as the number of rubles being turned in for conversion accelerated during the week these problems disappeared.[14]

Kyrgyzstan received immediate endorsement for its new stance from the multilateral institutions, led by the IMF, whose official position on the former Soviet republics had shifted 180 degrees over the previous twelve months, from opposition to support for independent currencies. On May 12, the IMF's Executive Board approved a SDR 16.125 million ($23 million) loan under the Systemic Transformation Facility, which had been set up less than three weeks earlier, and a SDR 27.09 million ($39 million) standby credit. The next day the World Bank announced its first credit to Kyrgyzstan, of $60 million through its soft loan arm, the IDA, with cofinancing of $70 million from Japan, the Netherlands, and Switzerland.[15]

The only real problems of the conversion period were relations with Kyrgyzstan's neighbors.[16] On the day that the som was issued, Uzbekistan closed its border with Kyrgyzstan and stopped bank transfers between the two countries. The reason given was that Kyrgyzstan ruble holders, afraid of not being able to spend their ruble banknotes at home, would flood neighboring countries with rubles, emptying the shops and pushing up prices. There is no evidence that a sudden ruble flight would have happened if Uzbekistan had not closed the border. There was an ongoing problem of rubles flowing into Uzbekistan from neighboring countries in order to purchase subsidized goods, but this reflected Uzbekistan's less-thorough price reforms and continued as long as Uzbekistan had artificially low prices and remained in the ruble zone. The immediate issue of settlement for trade and debts was resolved a month after the som's introduction, when the two countries agreed to use the U.S. dollar as the basis for bilateral interbank transactions and Kyrgyzstan acknowledged a debt of $13.3 million to Uzbekistan.

Meanwhile, Kazakhstan kept trade flowing by granting credit to its neighbor. The presidents of Kazakhstan and Kyrgyzstan held a cordial summit on June 7–8, at which President Nazarbayev was careful not to criticize the decision to introduce a national currency. The contrasting reactions of Uzbekistan and Kazakhstan suggest that the new currency was an excuse for Uzbekistan's border closing rather than the fundamental reason.[17]

Over the summer the som's exchange rate showed little clear trend. Initially it appreciated slightly against the ruble, and then started to depreciate in the late summer, but in the opaque market, these movements were obscured by bank-to-bank variations on any day. By September the market rates were around 160 rubles to the som and 6.3 som to the U.S. dollar.

Behind this vacillation of the currency, lay uncertainty over the government's commitment to a tight monetary policy. At the beginning of the year, negotiations between Kyrgyzstan and the IMF had almost collapsed on the economically important and politically sensitive question of the price of bread. President Akaev had rescinded a price increase in response to popular opposition, with the long-term implication that the budget deficit would remain large. In May, under cover of the introduction of the new currency, Akaev authorized a bread price increase, which was even bigger than the one he had overturned in February. This was a signal that the government would take tough decisons to keep the budget deficit under control, but it was not followed up on. The central bank allowed interest rates to rise substantially, but still provided backdoor credit to enterprises via the specialized banks (see Chapter 8). In September 1993, when the IMF was due to authorize release of the second tranche of its assistance, a major macroeconomic policy review was undertaken. The implementation of the recommendations of that review would be crucial to determining whether the som would appreciate as domestic inflation declined or whether the currency would follow the Ukrainian coupon into free fall.

TWILIGHT OF THE RUBLE ZONE

The ruble zone was being reduced to a group of countries torn by war or dependent on Russia politically. The latter group contained Belarus and Kazakhstan, the two former Soviet republics whose credit demands were viewed most favorably by Russia, and Uzbekistan, which was trying to minimize disruption by maintaining old trade patterns. For Kazakhstan, however, disputes over interrepublic debts grew more acrimonious in June 1993 as Russia pressured for reduction in Kazakhstan's intergovernmental debt and refused to link it to interenterprise debts (where Russian enterprises were net debtors to Kazakhstan enterprises). The situation escalated as the Kazakhstan government threatened to open direct negotiations with Asian republics in the Russian Federation,[18] and the Russian central bank responded by cutting off the supply of banknotes to Kazakhstan, leading to currency shortages in early July.

Tensions were exacerbated by the sudden announcement on July 24 by the chairman of the Russian central bank that pre-1993 ruble banknotes were being withdrawn. Russian citizens were allowed until August 7 to exchange old notes totaling up to 35,000 rubles for new, but foreigners were only allowed one day. Since many banks in Russia and in Central Asia failed to open on that day, Monday, July 26, the central bank's policy was confiscatory.[19] President Yeltsin, who was out of Moscow and apparently not informed of the decision, modified the terms when he returned to Moscow on July 26; the replacement ceiling was raised to 100,000 rubles, and the exchange deadline extended until the end of August. Old rubles continued to circulate in Central Asia and to be accepted as settlement for interrepublic transactions. Although relations with Kazakhstan and Uzbekistan were smoothed over and appeared to improve during August, the episode destroyed any residual trust in the Russian central bank.[20] Moreover, the basic decision was upheld, so Russia abandoned the old rubles for domestic transactions.

On August 19, President Niyazov of Turkmenistan had already announced that the country's new currency, the manat, would be introduced on November 1. During the first five days of November, all citizens over the age of eighteen could convert up to 30,000 rubles into manat at an exchange rate of 500:1. Enterprises' bank accounts were converted into manat at the same rate, but accounts over 50 million rubles were subject to special rules involving transfer of funds to restricted accounts. The limits on conversion rights of individuals and of enterprises represented a confiscatory element. The manat's exchange rate was set at two to the U.S. dollar. Neither of the (inconsistent) fixed rates was realistic as the manat immediately depreciated against the ruble and the dollar on the free market.[21] Turkmenistan's introduction of its national currency was widely interpreted as a reaction to the July measures in Russia, but it had been planned since the beginning of the year and is better explained as part of a broader move to economic independence by gas-rich Turkmenistan.[22]

At a September 1993 Moscow summit, Russia, Belarus, Armenia, Tajikistan, Uzbekistan, and Kazakhstan reaffirmed their commitment to ruble zone membership. The renewed ruble zone, referred to as the CIS Economic Union, obviously involved conceding monetary policy control to the Russian central bank, but the quid pro quo for the non-Russian participants was not publicized. The main purpose of this summit and another one held in October was to coordinate policy towards Tajikistan, and there is no reason to believe that Karimov or Nazarbayev saw their monetary declarations as having any more force than those made at the Bishkek summit a year earlier (just before they ordered the printing of national banknotes). In both Tashkent and Almaty, rumors of impending introduction of the national currency were ubiquitous; the only new twist by the autumn was a belief that the two leaders had a secret undertaking to make the move simultaneously.

Kazakhstan and Uzbekistan were adopting a wait-and-see approach, mainly waiting to see Russia's intentions. In October, following suppression of the parliamentary opposition to President Yeltsin, the reformers gained the upper hand in Russia. Aligning economic policies to those of Russia would now mean more rapid economic reform, especially with respect to price liberalization; a symbolic step in Russia was the complete freeing of bread prices. Also, Russia was aiming to reform its budget into a more federative one, which would reduce its ability to grant technical credits to CIS partners. Thus, developments in Russia in October were making the ruble zone less attractive to Uzbekistan, whose government was conservative on price reform, and to both Kazakhstan and Uzbekistan as recipients of technical credits.

On October 31 President Nazarbayev of Kazakhstan announced that Russia was not living up to commitments made by President Yeltsin at the recent summits. Specifically, Russia was not accepting payment in old rubles, and was demanding settlement of debts in gold or hard currency. Under these conditions, said Nazarbayev, Kazakhstan had no alternative but to introduce its own national currency within the next two or three months.

The week following Nazarbayev's announcement was characterized by monetary confusion. Uzbekistan announced that it would form a monetary union with Kazakhstan, but Kazakhstan denied this. Old (pre-1993) rubles, no longer valid in Russia or in Turkmenistan, flooded into Kazakhstan and Uzbekistan, as holders saw the conversion to new national currencies as probably their final opportunity to get rid of the potentially worthless banknotes. Traders were unwilling to accept the old notes, despite their continuing official status and market exchange rates dropped rapidly; old rubles exchanged for 4,000–4,500 per U.S. dollar in Almaty, more than double the previous week's rate, while in Tashkent five old rubles traded for one 1993 ruble. On November 5, Nazarbayev issued a decree freezing most bank accounts, so that any new deposits could only be used with government permission.

A week later Kazakhstan announced that its national currency would be introduced on Monday, November 15. Each resident was allowed one opportunity to exchange up to 100,000 rubles at the rate of 500 rubles per tenge. Also on November 15, Uzbekistan issued a temporary currency, the som coupon, at par with the ruble. Although the new currencies appeared on the same day, their different values made clear that coordination had broken down. The last-minute rush to introduce the new currencies led to a degree of chaos and rapid price increases in the face of uncertainty about the currencies' future.

In Uzbekistan shops closed toward the end of the week preceding the currency reform and did not reopen for the rest of November. During this three-week period, food could be bought at the market and some imports could be bought (at high prices) in the few dollar shops, but most nonfood items could not be purchased in Tashkent. The som coupons were first issued to pensioners and students, and then a few days later employees found that a third of their wages were in som coupons (and the remainder in bank deposits). The currency reform was essentially a withdrawal from the ruble zone, and the main measure declared 10,000 and 5,000 ruble notes void in Uzbekistan. People were allowed to deposit the void notes in bank accounts, which could be used for transfers but not to obtain cash.[23] The voiding of ruble banknotes was gradually extended to include smaller denominations. Bank accounts containing over 200,000 rubles were presumed to contain "illegal income" and were frozen for six months without interest, while inspectors dealt on a case-by-case basis with account holders seeking to prove that their bank balances were legally obtained. Even if the regulated accounts were opened up within a few months, in a high-inflation situation they would have lost much of their value. Thus, Uzbekistan's currency reform was confiscatory.

The som coupon was officially at par with the ruble, but it immediately depreciated against the ruble on the free market. The depreciation reflected in part lack of confidence in future monetary policy given the size of the budget deficit, and more immediately it reflected uncertainty.[24] The government announced that the som coupons were temporary, to be replaced by a permanent currency probably at the start of the next year.[25] Having just experienced a confiscatory currency reform, people were unwilling to hold new banknotes, which might soon be declared invalid without full compensation. The new ruble was the currency of choice, because it was convertible and could be used directly on shopping trips to Russia. People whose financial assets were too small to warrant saving in new rubles or dollars hoarded real goods. This led to shortages and petty countermeasures (for example, Tashkent metro users were limited to buying two tokens at a time because so many people were saving the metro tokens as a hedge against inflation). In sum, although the introduction of a national currency had been prepared for over a year (the som coupons actually bear the date 1992), it was not well implemented, with a very poor internal payments situation in the short term and severe damage to confidence in the monetary authorities, which would be a poor starting point for any subsequent monetary reforms.

After Armenia introduced the dram on November 22 and Moldova the leu on November 29, the ruble zone was reduced to a rump consisting of Russia, Belarus, and Tajikistan. Meanwhile, Belarus began negotiating full economic and monetary union with Russia.[26]

Tajikistan's position in the ruble zone in the second half of 1993 was unclear. The Russian central bank had ceased to provide new banknotes because the Tajikistan government's budget deficit was out of control; a common guess, quoted in the *Financial Times* (November 16, 1993, 3), placed the deficit at around 50 percent of GDP. The main medium of exchange was pre-1993 ruble banknotes, which by the end of 1993 were not accepted anywhere else, so it would have been perverse to consider Tajikistan to be in a common currency area with any other country.[27] It was, however, fitting that the only country in the former USSR with a communist government was still using banknotes decorated with Lenin's head.

The final act of the ruble zone played itself out during the second half of 1993. Once Russia had issued new banknotes and declared pre-1993 notes no longer legal tender, other ruble zone members were under constant threat that Russia might abrogate their right to settle intrazone debts in old rubles and thus make them completely dependent upon Russian assistance in building up a new ruble currency stock. Against this background, the September declaration represented a sharpening of choices. Staying in the ruble zone involved closer monetary policy coordination than before, and it became increasingly apparent that Russia interpreted this as monetary and economic union with macroeconomic policies determined in Moscow.[28] Only Belarus accepted the Russian interpretation as the basis for negotiation, while Kazakhstan and Uzbekistan (as well as Armenia and Moldova) felt they had no option other than to create independent currencies.

CONCLUSIONS

The CARs' macroeconomic policies have been heavily constrained by the slow process of their exit from the ruble zone. Initially they had no plans for independent currencies and shared in the general belief in the desirability of retaining the ruble as a common currency that would facilitate maintenance of old trade links. As the endemically inflationary nature of the ruble zone as institutionally organized in the post-USSR era became more apparent, some republics exited from the zone in order to pursue independent monetary policies. The CARs remained in the dwindling group of ruble zone loyalists, although they began to take preparatory steps for issuing national currencies, in case this should become desirable.

The main arguments for remaining in the ruble zone were the availability of Russian supplies at less than world prices and access to Russian credit. These were essentially short-run motives, because prices were being adjusted toward world prices and Russia might cut off access to credit. The long-run argument that replacing the ruble by fifteen currencies would disrupt trade among the former Soviet republics assumed second-order importance with the high inflation rates.[29] In the slightly chaotic situation of 1993, fed by continuing economic breakdown and distrust of Russian actions, the issuing of national currencies was a matter of when rather than whether, and any catalyst could set the process in motion.

That Kyrgyzstan was the first CAR to take the final step had some chance elements, but was also predictable insofar as Kyrgyzstan was the CAR most committed to economic reform. In this light, membership in a hyperinflationary currency area was uncomfortable, although once the step had been taken the Kyrgyzstan authorities were less forceful than their Baltic counterparts in adopting a tight monetary policy to bring down inflation. For less reformist countries, such as Uzbekistan, which had no real faith in the price mechanism to guide resource allocation, inflation was less of a pressing problem. For Kazakhstan, the carrot of Russian credit was an important reason to remain in the ruble zone, at least until mid-1993, but in the second half of 1993, the benefits appeared to be diminishing and ruble zone membership was leading the government to take measures inimical to economic reform (such as freezing bank accounts).

The two-year delay in addressing monetary issues was the main force imposing gradualism on the economic reform process in the CARs. Gaining macroeconomic control is central to a Big Bang approach to transition, and as long as they stayed in the ruble zone, the CARs effectively renounced the Big Bang option. Moreover, through the subsidies from Russia, the CARs who stayed in the ruble zone received material assistance in alleviating the costs of transition. Against this had to be weighed the cost of high inflation, which impeded the transition process, delaying long-term solution of the fundamental problem of falling incomes.

Introduction of an independent currency raised the stakes in the former Soviet republics. Now governments had the opportunity to gain macroeconomic stability, or to print money to pursue other goals; the Baltic republics and Ukraine illustrated the options. The key question facing the CARs in 1994 was, Which path would they take?

CHAPTER 12

Regional Relations: The Great Game, Part Two, with New Players

THE STRATEGIC interest of the great powers in the region make it a continuing powder keg. The Anglo-Russian conflict in the nineteenth century was known as the Great Game; in the 1990s the Great Game has resumed. Russia's ultimate aims in the nineteenth century were to break Britain's hold on India and to control a route to the Indian Ocean. The latter aim was revived with disastrous consequences when Soviet troops moved into Afghanistan in 1979. Since then the Soviet Union has ceased to exist, and Russia initially turned away from the region. Very quickly, it became apparent, however, that Russia had continuing interests in the region, and that the economic links established by the tsarist regime and over seventy years of communist rule provided a useful basis for creating a sphere of influence.

THE GREAT GAME, PART TWO

Between Younghusband's 1903–1904 mission to Lhasa and the collapse of the USSR in 1991, the Great Game was more or less in abeyance. Britain had a final opportunity to push back the southern border of the Russian Empire after 1917, when it had troops in Baku and in Ashgabat and a British agent, F. M. Bailey, was the most-wanted man in Tashkent, but the troops withdrew peacefully. Britain no longer had vital interests in Central Asia, and its main rival was now Germany, not Russia.

Russia took advantage of the Chinese Empire's weakness after the 1911 revolution to pull Outer Mongolia away from the Chinese sphere of influence. The Mongolian People's Republic, as it was officially known from 1924 until 1990, was unofficially referred to as the sixteenth republic of the USSR. Central Asia became an integral part of the Soviet Union during the 1920s, and any outside influence was strictly regulated. Fears that the region might come under undesirable foreign (religious) influence after the 1978–1979 Iranian Revolution or through the post-1979 Afghan War proved unfounded.[1] Indeed, the whole idea that the Islamic Soviet republics would be the major secessionists when the USSR began to disintegrate proved totally false.

Once the Central Asian republics had become independent, international relations were back on the agenda. The immediate response came from neighboring countries, from the United States as the only remaining superpower, and, more haphazardly, from the Western European countries. In 1992 these countries stepped into something of a vacuum as Russia was self-absorbed with internal problems.

China's interests appear to be largely defensive. It wants neither non-Chinese nationalism nor glasnost to spread from Mongolia, Kazakhstan, Kyrgyzstan, or Tajikistan to the Chinese frontier provinces. The revival of Islam and of Lamaist Buddhism in formerly atheist neighboring states is also a cause for concern in Beijing. Nevertheless, China is unlikely to adopt a purely defensive position, because it is tempted by the economic gains from trading with or providing transit routes to what it perceives as economically weaker neighbors.

Ethnic tensions increased in Xinjiang during the 1980s. Official reports were often silent or uninformative, but on several occasions (the best documented being in Kashgar in 1990) many people were killed by the security forces.[2] The similarities between Xinjiang and Kazakhstan are also highlighted by the growing concern about the effects of nuclear testing at Lop Nur in northeastern Xinjiang and pollution (in Xinjiang, a focus was Lake Bositang), and by the common view that the center was milking Xinjiang of its natural resources to benefit China's coastal provinces (despite an apparently large net flow of financial resources into Xinjiang). Between 1989 and 1991 Chinese leaders were deeply concerned about the failure of Gorbachev to assert Communist party power, although they maintained an official position of "noninterference" in another country's affairs (Garver 1993).

Trade between Xinjiang and the Asian Soviet republics, after being disrupted for two decades following the Sino-Soviet split, was revived in 1983. The trade during the remaining years of the USSR was not huge, consisting mainly of exchanging raw materials from Soviet Central Asia for Chinese consumer goods.

After the disintegration of the USSR, China adjusted to the new situation, quickly recognizing the successor states and signing trade agreements with each of the CARs. In March 1992 the Xinjiang Communist party secretary, Song Hanliang, called for "trade and economic and technological co-operation with various Central Asian countries." Introduction of air services between Urumqi and Almaty and Tashkent facilitated contacts, and trade flourished, especially with Kazakhstan.[3] Economic contacts are coming primarily from small traders, who are harassed by customs and other officials, but whose activities are not determined by government planners. Chinese consumer goods are plentiful in Kazakhstan and Kyrgyzstan; some of the profits have been used by Chinese businesspeople to establish joint ventures in Kazakhstan, to buy property in Kyrgyzstan, and to gamble in the casinos of Almaty. In 1992 China was by far Kazakhstan's largest trading partner outside the CIS, with trade growing from small amounts two years earlier (China's share of Kazakhstan's non-CIS imports increased from under 4 percent in 1990 to 44 percent in 1992) and, given the nature of the border trade, possibly understated in the official statistics.[4]

At the same time as economic links were blooming, repression was tightening in Xinjiang. The number of daily executions in Urumqi reached fifteen in January 1992, the highest since the early 1980s. Unrest was being fomented from across the border in the newly independent CARs; in February 1992 the Front for the Liberation of Uighurstan threatened cross-border raids from bases in Kazakhstan, and the September 1992 assumption of power in Tajikistan by a coalition including Islamic forces was even more worrying. The view that China must insulate itself from the Central Asian Republics was expressed by Wang Enmao, a former Xinjiang leader, now holding a senior position in Beijing, who shortly after the collapse of the USSR called for the erection of "a great iron wall" to protect Xinjiang against agents of hostile external forces (Harris 1993, 118).

Given these considerations, Chinese policy in the region is likely to be driven by developments in Xinjiang and in Central Asia. If the region remains calm, then trade should flourish between Xinjiang and the CARs. If separatist pressures mount in Xinjiang, the top priority will be to keep Xinjiang as an integral part of China, and trade or other concerns will be subordinate. The biggest concern for the eastern CARs is, If they become destabilized, will China try to reassert its claims to the Ferghana Valley?[5] Recent Chinese activity in the disputed Spratly Islands, off Southeast Asia, is a reminder that China is willing to use force to support territorial claims.

The position of the southern neighbors, Turkey, Iran, and Pakistan, is more complex. Turkey and Iran are in competition to create spheres of influence in the region. Iran has obvious links to the Persian-related speakers of Tajikistan and northern Afghanistan, while Turkish is intelligible to most of the other groups in former Soviet Central Asia. On the religious side, Moslems in the region are Sunni and have little in common with the Iranian Shiites. Officially the political leadership in the Soviet successor states looks to Turkey as the model of secular Islam, but it is unclear whether this has popular support, and the popular position may become radicalized with growing economic distress. The religious situation is further complicated by outside support for some radical groups, notably coming from Saudi Arabia.

At the same time as Iran and Turkey are competing for the hearts and the minds of the region, they are both members of the Economic Cooperation Organization (ECO), which is the main force for cooperation in the region. ECO's original members, Iran, Pakistan, and Turkey, were joined in 1992 by Afghanistan, Azerbaijan, and the Central Asian republics of the former USSR. ECO has a natural identity as a bloc of all the non-Arab Islamic states of western and central Asia, but whether it will become a major force or be divided by Turkish-Iranian competition for regional influence has yet to be seen. Even on narrower economic matters within ECO, there are nationalist undertones, as the three original members worry about which of them will gain greater or lesser economic influence: for example, should the essential transit route from Central Asia to the Indian Ocean terminate at an Iranian or a Pakistani port, and will Pakistan or Turkey become the preferred base for foreign firms seeking to supply Central Asian markets?

The country that lost the most influence in Central Asia with the disintegration of the USSR was India. Because of its political relationship with the Soviet Union, India was the most influential non-CMEA country in the region, at least up until the last Gorbachev years. With neither contiguity nor cultural ties, and little to offer in terms of economic relations, India's role collapsed. In 1990, India's trade with Kazakhstan was equal to that of China, but two years later it was less than a fortieth of China's trade. In 1993 India began to rebuild links more energetically, recreating some air links, and in January 1994 President Nazarbayev of Kazakhstan visited New Delhi, but India faces an uphill task in competing with other regional powers for influence in Central Asia.

Among powers outside the region, the United Kingdom has completely withdrawn and shows little diplomatic or economic interest.[6] Germany is now the best-represented Western European power in Central Asia, although the main German aim appears to be specific and defensive; by promoting local economic development, it hopes to forestall the claiming of German citizenship by the large population of German origin in Kazakhstan and Kyrgyzstan. Japan and the Republic of Korea also have some prominence, although more in commercial than political initiatives. The United States has the largest diplomatic representation in Central Asia, having moved quickly to establish embassies in all of the successor states to the USSR. The official U.S. position is to support foreign assistance for the transition economies, in order to reduce the likelihood of greater instability. The United States also clearly backs the adoption of the Turkish model of a secular Islamic country and hopes to forestall the spread of the Iranian model.[7]

In 1993 Russia began to reassert itself in the Caucasus and in Central Asia. The most obvious consequences were Georgia's application for CIS membership and Azerbaijan's decision to rejoin the ruble zone in the autumn of 1993.[8] Earlier in the summer President Yeltsin had taken a tough line with Ukraine's President Kravchuk, demanding that Ukraine hand over its nuclear weapons, its share of the Black Sea fleet, and the port of Sevastopol in lieu of unpaid debts. In Central Asia, Russia organized an alliance to enforce a military solution to the Tajikistan civil war.

Why did Russia undergo such a volte-face? In 1990–1991 the forces of reform, led by Boris Yeltsin, used decentralization as their main weapon against the conservatives who dominated the central institutions of the USSR. Yeltsin's own power base was in revived republic-level institutions, and he actively sought to cooperate with leaders of other republics. Thus he supported self-determination by the Baltic republics over the winter of 1990–1991, and cultivated close relations with the leaders of the most important republics, notably Ukraine and Kazakhstan. The new Union Treaty due to be ratified in August 1991 formalized the victory of the reformers, and provided the catalyst for the attempted coup by conservatives seeking to maintain the old Soviet Union. President Yeltsin's proposal for a union of the Slavic republics, which was extended to the loose and ill-defined Commonwealth of Independent States, was consistent with the idea of the republics' being equal sovereign states.

Through 1992 and much of 1993, Russian politics were dominated by the power struggle between President Yeltsin and parliament. In summer 1993 Yeltsin appeared to have gained the upper hand, a result confirmed in the military suppression of the parliamentary forces in late September and early October. Meanwhile, Russia started to act more assertively in the former USSR.

During the early part of 1993, Russia began using its control over credit and raw material supplies in a more discretionary fashion. Kazakhstan and Belarus were the most favored partners. In the spring, other republics were being driven away from Russian influence, as credit disputes provided the catalyst for Azerbaijan and Kyrgyzstan to exit from the ruble zone. Covert Russian support for Armenia in its April 1993 invasion of Azerbaijan and for Abkhazian rebels against Georgia threatened to destabilize the Caucasus rather than reestablish Russian influence.

As the summer progressed, Russian actions became more cohesive, and a doctrine of special relationship with the former Soviet republics was enunciated. President Yeltsin requested the United Nations "to grant special powers as a guarantor of peace and stability in the former countries of the USSR."[9] The "Monroesky Doctrine" was not accepted by the other powers interested in the region, but it did represent a significant move in the new Great Game. Hints of the desirability of forming a Transcaucasian Federation (under Russian protection) received positive responses from Armenia and Georgia, but Azerbaijan remained unwilling to accept Russian bases. In Central Asia the southern border of Tajikistan was stated to be in effect Russia's southern border, and the local regime was sustained by Russian subsidies and troops. In January 1994 Turkmenistan, under much pressure from Moscow, signed a defense pact, which included provision for Russian troops to patrol the border with Iran and Afghanistan.

Russian influence in Central Asia is based upon cooperation with the two regional powers. Kazakhstan is acutely aware of the special relationship imposed by the large number of ethnic Russians living in the country, and the leadership has retained close ties with Russia.[10] President Nazarbayev is also seeking to strengthen ties with Uzbekistan, perhaps to the point of economic federation, as a counterweight to Russian influence.[11] Uzbekistan has become the chief regional gendarme, handling local arrangements for keeping Tajikistan in the right hands (and also participating more openly in Afghanistan's civil war). The flexing of Uzbekistan's muscles causes concern among the smaller CARs, who fear irredentist claims. At the most extreme, some Uzbeks recall that the Tajik republic was part of the Uzbek SSR between 1925 and 1929 and would like to see the whole of Tajikistan reabsorbed into Uzbekistan. Less ambitiously, but equally contentiously, Uzbek nationalists cast covetous eyes on areas of Uzbek concentration in Kyrgyzstan, Tajikistan, and Turkmenistan.

Russia's December 1993 election, in which the liberal reformers did poorer than expected and the nationalist party led by Vladimir Zhirinovsky received 15 million votes, increased forebodings about Russia's intentions in Central Asia. Zhirinovsky was born and bred in Kazakhstan, and made no secret of his belief that the CARs should be returned to the Russian empire. At the same time rumors began to circulate that Russia was pursuing economic colonialism in the Causcasus (where Russia offered its services in settling the Nagorno Karabakh conflict in return for a 10 percent cut in Azerbaijan's offshore oil) and in the wider Caspian Sea area (where it was extorting high tolls for use of the only existing oil pipeline). The latter especially concerned Kazakhstan and Chevron, who were already having difficulty meeting planned sales from the Tengiz oil field because of physical losses from the leaky pipeline.

Whether Russia's resurgence will reawaken old rivalries, for example, with China in Turkestan, is still uncertain. The clearest conflict in 1993 was between Russia and Turkey. The June coup in Azerbaijan resulted in a pro-Moscow man's replacing the pro-Turkish Popular Front government. Russian action in Georgia, which turned President Sheverdnadze into a vassal, was in part aimed at securing military base rights, to prevent Turkish expansion in the Caucasus. A major prize in the Caspian area is the route for new oil pipelines, for which Turkey seemed the most likely terminus until Russia questioned these ideas in the second half of 1993. Turkey's response was to mutter about revising the 1936 Montreux Convention (guaranteeing shipping freedom through the Bosporus) to exclude oil tankers to relieve congestion and for environmental reasons. The old game has new moves as well as revised roles.

REGIONAL COOPERATION ARRANGEMENTS

With the breakup of the Soviet Union at the end of 1991, the Central Asian republics began to look south to establish new trade and other economic links. The potentially most important step was to join the Economic Cooperation Organization (ECO), which with Turkey, Iran, Pakistan, Azerbaijan, and Afghanistan forms a natural bloc of contiguous non-Arab Islamic nations. Less dramatic is the Caspian Sea Cooperation Council, involving Iran, Azerbaijan, Russia, Kazakhstan, and Turkmenistan (established in February 1992).[12] The ECO represents an attempt to promote cooperation within the region, while other organizations (including the Persian Speakers' Cultural Organization, which brings together Iran, Tajikistan, and the mujahiden of Afghanistan) appear more like pawns in the struggle among Turkey, Iran, and Pakistan to establish spheres of interest in Central Asia.

The links among Turkey, Iran, and Pakistan originate in cold war security concerns. The Baghdad Pact, sponsored in the 1950s by the United States and the United Kingdom, initially also included Iraq, and was renamed CENTO after Iraq withdrew in 1959. During the 1960s the role of the United States and the United Kingdom diminished, and CENTO became more like a regional pact than a Cold War artifact. An economic dimension was added by the creation of the Regional Cooperation for Development (RCD) in 1964, although the RCD did little before the mid-1970s. Following the 1973–1974 oil shock, the RCD was used as a vehicle to channel about $750 million in Iranian aid to Pakistan in the final years of the shah's reign.

In 1979, following the fall of the shah, CENTO was disbanded and the RCD disappeared. In 1984, largely on Iran's initiative, the RCD was revived and renamed the Economic Cooperation Organization (ECO). In the context of the Soviet occupation of Afghanistan and the Iran-Iraq War, the ECO clearly had a strategic impetus, although its practical role in the 1980s was negligible.

Following the end of the USSR, at a February 1992 summit held at the ECO headquarters in Tehran the Islamic former Soviet republics, Azerbaijan, Kyrgyzstan, Tajikistan, Turkmenistan, and Uzbekistan, became members. In the following month, Kazakhstan expressed its willingness to become a member. Afghanistan also joined ECO in 1992. The formal accession ceremony for all seven new members was held in November in Islamabad.

In February 1993 the ECO members announced the Quetta Plan of Action, aimed at achieving an integrated economy by the end of the century. A regional bank was to be established before the June 1993 Istanbul summit. The Quetta meeting, the first substantive ECO meeting since its expansion, also discussed plans for communications, transport, pipeline, and power grid networks. An initial contribution of $300,000 has been received from the three founding members, and ECO is seeking further financial support from the World Bank, UN agencies, and the Organisation of Islamic Conference (OIC).

From a geographical and cultural perspective ECO is in many respects a natural regional grouping. The members are contiguous, and include all the non-Arab Islamic countries west of India.[13]

The economic prospects of the ECO can be considered on two levels. The impetus for the enlargement and revival of the ECO was clearly the independence of the former Soviet republics. Their trade was heavily oriented toward the CMEA. One of their prime aims is to reorient trade, both to their southern neighbors and to overseas markets, for which a key prerequisite is to develop outlets to the oceans. ECO can provide the institutional framework within which such a reorientation will take place, with the landlocked Central Asian countries exporting a significantly increased amount of trade to and through Iran, Pakistan, and Turkey.[14] The institutional framework can help to coordinate the construction of infrastructure, such as railways, roads, and pipelines, as well as coordinating airline and communications services. The regional bank could also facilitate trade by reducing the financial obstacles. In general, these trade-facilitating measures should be mutually beneficial, although the value of any individual expenditure has to be assessed and compared with the cost.

The second level of discussion, which will inevitably arise, concerns the desirability of forming a preferential trading area. Here the assessment is much more likely to be negative. The economies are largely competing rather than complementary. If they reduce tariff and nontariff barriers to intra-ECO trade while retaining significant barriers to trade with third countries, the dominant effect will be trade diversion, and expensive trade diversion at that. The nearest historical parallel lies in the many Latin American integration schemes over the past three decades, which were supranational extensions of import-substituting industrialization policies. All of these schemes broke down essentially because while members were happy with the logic of creating a bigger protected market for their own products, none of them wanted to buy their partners' expensive or low-quality products. Within ECO there is likewise little scope for artificially promoting trade among members—except at a large cost in resource misallocation.

Since their countries became independent, the leaders of the CARs have made various declarations about promoting customs unions or other preferential trading arrangements. In January 1994 the presidents of Uzbekistan and Kazakhstan signed an agreement in Tashkent to create a single economic space for the two republics, allowing free movement of goods, capital, and labor, and coordination of budgetary tax, price, customs, and currency policies. The farce of "coordinated" introduction of national currencies in November 1993 and the two countries' divergent economic policies since 1991 give little reason to expect realization of this program. On February 1, 1994, Kazakhstan, Kyrgyzstan, and Uzbekistan attempted to give content to earlier declarations about creating a Central Asian Economic union by removing customs on their common borders (reported in *Transition 5*, February/March 1994, 18), but this did little more than legitimize the reality of lightly patrolled borders. Thus, over two years after independence, there had been much speculation but no content to creating Central Asian preferential trading arrangements.

The economically soundest way to proceed on the trade policy front is to liberalize trade flows on a multilateral basis, except where there may be some market power involved. Thus, there may be a role for government agencies in marketing oil, gas, mineral, and cotton exports, but otherwise these small countries would be best served by Hong Kong–style trade policies of minimal intervention. One guide to the extent to which individual CARs are thinking in this direction is their attitude toward the General Agreement on Tariffs and Trade (GATT). Acceding to the GATT guarantees nondiscriminatory access to other GATT signatories' markets, while imposing obligations to abide by the same rules in one's own trade policies. By early 1994, Kazakhstan, Kyrgyzstan, and Turkmenistan had established observer status, while Tajikistan and Uzbekistan had no ties to GATT.[15]

In the context of liberal external trade policies, removing obstacles to trade within ECO will provide added benefits, especially to the landlocked members whose major concern is to get their products through the first or last stages of the journey to and from tidewater with the minimum of cost, red tape, and delay. Thus, by securing cooperation on key infrastructure projects and promoting trade facilitation, ECO could develop as an important regional organization. Trade between the former Soviet republics and the three coastal members will grow quickly (from a low base), and ECO can provide a framework for stimulating this growth. It could also provide a forum for representing common interests. On the other hand, if ECO attempts to create a customs union aimed at helping protected industries that are unable to compete in world markets, then it could join LAFTA, LAIA, and many other regional trading arrangements in the dustbin of history.

CONCLUSIONS

Economics is closely linked to political prospects. The political and economic situation is unstable, with the only certainty being the impossibility of a return to the status quo ante 1992. All of the former Soviet republics have experienced large drops in national income, which have probably not yet reached bottom. Nevertheless, fears of a revolution like that of Iran in 1978–1979 are likely to be misplaced. Soviet Central Asia did not experience the sudden forced modernization that the shah put Iran through in the 1960s and 1970s; the comparable events in the USSR occurred in the 1920s and 1930, in the face of strong opposition in Central Asia at the time, but the current generation has grown accustomed to the amenities and nature of a posttraditional society. Less dramatic Islamic fundamentalism will, however, find a fertile breeding ground if economic deprivation increases and people lose hope in the future: this is the model of Gaza, and of the poor in Algeria and Egypt. Promoting a more tolerant or secular Islamic state, which does not need to rely upon repression of "fundamentalists"—along the model of Turkey or Malaysia—will depend very much upon economic performance.

Assuming the absence of dramatic revolutionary change, Central Asia's international relations are likely to be dominated by more traditional struggles for spheres of influence. The outcome of such struggles will have an economic dimension, in that political influence is likely to be correlated with trade patterns. Thus, if Russia is successful in reestablishing itself as the sole dominant power in the region, this is likely to be reinforced by discouraging new transport and trade links. Similarly, competition between Iran and Turkey will be tied in with decisions over transport and pipeline links to the Indian Ocean or the Mediterranean Sea.

Russia is by far the best-placed power in Central Asia. Seventy years of Soviet rule created strong economic levers. Moreover, by the end of 1993 Russia was showing greater eagerness to reassert itself, while other great powers (especially the United States and the European Union) were showing that although they might not approve, they were not prepared to do anything to stop Russia.[16] A return to the total domination by trade with Russia that existed prior to 1992 is, however, implausible. The Central Asian countries are sovereign states, even if they are weak in comparison to neighboring states. Membership in the United Nations, the IMF/World Bank, and regional banks (the EBRD and the Asian Development Bank) provide exposure to international trade possibilities and access to aid and advice for diversifying trade patterns.

In the absence of crude border-closing measures, the reverse relationship between economics and international relations will become more important. Once the rail link is completed in the mid-1990s, Turkmenistan's economic relations with Iran will strengthen, together with ties via Iran or Azerbaijan with Turkey. For Kazakhstan, Kyrgyzstan, and Tajikistan, China will inevitably become a major trading partner. Already in 1993 there were signs that these developments in western and in eastern Central Asia are coming together as improved airlinks have created a "new Silk Road" from Istanbul via Baku, Tashkent, and Almaty to Urumqi, and with the extension of the land transport network these international links will surely expand. The consequences will be to diversify not only economic but also political links beyond the region.

━━━━━━━━━━━━━━━ **CHAPTER 13** ━━━━━━━━━━━━━━━

Regional Problems and National
Economic Differentiation

BEFORE INDEPENDENCE the Central Asian republics of the Soviet Union were considered as a unit. The commonality imposed by geography remains, and some of the shared problems require, to a greater or lesser extent, joint action. On the common problem that has been the focus of this book, the economics of transition and development after the collapse of the USSR, joint action has been minimal and counterproductive when it did happen (notably in retaining a common currency). By the end of 1993 the CARs were clearly differentiated in terms of their progress in transition and in their development strategies.

This chapter first addresses the question of which regional problems still require joint action even though the CARs are independent states. The second and third sections ask why the differentiation in economic strategy occurred so sharply and so quickly. The central point of these sections is that in a complex system, a small change can have a cumulative effect; in the context of economic reform, the process develops a momentum once it has begun, or obstacles multiply once a decision to avoid rapid change has been made.

SHARED PROBLEMS REQUIRING JOINT ACTION

The borders between the CARs are all artificial. They do not follow geographical demarcations, nor do they closely parallel ethnic divisions. The region does, however, have a geographical unity, and the CAR's borders with other countries are reasonably distinct, at least in the south and west.

The dominant source of unity is the dependence on the Amudarya and Sirdarya river systems. Abuse of this natural resource in the second half of the twentieth century has led to one of the world's greatest ecological disasters, the shrinking of the Aral Sea, which demands speedy and drastic action even to arrest the decline, let alone to reverse it. All five of the CARs exploit the waters of the river system, so a solution requires negotiation on sharing the burden of reducing water use. Although the main users are Uzbekistan, Turkmenistan, and Tajikistan (and the Chimkent region of

Kazakhstan), Kazakhstan is also involved because it suffers as much as any CAR from the ecological disaster due to the wind patterns and the exposure of its agricultural sector to climatic change.

A second common feature is the landlocked nature of the CARs and the northward orientation of all transport and communications systems. The CARs obviously have much to gain from coordinated planning of new networks, especially in establishing rail and road routes to the sea and in constructing oil and gas pipelines. Such coordination is likely to be on an ad hoc basis. Pipelines from the Caspian Sea area, for example, are of importance only to Kazakhstan and Turkmenistan. Rail links, by contrast, have a regional significance. The only eastward link (apart from the circuitous Trans-Siberian route) is the Kazakhstan-Urumqi line joining the Chinese network, and the only southward link in the foreseeable future will be the Turkmenistan-Meshed line joining the Iranian network; both of these rail links, which connect to Indian Ocean and Pacific Ocean ports, have an importance for all CARs, but use by all CARs will require agreement on transit rights and costs.

A more debatable area for joint action is in the political realm, or more narrowly, in economic diplomacy. As described in Chapter 12, the CARs are the board upon which surrounding powers play their games. This may provide scope for opportunistic alliances with outside powers by individual CARs, or it may be that none of the CARs has much room for maneuver in light of Russia's still dominant position. Since independence, there have been many appeals to regional unity (and to a shared cultural heritage) but few concrete steps. Moves to establish a customs union involving some CARs are misguided and probably doomed (see Chapter 12). Participation in a wider organization, ECO, could provide some counterweight to the overbearing Russian (and to a lesser extent, Chinese) economic influence, which could be particularly important in offering alternative transport routes.

ECONOMIC DIVERSITY

In explaining the CARs' differentiation in progress along the path of economic reform, variations in resource endowment seem to matter relatively little. Turkmenistan and Kazakhstan both benefited by the move from Soviet to world prices and by having primary products that could be exported in more or less undiminished quantities. Nevertheless, they are at opposite ends of the reform spectrum. Economic policy decisions appear to have been more critical, which is surprising in view of the degree to which the CARs' leaders had shared backgrounds and fairly similar outlook.

TABLE 13.1

Unemployment in Transition Economies, 1991 and 1993

	Number (thousands)		Rate (percent)	
	Dec. 1991	Aug. 1993	Dec. 1991	Aug. 1993
Eastern Europe				
Bulgaria	419.1	603.0	11.5	16.0
Czech Republic	232.0	158.6	4.4	3.0
Slovak Republic	319.4	344.8	12.7	13.5
Hungary	406.1	675.0	7.4	13.0
Poland	2,155.6	2,829.6	11.8	15.4
Romania	386.0	1,029.8	3.1	9.0
Baltic States				
Estonia	0.9	16.2	0.1	2.3
Latvia	1.8	73.1	0.1	5.0
Lithuania	4.7	32.4	0.3	1.6
CIS				
Armenia	—	93.2	—	5.5
Belarus	2.0	62.0	<0.05	1.3
Kazakhstan	4.5	36.8	0.1	0.5
Kyrgyzstan	0.2	2.8	<0.05	0.1
Moldova	0.1	10.2	<0.05	0.5
Russia	69.0	713.9	0.1	1.0
Tajikistan	—	13.7	—	0.7
Ukraine	6.8	78.1	<0.05	0.3
Uzbekistan	—	15.0	—	0.2

Source: Transition 4, December 1993.   (— = data not available)

Leaders of all of the CARs expressed a commitment to economic reform (they had little alternative because the old system had already disappeared), while seeking to maintain political "stability" (that is, their own fairly autocratic rule). Thus, the political context was quite different from that in Eastern Europe, and to a lesser extent in the Baltic states, where the general desire for rapid overturning of the old political and economic system provided a most favorable setting for Big Bang economic reforms. One indicator of the economic caution of the CAR governments is the unwillingness to countenance open unemployment. The Eastern European countries have had high unemployment rates since the late 1980s, associated with drastic restructuring of their economies. All of the Soviet republics had negligible unemployment in December 1991. In 1992–1993 unemployment rose in the Baltic states, and to a lesser extent, in Russia; elsewhere in the CIS, including the CARs, although the number of unemployed increased, the unemployment rate remained tiny in the context of major economic restructuring (Table 13.1).

The non-Baltic former Soviet republics all fall into the category of politically stable economic reformers, but the progress in economic reform has been on a continuum that is increasingly becoming polarized.[1] At one extreme is Ukraine, where the reform process has been effectively halted as representatives of the old economic system won the policy debate. Turkmenistan and Uzbekistan appear to be following the Ukrainian path. Although they initially set up privatization processes and liberalized prices, when faced by serious choices, they were unwilling to see enterprises close down, and reforms ground to a halt (already in 1992 in Turkmenistan, and by mid-1993 in Uzbekistan). The governments of Kazakhstan and Kyrgyzstan have also been concerned about growing inequality and unemployment, but they kept the reform process moving through 1993 and it appears to be developing its own momentum.

Early decisions on whether to embrace economic reform with some real enthusiasm, or whether to worry more about the potential economic disruption, were crucial. The extent of the implementation of the January 1992 price reform is a good leading indicator of future developments (Table 4.4). Although the differences in percentage of freed prices and in how much the price of a loaf of bread was allowed to increase may seem of secondary importance, these decisions set in motion a logic of future economic policy decisions. If prices were kept artificially low, while all the countries remained in the ruble zone, then there had to be measures to prevent residents of other republics from buying the subsidized products. Thus, more limited price reform led inexorably toward controls, while price deregulation removed the need to worry about this type of arbitrage and allowed governments to concentrate on progressing further with economic reforms.

THE MOMENTUM OF ECONOMIC REFORM IN TRANSITION ECONOMIES

Economic reform in transition economies often develops its own momentum. In China since 1979, Vietnam since 1986, and Mongolia since 1990, economic reform has moved forward while the governments have remained stable. At times, notably in China, the reform process has moved ahead without any obvious government push, mainly because the central government was willing to let go in certain spheres (see Chapter 10). On the other hand, retreat from reform can also develop its own momentum when conservatives hold on to economic control.

Ukraine's experience in the early 1990s illustrates how one thing leads to another when economic conservatives are in charge. During the final months of the USSR, Ukraine was characterized by popular pressure for independence, but relatively little pressure for economic reform. The leadership that harnessed the desire for independence remained under the influence of advocates of gradual economic change (for example, managers of state enterprises). Already in 1991 Ukrainian economic policy consisted of unrestrained creation of credit in response to enterprises' requests. Shortages of banknotes led to the issue of coupons, and in 1992 both the coupons and Ukrainian ruble bank drafts depreciated against the ruble. In November the lack of any connection between the coupon and the ruble was legitimized by declaring the national currency independent of the ruble zone.

In 1993 as open inflation accelerated and people lost trust in the coupon as a store of wealth, they sought external havens for their financial assets. To counter the capital flight and retain some control over foreign exchange earnings, the government tightened regulations, forcing exporters to surrender part of their earnings at a predetermined rate. This only discouraged exports further and encouraged practices such as underinvoicing (of exports), overinvoicing (of imports), and barter trade. In August the coupon fell to over 19,000 to the U.S. dollar.

With inflation running at over 100 percent per month, President Kravchuk tried in November to deal with inflation and currency depreciation by decree. Foreign exchange transactions were permitted only for government-approved imports or exports, at an exchange rate fixed by the central bank; wholesale and retail prices were brought back under control; and the state order system was reinstated, with most enterprises required to sell part of their output to the state at a fixed price. Although apparently widely ignored, the November decrees amounted to an attempt to reimpose the old economic system, and economic reform was truly dead.[2]

The speed of Ukraine's economic collapse is remarkable. It is qualitatively different from the transitional output losses suffered by other formerly centrally planned economies. In Poland, for example, a sharp output decline after the 1990 Big Bang was an inevitable concommitant of the huge change in output mix that had to take place, but by 1993 the transitional decline was over, and the country could look with some confidence toward future economic growth. Ukraine, by contrast, saw its GDP fall by some 20 percent annually from 1991 to 1993 while its long-term economic prospects were becoming poorer and poorer.

Ukraine illustrates the dangers of gradualism in economic reform. If gradualism is allowed to become a justification for preventing any economic change, then it can lead to rapid economic collapse. Nevertheless, gradualism has sometimes succeeded; how have the Asian gradualists differed from Ukraine?

A major reason why reform processes develop their own momentum is that they create vested interests in favor of reform, which outweigh the

original vested interests opposed to change. In China and Vietnam a crucial early reform was in agriculture, giving a stake in the reform process to
a large part of the population. In a crucial sense these initial steps were
radical rather than gradual, because by changing the incentive structure
the reforms unleashed a sudden increase in level and change in composition of agricultural output. The rural sector then provided demand for
consumer goods and construction materials, as well as generating capital
and surplus labor, which could be released for light industry. Through the
1980s the rural population, still the vast majority, provided solid support
for continued economic reform, even though the benefits were increasingly
going to east-coast urban centers. In China farmers were experiencing declining relative incomes in the early 1990s and were expressing discontent,
but by then other important pro-reform groups had been established.

Agriculture cannot play quantitatively the same role in Central Asia
because it is far less important, but in Mongolia, Kyrgyzstan, and Kazakhstan, privatization of the herds may have played a positive role in
mobilizing support for reform. By contrast, agriculture in Uzbekistan and
Turkmenistan is dominated by irrigation, which makes it difficult to privatize and requires continuing government intervention to maintain the
irrigation system.

Another factor creating at least temporary support for economic reform
in the CARs was the sudden availability of foreign products. In 1992 the
new goods included obvious luxury items, but also the ubiquitous Snickers
and tapes of Western pop music. The latter surely represented a popular
revolt against the low quality of Soviet goods and the drabness of Soviet
life. At a minimum this created a group of people in their teens and twen-
ties who had no wish to return to the past (even if the most popular Western song in 1993 was "Yesterday, All My Troubles Seemed So Far
Away"), but it probably embraced far more people.[3]

Describing what has emerged still leaves open the question of why the
CARs have become differentiated in their economic reform progress. Because of their similarities, the question cannot be convincingly resolved
by cultural explanations. Personalities may have played a role, but the
leaders all had similar traits, including authoritarian tendencies and lack
of real understanding of what market economies involved. The nature
of the economies, and in particular the role of irrigation agriculture,
seems more important, but we must beware of building grand explanations on the basis of five observations (of which one is a special case due to
civil war).

Just as there is a danger of putting too much weight on any explanation,
there is also a danger of overdetermination. Economic historians used to
draw up long lists of advantages that explained why the first industrial
revolution occurred in England rather than, say, France, but the modern

tendency is to emphasize the smallness of the initial differences and how once the growth process got started in England it became self-reinforcing. On a more general plane, this is a central theme of the new growth theory, which has captured many economists' interest since the mid-1980s.

CONCLUSIONS

The Central Asian republics became independent with little preparation and a mixed inheritance. The overwhelming problems of a collapsing economic system, inflation on the verge of hyperflation, and horrendous environmental degradation required different approaches, which the new governments were ill equipped to evaluate. Environmental action, especially on the Aral Sea, must be coordinated. The task of creating new communications networks to supplement the old Soviet system will benefit from cooperation. A common approach to monetary policy, on the other hand, proved to be mistaken, and essentially wasted two years in the process of economic transition and establishment of a firmly based development strategy. Devising a new economic system poses common questions, which must be solved by each government individually; with the establishment of national currencies, these questions can be seriously addressed in the mid- and late 1990s.

The years covered by Parts Two and Three of this book, 1992 and 1993, were critical years for the CARs. They represent the first phase of transition insofar as it took this period for the CARs to take the plunge and withdraw from the ruble zone. At the same time, the future pattern of economic development was to some extent set. The cumulative process described in the previous section suggests that Kazakhstan and Kyrgyzstan may already be on the right track, and the momentum may keep them on that path. Uzbekistan and, even more so, Turkmenistan appear to have set off down a wrong trail, which may be difficult to deviate from. Tajikistan has still to set out on any post-Soviet economic path.

In a situation of autocratic regimes and powerful neighbors seeking to stamp their own influence on the CARs' economic development, it would be foolish to pretend that any forecasts are reliable. The continued existence of the CARs as independent sovereign states is by no means certain, and destructive ethnic conflict among CARs or internal strife cannot be ruled out. Assuming that the CARs do survive in reasonable peace, they will remain tied by their shared problems, but on the economic front a differentiated future of some economic success stories and some failures is the prospect for Central Asia.

National Income Comparisons for the Soviet Union and Its Successor States

It has become commonplace to add a footnote about the unreliability of national income statistics for the successor states of the Soviet Union. Some of the difficulties have been referred to in the text, but it is important to identify the sources of the unreliability and their implications for using the available estimates.[1] Some problems arise from changing objectives and lack of resources in statistical offices, but even with perfect statisticians, insurmountable conceptual problems surround some uses of economic aggregates for the early 1990s. This appendix analyzes the main sources of confusion.

Estimates for 1989–1990

Estimates of the USSR's national income in comparison to that of other countries varied tremendously. The main reason for this wide range was disagreement over the appropriate ruble-dollar conversion factor. Beside this, problems of converting net material product into GDP or GNP and basic questions of data quality were insignificant. Assessments prepared by the U.S. Central Intelligence Agency used a purchasing power parity (PPP) exchange rate and came up with estimates of per capita GNP over $9,000, while the study by the IMF, World Bank, OECD, and EBRD prepared for the 1991 Houston summit using the commercial exchange rate of 1.76 rubles/$ estimated a per capita GNP of $1,780 in 1989.

The USSR had no market-determined exchange rate. The official rate of 0.59 rubles/$ was clearly an overvaluation; applying it to the official ruble-denominated measures of Soviet output, adapted to international national accounting concepts, would yield a 1990 per capita income of $6,180. The commercial rate of 1.76 was introduced in November 1990 for the specific purpose of making export proceeds at least as attractive as domestic wholesale prices. If it achieved this (which it is widely believed to have done), then the commercial rate is an undervaluation and the per capita income of $2,070 at this rate may be considered a lower-bound estimate.

An alternative to using either of these essentially arbitrary exchange rates is to use actual transaction rates. Until the summer of 1992 the ruble had multiple exchange rates against the dollar. The Socio-Economic Data Division of the World Bank has tried to establish foreign trade price differentials (FTDs), which could be used as a more reliable conversion factor, in that they would provide a trade-weighted average of the multiple rates. Using FTDs led to a GNP per capita between $3,840 and $4,350, depending on how oil royalties and turnover taxes are treated. These figures must be treated with caution, because for Soviet policymakers the distinction between fiscal and monetary measures was immaterial, but it is crucial for separating out indirect tax and multiple exchange rate components of FTDs.[2]

The preferred solution in making internationally comparable GNP estimates for 1989–1990 has been to rely on PPP exchange rates. This has its problems because the USSR was never part of a PPP exercise involving market economies. The World Bank has used Poland as a bridge between a PPP-based CMEA study of 1986 and the International Comparisons Program (ICP), which gives a 1990 per capita GNP for the USSR of $2,870 and an implicit exchange rate of 1.27 rubles/$. Although this figure is higher than estimates using the commercial exchange rate, it is much lower than estimates based on the official exchange rate or previous estimates based upon PPP.[3]

In addition to the new USSR figure of $2,870, the World Bank has provided new estimates for the individual republics (see Table 4.1 for the figures for the five Central Asian republics). The World Bank has adjusted the official estimates of republics' GNP per capita relative to the USSR on the basis of its missions to eight republics and internal statistical analysis. The biggest change is to significantly increase Kazakhstan's relative income.[4]

Estimates for 1991

Estimates being quoted for 1991 are based on extrapolations of 1990 figures using various growth rates. During 1991, however, basic data issues became more serious. With the loosening of central control, economic behavior changed, as did the reporting of production. Private and illegal activity increased, but was underreported.[5] Especially after the August coup, there was a wave of spontaneous privatization (or expropriation of public assets), which increased the difficulty of keeping track of output changes.

Pricing issues start to be significant in 1991. With controlled prices, there was certainly repressed inflation, so using official indices of (open) inflation to deflate nominal output figures will overstate real output growth in 1991. After the January 1992 price reform, the gap between prices in state stores and in markets fell substantially, implying that some of the 300 percent price increase in January was merely a replacement of repressed by open inflation.[6]

The Independent Central Asian Republics

In 1992 pricing issues became more obviously a major problem in making income comparisons. First, the change in relative prices within an economy making the transition from central planing to a more market-oriented system leads to index number problems, which are now well-recognized, but difficult to deal with; in general, using base-year weights tends to allocate too much of the nominal income growth to inflation and too little to real output growth. Together with the shift in incentives from overreporting to underreporting, this suggests that the real income drops are likely to be overestimated. Second, the onset of high and rising inflation rates led to rapid depreciation of the ruble, so that even after a unified ruble-dollar rate was established in July 1992, it was unsuitable for making international comparisons. Third, the old USSR relativities for determining individual republics' incomes became anachronistic as inter-republic trade moved from CMEA to international prices, with terms of trade benefits for some republics and losses for others.

These added problems compounded the increasingly serious basic data issues. The Soviet republics were not fully aware of the output on their territory because some activities were run as all-Union activities organized directly from Moscow. This especially applied to defense-related projects, whose output is likely to be less important now, but many of the factories in this category also produced for the civilian market. These activities should now be included in the republics' national accounts, but that will make time series comparisons difficult and render the method of extrapolation by growth rates dubious.

The implication is that 1992 and 1993 income estimates will be even less reliable than those for 1991. Moreover, intertemporal comparisons over these years are fraught with danger. For example, Turkmenistan's real output (that is, quantities produced, aggregated by any reasonable weights) almost certainly declined in 1992, while real expenditures (that is, quantities consumed and invested, aggregated by any reasonable weights) increased because of the improved terms of trade. Thus, concepts of "economic growth" have to be carefully defined, and normally assumed identities may not apply. These are essentially transition problems, which should diminish over time.

The long-term solution is obvious. As the conceptual problems diminish with the end of the transition period, the quality of the data will depend more and more on the competence of the statisticians who assemble them. The republics will have to build up their national statistical offices and train their staff to collect and process economic statistics in a market setting, but that will take time and resources.

The National Income Accounts and Material Well-Being

In market economies the use of per capita national income as a proxy for material well-being is imprecise, but defensible. Since for most countries gross national product (GNP), gross domestic product (GDP), gross national expenditure (GNE), and national income all follow similar time paths, any of these aggregates divided by population would provide some guide to the rate of increase in economic well-being.[7]

There are well-known caveats. Economic growth brings bads as well as goods, illustrated by the pollution in rapidly growing cities, such as Bangkok or Taipei, and may be unsustainable if it is achieved by running down the natural capital stock, which is not included in the national accounts as depreciation. On the other hand, the rate of growth may be understated in national income accounts because inflation is overestimated as a result of the rapid rate of introduction of new products (a similar index number problem to that described above) and improved models of old products.

Bailey (1991), writing before the end of the Soviet Union and thinking of other continents, has argued that economic liberalization improves economic well-being in ways not captured in the national accounts: "When a country liberalizes, a flood of imports enters the country, giving consumers the opportunity to buy modern foreign products that had previously been unavailable. Marketplaces that were previously rather colorless come alive with a diversity of goods. In many cases long waiting lines for necessities disappear" (13). This description is even more appropriate to the former Soviet Union than to the countries Bailey is writing about (Chile, Ghana, Mauritius, and Turkey).

Bailey goes on to emphasize that using GNP growth as the standard measure understates the gains from trade.[8] Bailey illustrates the undermeasurement of the gains from international trade with a hypothetical example of a country that exports only cotton, imports food (vegetables), and produces manufactured goods (refrigerators) behind prohibitive trade barriers. The hypothetical country sounds like a CAR except that the cotton and vegetables are traded domestically at world prices; the domestic price of refrigerators is five times the world price. After trade liberalization all domestic prices are equal to world prices, and the local currency is devalued by 50 percent. Table A.1 summarizes preliberalization and postliberalization prices and quantities for the three goods produced in Baileyland.

TABLE A.1

Prices and Quantities in a Hypothetical Liberalizing Economy

	Preliberalization			Postliberalization		
	Cotton	Vegetables	Refrigerators	Cotton	Vegetables	Refrigerators
Price	100	100	500	200	200	200
Output	100	50	10	120	110	0
Exports minus imports	50	−50	0	70	10	−80
Consumption	50	100	10	50	100	80

Source: Bailey 1991, table 8.

Notes: Prices are in domestic currency units; output, exports, imports, and consumption are quantity measures, with units selected so that the preliberalization world price is 100 domestic currency units.

In Baileyland higher prices for cotton and vegetables have stimulated output growth, while lower prices for refrigerators have wiped out the industry. Nominal GNP has increased from 20,000 to 46,000 currency units. The GNP deflator is 2.0 (the price of all current outputs has doubled), so real GNP has increased by 15 percent. Using consumption weights to calculate the price index would indicate much larger gains in "apparent real income"; the Laspeyres price index (using preliberalization consumption weights) is 1.6, which gives a real growth rate of 44 percent, and the Paasche index is 1.2 (not 1.44, as in Bailey [1991, 23]), with a growth rate of 92 percent. Using an "ideal" index, averaging the two, gives a postliberalization real income of 32,857 currency units, that is, a growth rate of 64 percent. Thus, in this example, a consumption-weighted deflator yields a growth rate over four times higher than the conventional measure using the production-weighted deflator. "The conventional growth measure entirely excludes the part (of the gains from trade) that goes with increased imports of consumer goods" (Bailey [1991, 22]). Moreover, this is in addition to the new model or quality effects; the imported refrigerators are likely to be superior to the no-longer-sold domestic models.

Nobody has attempted to measure these benefits to consumers in the transition economies of the 1990s. The standard growth measures are easier to compile, despite the huge difficulties in the USSR and the CARs, although it is often unclear precisely how the price deflators are really constructed. Nevertheless, the producer bias of the workers' states is being subtly reinforced in the postreform national accounts by the emphasis on output measures. Casual observation strongly suggests, however, that consumers in the CARs place a huge value on their newfound ability to obtain imported consumer goods.

Finally, the significance of the word "material" in the notion of material well-being should be stressed. The centrally planned economies performed worst at providing differentiated consumer goods that matched their citizens' preferences, but they did much better at satisfying basic needs. Compared to any plausible counterfactual, the CARs' citizens benefited from being inside the USSR in terms of health care, education, and housing. Standards of health care provision have fallen dramatically since independence, as subsidies have been removed and the provision of medical inputs has been disrupted. Other public services also face the prospect of serious decline; law and order had visibly broken down in 1993 in some areas. Although national accounts (unlike the old Soviet measures of material product) include such services in GNP, there is no good output measure for health, education, policing, the arts, and so forth; the most common proxy is simply to measure inputs (cost of teachers, police, etc.). In all of these areas, the CARs may have become poorer since independence, although where culture is concerned, economists have little to contribute.[9]

Conclusions

The major statistical issue in the final years of the USSR was how to make international comparisons, and the key question was the appropriate exchange rate. Table 4.1 presents plausible estimates of the CARs' income levels in 1990. Since then, the main issue has been the rate of economic growth in the individual CARs. There are huge measurement problems and some predictable biases. Estimates of the post-1990 decline in output must be viewed as approximations, which are better than nothing, but which are to be used with caution, especially in drawing conclusions as to welfare. Terms of trade changes and loss of interrepublic transfers created a substantial wedge between GNE and GNP. Since the former is measured by adjusting GNP for trade flows, both GNE and GNP are based on output measures, which understate the benefit to consumers from price and trade liberalization. Thus, material well-being has surely declined by less than the measured fall in GNE per capita, but we do not know by how much less. Against this, nonmaterial aspects of well-being have probably declined (apart from increased freedom and national independence), and income inequality has likely increased.

Ten Economic Lessons from
the Former Soviet Union

1. Most economists underestimated just how poor centrally planned economies were at producing consumer goods in line with people's preferences. The Soviet economy was terminally ill by the late 1970s, and half-hearted perestroika under Gorbachev did not cure it. Even more drastic reforms in Hungary and workers' self-management in Yugoslavia failed to work anywhere near as well as more market-oriented economies. This underestimation represented a failure by most economists to appreciate how powerful neoclassical analysis is in the long run.

2. Neoclassical theory is less useful in explaining the huge output losses incurred during the transition from central planning to a more market-oriented economy. Drastic changes in the output mix take time, and labor markets do not clear; that is, in the short run, markets are imperfect.

Another shortcoming of neoclassical economics is its lack of emphasis on the role of governments in providing the framework for markets. Outside observers underestimated the extent of government failure in newly independent countries. Creating a government structure is not simple, especially in areas of macroeconomic and foreign policy, where the CARs had absolutely no experience. Lack of an efficient structure has, however, hindered implementation of key policies necessary for the functioning of a market economy (for example, contract law, antimonopoly provisions, bankruptcy law, financial sector supervision).

3. The drop in output was exacerbated first by the breakup of Comecon, and then by the disintegration of the former USSR. This economic effect is unsurprising, but a deeper lesson is that economic history should not be ignored. Stories from the successor states of the Austro-Hungarian Empire, for example, of boxcars being held at the border for fear they would not return, have counterparts in the republics of the former Soviet Union. Especially with public assets, which are difficult to value, possession is nine-tenths of the law, so self-interested (or self-protective) behavior cannot be condemned or easily avoided, but breaking up a rail network (or the Aeroflot fleet) imposes costs.

Another lesson from post-1919 for post-1991 is the propensity of successor states to lose control over their newly independent currencies (Dornbusch 1992; Garber and Spencer 1994). Those who do not learn from the mistakes of history are condemned to repeat them.

4. The apparently most useful and in practice most irrelevant branch of economic theory to the CARs' situation has been the optimal currency area literature. This literature could be interpreted as justifying the ruble zone as an optimal currency area, but in 1992 staying in the ruble zone was a disaster because monetary policy was not optimal. Russia's failure to control its budget deficit and the existence of multiple centers of money creation posed insoluble problems for monetary control.

5. Customs union literature, however, is useful to counter the common idea that the CARs should seek to maintain a customs union. The best trade policy for a small economy is free trade, and that leaves no room for discriminatory trade policies. Few countries pursue this ideal, largely because vested interests prevent removal of trade barriers, but the former Soviet republics are fortunate to be starting with a clean slate.

One lesson that could be emphasized for the CARs is the failure of the policies of import-substituting industrialization adopted almost universally by developing countries in the 1950s. Several successor states are now reacting to the overspecialization of the Soviet economy by trying to be self-sufficient in almost everything; if this aim is supported by protectionist trade policies, it will be a recipe for long-run economic stagnation.

6. International advisers have a role to play, and this was especially true for the CARs with little experience of macroeconomic management. But foreign experts can be wrong. The IMF, for example, in early 1992 pushed the newly independent republics to retain the ruble zone, and discouraged conflicting advice as liable to confuse policymakers. A year later the IMF was advocating national currencies with floating exchange rates.

The lesson is that two-handed economists are desirable, despite the jokes and despite the desire by policymakers to be told the right answer. Economics is imprecise, and most policy choices involve uncertainties as well as trade-offs. The argument that policymakers in the CARs will be confused by conflicting advice is patronizing; it is their job to sift out appropriate from inappropriate advice.

7. Foreign investors will not come rushing into a country just because they are now permitted. This is also a lesson from China, where direct foreign investment grew very slowly for half a decade after the 1979 Joint Venture Law, then fluctuated during the second half of the 1980s, and only really took off in the 1990s. The Chinese also found that you do not always get what you want: officials sought hi-tech joint ventures with impressive hardware, but most joint ventures have been in labor-intensive activities.

This fits with China's comparative advantage, and the managerial and export-marketing expertise have been the most valuable components of the foreign investment package.

8. Sequencing was the big debate immediately after the changes in Eastern Europe in 1989. The main lesson from Latin America and from Poland is that macroeconomic stabilization must come first. The CARs have not yet added much to this debate, although as separate national currencies are created and independent monetary policies are pursued, they will present a controlled experiment.

9. Privatization was also hotly debated, and many schemes devised. Privatization in practice has so far come "from below," that is, by buying small-scale enterprises or by starting from scratch. Large state enterprises have been more difficult to privatize, because of valuation problems and concerns about equity. In the absence of extensive privatization from above, however, many ex-Soviet republics are experiencing privatization from within, as managers, employees, or officials appropriate state property. This is almost surely the worst form of privatization on both efficiency and equity grounds. The lesson is that privatization schemes should be persevered with despite the difficulties; almost any privatization from above would be better than privatization from within.

10. Agriculture first (the Chinese model) is a good strategy because planning worked poorly in this sector and increased agricultural output has many beneficial linkage effects. Full privatization is less important than allowing farmers to enjoy any additional output. Agricultural reform will work better in rice-growing areas than in wheat- or cotton-growing areas, where there are costs from breaking up large production units, but the responsiveness of reformed agriculture is universally positive and rapid.

Notes

Chapter 1

1. Representatives of Tatarstan, an autonomous republic that has assumed many attributes of a sovereign state in the early 1990s, have been invited to CAR leaders' meetings. The Tatars are the largest ethnic group in Central Asia without their own country (Table 1.2).

2. Evolving views on the economics of transition can be traced through the annual surveys of the International Monetary Fund (IMF), the UN Economic Commissions for Europe (UN-ECE) and for Asia and the Pacific (UN-ESCAP), and the European Bank for Reconstruction and Development (EBRD), as well as in the World Bank's *Studies in Transition* and the EBRD-sponsored journal, *The Economics of Transition*.

3. Chen, Jefferson, and Singh (1992), Sachs and Woo (1994), and Pomfret (1994b) draw different lessons.

4. Many textbooks on economic development include surveys of the evolution of the subject and of the empirical evidence; my own interpretation is in Pomfret (1992).

Chapter 2

1. Chinese influence waxed and waned, depending as much on conditions in the Chinese heartland as on conditions in Central Asia. The extent of Chinese control peaked during the Han dynasty, when in the first century, Chinese forces reached the Caspian Sea. The next high point was under the Tang dynasty, when China ruled directly or through vassals over much of Central Asia until defeated in battle by Islamic forces in 751.

2. The term was popularized in English by Rudyard Kipling in his novel *Kim*. My favorite books on the Great Game are Hopkirk (1990) and the amazing memoirs of F. M. Bailey (1946).

3. Northern Kazakhstan received over a million peasant immigrants between 1906 and 1915. By 1926, over 2.2 million Slavs lived in Kazakhstan, but only 600,000 in the rest of Central Asia (Clem 1992, 31–34).

4. There is little published material on the economy of Soviet Central Asia; Rumer (1989), McAuley (1992), and the chapters on Kazakhstan and on Central Asia in Williamson (1993) are the most recent studies. Lewis (1992) has assembled a collection of articles by geographers written during the final year of the USSR. In April 1992 the IMF published a series of economic surveys of the successor states to the Soviet Union, which focused on the current situation (a follow-up series of more substantial surveys appeared in 1993). The chapters on Central Asian countries in Europa Publications (1992) contain useful historical synopses. In 1993 the World Bank started to release country studies of the CARs (World

Bank 1993c, 1993d, 1993e, 1993f); these tend to be more prescriptive than analytical and contain little historical background, but they include much recent information. The World Bank's statistical compendiums (1993a, 1993b) are invaluable.

Chapter 3

1. This book does not pretend to undertake an adequate analysis of the evolution or working of the Soviet economic system. See Nove (1969, 1976, 1986) for in-depth analysis; for evaluations of the Soviet economy on the eve of the disintegration of the USSR, see Ericson (1991) and IMF et al. (1991).

2. Rumer (1989, 85–104) reviews the history of schemes to divert water from Siberia to Central Asia. This and other Aral Sea issues are dealt with by Sinnott (1992).

3. Under the Soviet system, the ministry in Moscow allocated shares and enforced these decisions. According to rumors, the ministry still retains some detailed hydrological information, which it does not wish to make available to the national governments of Central Asia because doing so would lead to conflict.

4. About thirty "nonmilitary" nuclear explosions were also conducted in Kazakhstan, but little is known of their impact.

5. Reported in "The Caspian Also Rises," *The Economist*, April 23, 1994.

6. The broader relationship between the Soviet system and environmental problems is discussed in IMF et al. (1991, 3:1–29).

7. The health assessment mission by three foreign experts in February 1992 reported that production of air pollutants in Chimkent (Kazakhstan) was 375 kg per capita per year, compared to 100 kg in New York (Chen, Rohde, and Jolly 1992, 1199).

8. Corruption was, of course, not limited to the southern republics but was endemic in the Soviet Union during the Brezhnev era. The distinctive feature in the CARs and Caucasus was the networks based on family or clan loyalties.

9. The figure is given in Aslund (1989, 151), quoting *Pravda*, January 23, 1988. Rumer (1989, 149–59) provides horrifying descriptions, based on post-glasnost Soviet investigative journalism, of the activities of local autocrats in Uzbekistan.

10. After another outbreak of violence in June 1989, when five people died in riots in Novy Uzen directed against settlers from the Caucasus, Kolbin was transferred to Moscow, and an ethnic Kazakh, Nursultan Nazarbayev, became first secretary.

11. Within Kazakhstan cotton production is entirely in the south, and concentrated in Chimkent oblast. Thus, while the cotton economy and the associated water resources in the Amudarya/Syrdarya system are of less importance to Kazakhstan as a whole than to other CARs, they have important regional implications within the country.

12. Lewis (1991, 145) provides data on cotton yields, which appear to have peaked in Turkmenistan during the late 1960s and elsewhere in Central Asia during the 1970s. In every republic yields per hectare were substantially higher in

1971–1975 than in 1986–1988—by over 15 percent in Uzbekistan and 18 percent in Turkmenistan, the two biggest producers.

13. Turkmenistan's dominance is understated by the quantity figures, because a large part of Kazakhstan's natural gas reserves is believed to be sour high-sulphur gas, which is relatively expensive to produce and treat.

14. Of the CARs' total trade, 85–90 percent was with other Soviet republics, while for the Canadian provinces the (weighted) average share was 44 percent.

15. The CARs' exposure was unique among peripheral CMEA members. In Eastern Europe Stalinist development strategies created more diversified national economies. When in the late 1950s and early 1960s Soviet leaders shifted the emphasis from national self-sufficiency to specialization within the CMEA, this was resisted by Poland, Hungary and Romania; especially controversial was the Galati steel project, which Romania pressed ahead with in 1961 over Soviet objections, even to the extent of buying machinery and equipment in Western Europe. The CARs, with no pretense of sovereignty, could not pursue economic diversification against the wishes of planners in Moscow. The closest parallel is Mongolia, but its development was integrated into CMEA plans only after the mid-1970s.

16. IMF, *Common Issues and Interrepublic Relations in the Former USSR* (Washington D.C.: IMF, April 1992), 7, 53.

17. Data are from Lewis (1992, 272). These figures are symptomatic of a differentiation that had emerged during the last three decades of Soviet rule; by many measures modernization in the five Central Asian republics had proceeded furthest in Kazakhstan and Kyrgyzstan and least in Tajikistan and Turkmenistan. It must be emphasized, too, that the participation rates do not indicate equal opportunity; none of the CARs has a female president, and few leading political or administrative personnel are women.

18. Rumer (1989, xiv) claimed that "the Armenian-Azerbaijanian conflict is nothing more than a small ripple on the surface; the real storm will come from the Islamic peoples of Central Asia."

Chapter 4

1. See the discussion accompanying Table 3.1 and Appendix 1. Ofer (1987) discusses Soviet growth up to Gorbachev.

2. DDR leader Honecker strongly advocated military action to suppress Solidarnosc, correctly perceiving the potentially fatal threat to the old regime, but the Soviet leadership prevaricated, and Jaruzielski's domestic solution of imposing martial law was accepted.

3. Gorbachev's reputation in the West was based overwhelmingly on his non-confrontational foreign policy, to a small extent on his introduction of glasnost, and hardly at all on his economic policies. His external reputation peaked in 1989, when he acquiesced in the peaceful revolutions in Eastern Europe, and was cemented by the December 1989 Malta summit with President Bush, which officially ended the cold war. Although Gorbachev enjoyed strong support from Western leaders over the next nineteen months, this brought him little concrete assistance

that he could show off at home. Domestically, Gorbachev's reputation went steadily downhill as the economy deteriorated, and as he lost control over internal security (usually dated from the Nagorno Karabakh crisis of 1987–1988). Western misperceptions of his reformism arose from a facile extension of his admirable foreign policy, based on the assumption that his domestic policies must also be admirable (that is, reformist, in the direction of political pluralism and a market economy), and from turning a blind eye to both the obvious domestic failures (for example, the antialcohol campaign and the failure to implement the Shatalin Plan) and the authoritarian atrocities (for example, Black January in Baku). This inflated positive view of Gorbachev as reformist became confused with a mistaken belief in his domestic popularity and indispensability.

4. "Repressed inflation" refers to a situation where excess demand is not fully eliminated by price increases. "Open inflation" is defined as the actual rate of price increases. In the USSR, excess demand led to queues and to black markets; despite the growing inflationary pressures during the 1980s, price indices registered artificially low rates of inflation because official prices were fixed.

5. The standard Soviet practice was to appoint Russians as the second secretary of the Communist party and as head of the KGB in each CAR and as commanders of the Central Asian military districts. Heller and Neckrich (1986, 699–70) describe the mechanisms of control over non-Russian Soviet republics during the Brezhnev era.

6. Aslund (1989, 106) explains the lack of reform in the Central Asian republics by their abundant labor (central planning was relatively efficient at labor absorption, but less efficient when labor was scarce, as in the western USSR) and by their low development level (where quality was less important than meeting basic needs). These explanations do not fit the Chinese experience, where reforms were often started in poorer areas and where labor abundance was universal in the late 1970s. The parallel between the Central Asian republics and China lies in the slow spread of Chinese reform experiments to culturally subdued provinces, such as Tibet and, to a lesser extent, Xinjiang and Inner Mongolia.

7. As Aslund (1989) emphasizes, this was not the first contradiction in perestroika. In 1986 Gorbachev advocated an "optimal relationship between the central management and the operative independence [of enterprises]" (p. 113), and in 1987 he announced plans to merge thirty-seven thousand industrial enterprises into a few thousand associations, while speaking of the need to avoid monopoly practices (p. 119).

8. Ellman and Kontorovich (1992). Ellman points out (p. 118) that Soviet budget figures are difficult to sort out because military expenditure was disguised in published figures.

9. Morrison (1991) portrays Gorbachev as a vacillator who tried to occupy the (shifting) middle ground. In the final months of the USSR, he sided with the conservatives in the winter of 1990–1991 (surrounding himself with the men who would lead the August 1991 coup), and then with the reformers in the spring of 1991, and ended up being trusted and supported by nobody. Gorbachev also seemed preoccupied with issues of political power, center-republic relations, and foreign policy, while only having a hazy understanding of economics.

10. Although the president of Azerbaijan signed the December 1991 Almaty

declaration establishing the CIS, membership in the CIS was never ratified by the Azerbaijan parliament. As discussed in Chapter 12, both Georgia and Azerbaijan reversed their opposition to CIS membership during the second half of 1993.

11. The country chapters in Part Two give some information about the political situation in each CAR on the eve of independence. The diary of Tiziano Terzani (1992), an Italian journalist traveling across Central Asia during the late summer and autumn of 1991, provides an illuminating snapshot of the region as a whole.

12. Koen and Phillips (1993) analyze price behavior and its consequences in Russia during 1992.

13. Leszek Balcerowitz, the architect of Poland's Big Bang, coined the term "pure socialist production" to describe products that nobody wanted (steel of the wrong grade, redundant tanks, ugly, ill-fitting shoes), and some estimates placed pure socialist production as high as 10 to 20 percent of Eastern European centrally planned economies' GDP. This output could be lost without reducing welfare. In practice, however, "pure" socialist production rarely had zero value; consumers would eat Comecon chocolate when no other was available, even if nobody wants it now that Western chocolate is on sale, which means the value of the old chocolate was somewhere between zero and the world price of chocolate, but who knows where in this range. A further consideration for the CARs, less relevant to the independent Comecon members, is that an individual CAR could benefit from output produced on its territory and exchanged for goods from other republics; the Tajikistan aluminium smelter and the Kyrgyzstan sugar refinery probably had negative value-added, but still generated incomes within the respective CARs, while the costs of inefficiency were spread over the USSR.

14. The CARs are among the former Soviet republics for which progress has been slowest. In both the World Bank's *Statistical Handbook 1993: States of the Former Soviet Union* and the IMF's Supplement to *International Financial Statistics* on the former Soviet Union (published in late 1993), the number of blank entries is exceptionally high for the CARs.

15. Kazakhstan's 1990 GNP per capita was similar to that of Brazil (the highest in Latin America), higher than that of any African country or any Asian country apart from Japan, the NIEs, and Saudi Arabia, but lower than that of almost all European countries (including Russia). The other four CARs, with GNP per capita between \$1,130 and \$1,690 were bunched with Peru, Thailand, Tunisia, and Turkey in the international rankings.

16. The price reforms of February and April 1991 were crude and rather inept attempts to combat repressed inflation and the monetary overhang by redenominating prices and assets and did not address the fundamental problem of distorted relative prices.

17. At a minimum, even if income disparities were not widening, there was great uncertainty. Such uncertainty about the distribution of costs and benefits of reform may explain the widespread hostility to rapid reforms (so-called shock therapy) even when the old system had been discredited. Fernandez and Rodrik (1991) have argued that such ex ante hostility can be transformed into ex post support if the uncertainty is dispelled; nothing succeeds like success, and initially unpopular reforms in South Korea (early 1960s), Chile (1970s), and Turkey (early 1980s) subsequently became popular.

18. Interfax, CIS Statistical Committee, *Statistical Report no, 9, Special Issue* (November 12, 1992). The dietary changes were also observed by three foreign experts on a health assessment mission to the five CARs in February 1992: "Most family meals consist of bread and potatoes; beyond reach are vegetables, fruits, milk and meat" (Chen, Rohde, and Jolly 1992, 1197).

19. President Karimov issued a decree closing the kebab stands in Tashkent for several days in July, which was unlikely to have any impact on the spread of a water-borne disease like cholera. On several occasions in the late summer and autumn borders were closed, as governments blamed their neighbors for allowing infected people to carry diseases into their healthy countries. The introduction of such quarantine measures was often at short notice; in September 1993, I was in a plane coming from Urumqi that was refused permission to land in Almaty as it began its approach.

20. Fischer (1992, 43–46) discusses payments union issues and reviews some specific proposals.

21. Such trade between partially liberalized economies is already apparent across the China-Mongolia-Russia and China-Kazakstan borders, although the absolute value of this international trade is limited by the state of transport facilities.

22. An early decision of the reformist government in Mongolia was to commission a steel mill from a Japanese company, C. Itoh. In late 1992, even before the mill was completed, Mongolia was experiencing difficulties in finding the hard currency to service the soft loan with which the mill had been financed. Faced by the choice of using foreign exchange to import food and fuel or to service the debt, the government was tempted by the first option but received warnings from the Japanese government about the potential adverse consequences in terms of access to future aid and capital if financial obligations were not met.

23. Widespread protests followed the January 1992 price increases, including strikes in major industrial centers (for example, by Karaganda coal miners in Kazakhstan) and violent demonstrations in cities (for example, two students were reported killed in Tashkent).

24. Although the list includes most of the major food and drink items in the Central Asian diet, the sample is arbitrary (for example, if bread, sugar, and rice had not been included, Almaty's sum of ranks would have been less than Moscow's). Moreover, a simple ranking ignores whether prices are similar (eggs), whether they have a wide range (sugar or butter), or whether they are bipolar (milk and flour) or tripolar (vegetable oil). The sum is unweighted, yet some goods are more important consumption items than others (but consumption patterns also differ; for example, rice is more important in Tashkent than in Moscow). Finally, there is no way of knowing the reliability of the data; for example, do they refer to goods of similar quality? Using the indicator as a guide to price reform by assuming that higher prices mean freer prices is to ignore other causes of spatial price differences.

25. By its nature such behavior is underreported and difficult to document, but it appears to have happened on a large scale in Russia after the August 1991 coup and to have been a dominant feature of the Albanian economy in 1991–1992 (Aslund and Sjoberg [1992], call Albania a "kleptocracy"). Privatization from

within may be beneficial if property rights pass to competent managers familiar with the business, but more likely is indiscriminate asset stripping as any alienable asset obtained at no cost is worth having even if its value to the stripper is much less than its value to the firm as an entity. Russian survey data reveal exceptionally strong managerial control, with the support of workers, and few outside share-holders in privatized enterprises (Boycko, Shleifer, and Vishny 1993, 165–72).

26. The Chevron agreement is the largest-ever deal between a Western company and the USSR or any of its constituent republics.

27. A small number of joint ventures predate the breakup of the USSR, of which the most important involves a South Korean consumer electronics company in Kyrgyzstan. In 1993 some bigger initiatives were reported, especially involving South Korean firms; Daewoo received authorization from the South Korean government in March to invest $100 million in building a car plant in Uzbekistan, which would be the biggest South Korean investment in the CIS (*Far Eastern Economic Review*, May 20, 1993, 56).

28. Although they are usually separated, this is an element of price reform, because the interest rate is a price, and one of the most important. A well-functioning capital market has many interest rates adjusting for term and for risk. Commercial banks specialize in screening borrowers for risk; they profit from making loans, but incur losses if the borrower defaults. Training loan officers takes time, but is faster than waiting for the emergence of the larger number of competent lenders implicit in bond or equity markets. Bond markets should also come early in the sequence of financial reforms, and should at least involve high-profile borrowers, such as the government; this broadens the capital market, but is also important for permitting more sophisticated monetary policy.

29. In Uzbekistan, government expenditure as a share of GDP increased from 35 percent in 1987–1989 to 46 percent in 1990 and 55 percent in 1991, mainly because of increasing explicit subsides (accounting for about a quarter of all expenditures by 1992). Meanwhile, government revenue as a share of GDP remained more or less stable at 25–28 percent over the period 1987–1991.

30. Uzbekistan also hopes to benefit from gold sales as a source of government finance.

31. The situation was further confused by CIS members' decision to have an origin-based VAT, which discourages exports and leaves countries open to reductions in the price of imports due to other countries' VAT revisions. Once one country cuts VAT rates, others are tempted to follow, reducing their tax revenues. By contrast, the more usual destination-based VAT with a zero rate for exports leaves countries' trade positions unaffected by VAT changes elsewhere.

32. These issues are addressed in greater detail in Tanzi (1993). Indiscriminate decentralization of spending responsibility to subnational jurisdictions while additional revenues accrue at the national level is a related problem, which is intertwined with center-region power struggles in the larger Soviet successor states. Wallich (1992) and Wallich and Nayyar (1993) analyze fiscal federalism issues in Russia; they have also become important in Kazakhstan and Uzbekistan. In 1992 the size of the budget deficit was obscured by severe data problems. When an early IMF mission to one CAR expressed shock at the size of the budget deficit, the government officials went away and returned the next day with a new set of gov-

ernment accounts showing a far smaller deficit; the mission had no way to adjudicate between the two sets of figures. By 1993 the IMF representatives had a much better idea of the magnitude of revenues and outlays, so pure invention was less feasible and the ruses discussed in the text became more important in reducing the size of the published budget deficit.

Chapter 5

1. There is also a large Uzbek community in northern Afghanistan, and a substantial Uzbek minority in Turkmenistan.

2. The *Far Eastern Economic Review* (November 19, 1992) claimed that two hundred thousand Russians a year had left Uzbekistan since 1988.

3. *Far Eastern Economic Review*, November 19, 1992.

4. In May after Kyrgyzstan introduced its national currency, Uzbekistan closed the border to prevent an inflow of rubles. In September the border was closed to prevent the spread of cholera. These measures primarily affected the Fergana Valley, because road and rail communications between Uzbekistan and Bishkek pass through Kazakhstan.

5. Uzbekistan imported 6 million tons of crude oil in 1990, with 5.5 million coming from Russia. In 1992 Russia supplied only 3.8 million tons, while imports from other sources were roughly constant. In 1993 the contracted volume of oil to be supplied by Russia was 3 million tons, but actual deliveries were less.

6. In 1989 ninety tons of gold were mined in Uzbekistan, about 30 percent of the USSR's production, but by 1991 this had fallen to seventy tons. Newmont Mining Corporation of the United States signed an agreement in spring 1992 to treat low-grade gold ores at a mine in Muruntau (four hundred kilometers west of Tashkent), and the European Bank for Reconstruction and Development (EBRD) has authorized funding for the project.

7. The copper comes from two open-pit mines, both with an ore content of 0.4 percent copper, which is low by international standards. According to a World Bank (1993c, 163) report, the larger copper mine, Kalmakir, may be competitive because some gold is also retrieved from the ore, but Uzbekistan's lead and zinc mines are not competitive by international standards.

8. The car project is a fifty–fifty joint venture to remodel a plant at Asakha (in the Andijan region of the Fergana Valley) formerly producing trailers, so that it can produce a small car (Tico), a seven-passenger microbus (Damas), and a 550-kilogram small truck. In the first stage bodies and components will be manufactured and cars assembled at the plant, while tires, seats, windshields, and other parts will be purchased from local suppliers. In the second stage (to be completed by 2000) engines and transmissions, previously imported from Korea, will be built in Asakha. The Tico sells for $4,500, including standard air conditioning and good fuel consumption (4.1 liters per one hundred kilometers); three thousand units were imported from Korea in 1992–1993 in order to establish a sales network and consumer familiarity.

9. Uzbekistan has two other motor vehicle joint ventures. Mercedes is involved in building a factory to manufacture trucks in the Khorezm region, and AutoVAZagregat Enterprise in Samarkand (a Russian-Uzbek joint venture) has

begun assembling buses. In May 1994 BAT announced that it would invest $200 million in Uzbekistan's tobacco industry over five years, in an arrangement similar to that negotiated by Philip Morris in Kazakhstan in 1993 (see note 16 to Chapter 6). BAT was simultaneously negotiating a similar deal in Kyrgyzstan (*Financial Times*, May 17, 1994, 20).

10. This was highlighted after Kyrgyzstan's creation of an independent currency in May 1993, when many rubles left Kyrgyzstan, and most of them appeared to go to Uzbekistan. The Uzbek government sharply criticized Kyrgyzstan, closed the border, and halted bank transfers between the two republics. Some of the dispute was political, but on economic grounds Uzbekistan's attack was founded on weak logic for the ruble flow into Uzbekistan was more due to Uzbekistan's regulated prices offering ruble bargains which were not available in Kyrgyzstan's other large neighbor, Kazakhstan.

11. The housing market remains imperfect and segmented. After a brief period of trading, the government issued a decree in March 1993 banning sale of housing and other buildings. The reason was to forestall purchase of housing by foreigners and especially by other CIS nationals. Continuing strict regulation of residence also impedes a free housing market. Rents are not regulated, but in the most active part of the rental market, foreigners seeking good-quality housing, there is excess demand. The elite who had the best housing were able to rent the few high-quality units at very high prices to the new expatriate community; in late 1993, foreigners were paying rents as high as $4,000 per month for apartments in the best part of town.

12. Some of the exports were diverted to CIS markets, especially Russia, in 1993 as CIS prices came more in line with world prices; exports for rubles were not subject to the 35 percent tax.

13. Among consumer goods the biggest price differential was in tea, whose regulated price was 5–8 percent of the market price in late 1993.

14. The heavily subsidized pharmaceutical imports provided some examples when the country ran out of vaccines in 1993. Another critical area was the subsidized imports of irrigation equipment, where some types of pumps became unavailable. With artificially low domestic prices, there was excess demand for imports and no good mechanism for establishing priorities within the product group.

15. The Tashkent Exchange began trading on January 1, 1992. After initial active turnover, especially of Russian shares, the exchange stagnated in 1993, in part because an amendment to Article 78 of the Criminal Code allowed heavy penalties for speculation, which was vaguely defined.

16. On the background to the "zero option" agreement see Armendariz de Aghion and Williamson (1993).

17. Credits from the Russian central bank are reported to have been 180 billion rubles in the first half of 1993 (Economist Intelligence Unit, *Country Report: Uzbekistan*, 3d Quarter 1993, 72). Besides the EBRD funding for the Newmont gold-mining project, Uzbekistan had received a $26.8 million loan from the Islamic Development Bank and $15 million in export credits from the United States by mid-1993. Relations with the United States deteriorated, however, after a U.S. embassy official was publicly beaten up at Tashkent airport in May. The IMF and

World Bank have been slow to authorize loans to Uzbekistan because of the lack of progress in economic reform. The first World Bank loan agreement ($21 million for institution building) was signed in September 1993.

18. The term "Oriental Despotism" has stuck because Wittfogel (1957) retained it as his book's title for historiographical reasons, even though he opens the book by saying that he prefers the term "hydraulic society" (p. 2). His analysis of hydraulic societies as responses to arid environments that involve "large-scale and government-managed works of irrigation and flood control" (p. 3) seems more appropriate to Central Asia than to anywhere else in the modern world. Wittfogel's own examples, however, are mostly historical, without reference to the CARs' cotton economy (even when he turns to a more polemical application to the USSR). Wittfogel's technology driven explanation of how hydraulic societies are bureaucratic with supreme autocratic leadership could apply to any of the CARs, but it fits best the most cotton dependent of them, Uzbekistan.

Chapter 6

1. Even before independence, President Nazarbayev had already made state visits in 1990 and 1991 to North American, Western European, and Asian countries.

2. Figure quoted in the Kazakhstan section of *Eastern Europe and the Commonwealth of Independent States 1992* (London: Europa Publications, 1992), 464.

3. Measured by number of nuclear warheads, Kazakhstan, with 1,410, became the world's fourth-largest nuclear power after the disintegration of the USSR. The government has pledged that Kazakhstan will be a nonnuclear state and is committed to destroying or removing from its territory all nuclear warheads by the end of the century.

4. There was also some immigration of Kazakhs from Xinjiang Province in China, especially in the early 1960s. Postindependence official figures on ethnic composition have included Kazakhs outside the country (mainly in Mongolia and China) who are eligible for Kazakh citizenship, which in conjunction with the emigration of Slavs and Germans inflates the percentage of ethnic Kazakhs.

5. The significance of this event in Kazakh consciousness was reflected in the erection after independence of a memorial plaque in the square where the incident occurred.

6. The two-language hierarchy was codified in the same way in the January 1993 constitution, which also specified that the president must be fluent in Kazakh.

7. In the late 1980s Kazakhstan produced 12 percent of grain, 23 percent of wool, 8 percent of meat, and 4 percent of cotton in the USSR (1986–1989 averages, from IMF et al. [1991, 1:218]).

8. The World Bank considers about 30 percent of the land brought into cultivation during the Virgin Lands campaign unsuitable for cultivation and maintains that its use contributes to soil degradation. World Bank, *Kazakhstan: Country Economic Memorandum*, Report no. 10976-KK (Washington D.C., November 1992), 129.

9. See "Toil and Trouble: Problems Loom over Failure to Deal with Land Issue," *Far Eastern Economic Review*, December 3, 1992, 23–26.

10. Estimate by Serik Akhanov, deputy director of the Supreme Economic Council, quoted in *Far Eastern Economic Review*, December 3, 1992, 26.

11. See, for example, IMF et al. 1991, 1:216–17, table 16.

12. See discussion in IMF, *Economic Review 5: Kazakhstan* (June 1993), 10.

13. David Tarr, "How Moving to World Prices Affects the Terms of Trade in 15 Countries of the Former Soviet Union," World Bank Working Paper, WPS 1074 (January 1993).

14. Figures from State Committee on Statistics and Analysis of Republic of Kazakhstan, *Statistical Bulletin no. 2* (1992), 41–44; and IMF, *Economic Review 5: Kazakhstan* (June 1993), 91. The aggregates hide substantial changes in trade patterns between 1990 and 1992, with both exports to and imports from Eastern Europe and Cuba dropping sharply. Imports from developing countries in Latin America and in Asia (except China) fell from about a tenth of the total to almost zero, while imports from China soared from 3.7 percent to 43.7 percent of all imports. These changes in trade patterns reflect adjustment from political obligations to market conditions, with exports going increasingly to the high, income countries of Western Europe, North America, the Middle East and Asia, and import of consumer goods coming increasingly from China (with the industrial countries' share of imports holding constant).

15. Chevron began pumping sixty thousand barrels a day from the Tenghiz field in May 1993, with a promise to double output by the year's end. The sole outlet for the oil is a leaky pipeline across Russia to the Black Sea, and by the end of 1993 only thirty thousand barrels a day were passing through it as the Russian authorities cited environmental and other reasons for limiting access. Meanwhile Russia was raising fees and demanding an equity share in future oil deals, while pressuring Azerbaijan and Turkmenistan not to participate in new pipeline schemes terminating in the Mediterranean or the Gulf.

16. The DFI is not just energy related. In autumn 1993 Philip Morris paid $24 million for 49 percent of the shares of the Almaty tobacco factory. The U.S. firm plans to invest $200 million in modernizing the plant over three years, after which it will become sole owner.

17. This was exacerbated by fears of cross-border arbitrage of subsidized products. In August 1993 petrol could be bought in Kazakhstan for 500 rubles per liter, while the freer price in Kyrgyzstan was higher, and in Uzbekistan the controlled price was only 100 rubles.

18. When Kyrgyzstan introduced its national currency in May 1993 Kazakhstan's reaction was more muted than the critical response from Uzbekistan, and President Nazarbayev was careful not to object to the principle of an independent currency.

19. Economist Intelligence Unit, *Country Report: Kazakhstan*, 3d Quarter 1993, 46.

20. Starting in April 1994, 3,500 medium-sized enterprises (those employing at least five hundred but fewer than two thousand workers) were to be sold to the IPFs at auctions held every few weeks until July 1995, at which point shares in the funds could be traded. Thirty-eight large industrial enterprises (with two thou-

sand or more employees each) were also due to be sold in 1994. *The Economist*, April 30, 1994.

21. The IMF (*Economic Review 5: Kazakhstan* [June 1993], 31 and table 29) estimates that the average effective lending rate was 21 percent per year.

22. Within industry employment increased in the energy sector in response to the change in relative prices.

23. According to IMF estimates for 1991 and 1992, Kazakhstan was the only former Soviet republic to reduce the government budget deficit as a share of GDP. *World Economic Outlook*, May 1993, 59.

24. These limits are fairly elastic, but at some point a ruble zone member creating excessive credit will experience currency shortages and issue a parallel currency, which will take on more characteristics of a national currency, ultimately depreciating against the ruble. This has been the experience of the Ukraine in 1992, of Azerbaijan in the first half of 1993, and of Georgia in summer 1993.

25. The 1994 budget aimed at reducing the deficit to 4 percent of GDP by increasing revenue through better collection of trade taxes and establishment of a broader base for the VAT and income tax (by reducing exemptions) and by reducing expenditures through more targeted social expenditures and decreased enterprise subsidies.

26. While an incorruptible public administration is best of all, there appear to be more and less preferable forms of corruption. The comparison is often made between Chinese and Indian corruption. In the People's Republic of China officials are keen to promote economic activity from which they can benefit, while in India public officials' main opportunity for personal gain appears to occur at the approval stage, which slows down the introduction of new economic activities and encourages excessive devotion to lobbying (rather than production) by businesspeople. Although corruption is widespread in both countries, Kazakhstan appears to have more of the Chinese attitude, while Uzbekistan is closer to the Indian model.

27. The other end of the Chinese link is the city of Urumqi, which quickly established air, rail, and bus links with Almaty. By 1993 trilingual signs (in Chinese, Uighur, and Russian) lined the road from Urumqi airport into the city, and in the town center the money changers' first word was "rubly," rather than the "change dollars" heard everywhere else in China.

28. These concerns are exacerbated by growing awareness of the environmental costs of the Soviet economic system, which were largely hidden under the Communist regime.

29. Through 1992 there was continuing unrest in the large mining town of Karaganda, including a thirty-two-day strike. The miners are well-organized (the main enterprise is the largest in Kazakhstan, employing seventy thousand people) and facing falling real wages. The coal mine uses obsolete techniques and seams are being exhausted so contraction is likely, but there are few alternative employment prospects in the city.

30. In July 1993 the IMF announced its first assistance, an $86 million credit to Kazakhstan under the Systemic Transformation Facility. Following the introduction of the tenge in November 1993, with IMF technical support, the International Monetary Fund approved in January 1994 a second drawing under the STF of $85 million plus a standby credit of $170 million available over the

next twelve months. Meanwhile the World Bank approved a $62 million environmental protection project. The Japanese government announced parallel financing to the IMF loans and the U.S. Environmental Protection Agency backed a $25 million scheme to study the Caspian Sea's ecology. The IMF estimated (Press Release no. 94/2, January 26, 1994) that these projects brought commitments of financial assistance to Kazakhstan of over a billion dollars, which is a strong endorsement of the government's policies even if disbursements fall short of this total. In January 1994 Kazakhstan became the first CAR to be admitted to the Asian Development Bank, another international seal of approval after the parallel applications of Kazakhstan, Kyrgyzstan, and Uzbekistan had been held up for months.

31. See, for example, "The Rigging Game," *Far Eastern Economic Review*, March 31, 1994, 26.

Chapter 7

1. In 1989 the GBAO contained 164,000 people spread over sixty-four thousand square kilometers.

2. The interpretation is highly politicized. The leaders of Uzbekistan and Kazakhstan defend their support for the Tajikistan government in 1993 as necessary to stop the spread of Islamic fundamentalism. The specter of fundamentalism next door has also been used by the Uzbekistan government to justify domestic repression.

3. Niyazi (1993) gives an account and analysis of the February 1990 riots.

4. The forces were those of warlords in the Kulyab region of southeastern Tajikistan, supported by helicopters and aircraft supplied by Uzbekistan (the Kulyab region is Rakhmanov's home and also a center of the Uzbek minority). After Dushanbe was taken, supporters of the September-November government were hunted down, and a reported three thousand to five thousand Islamic fundamentalists and democrats were massacred. *Far Eastern Economic Review*, January 28, 1993, 18.

5. Here, the Tajikistan civil war becomes intertwined with the Afghanistan civil war. The Tajikistan opposition receives no support from the Uzbek warlord, Rashid Dostam, who controls most of northern Afghanistan from his capital, Mazar-e-Sharif, but other mujahideen leaders are providing weapons, money, and training to Tajik fundamentalists in the mountainous northeastern part of Afghanistan. There is also speculation about involvement of Iranian and Pakistani advisers. *Far Eastern Economic Review*, June 3, 1993, 24.

6. Ethnic Russians also occupy the leading positions in Tajikistan's own government forces. In a February 1993 interview with a Dushanbe newspaper (*Chumkhurjat*, February 4–5), the defense minister, Alexander Shishliannikov, admitted that he did not know the Tajik language yet, although he was trying to learn, and that in the army Russian continued to be used because many of the officers and warrant officers did not speak Tajik.

7. The Tajikistan government was becoming increasingly intolerant of opposition (mirroring developments in Uzbekistan). Journalists were executed and imprisoned, and criminal charges were laid against Nabiyev's opponent in the November 1991 elections. Nabiyev himself died of natural causes in April 1993.

Other leaders came to less peaceful ends; two of the main warlords shot each other dead under mysterious circumstances in March 1993.

8. Numbers are hard to obtain. The *Far Eastern Economic Review* (November 12, 1992, 24) reported that over 350,000 Russians, Germans and Ukrainians had fled between 1989 and 1992, which is a large proportion of the 480,000 people classified in these three ethnic groups in the 1989 census.

9. IMF, *Economic Review: Tajikistan* (1992).

10. Apart from hydropower, Tajikistan is totally dependent on imports for energy sources. The country has negligble oil or natural gas reserves (Table 3.4) and no oil refinery, so it imports all of its oil products (from Russia, Uzbekistan, and Kazakhstan) and almost all of its natural gas and coal.

11. Gold output figures were classified data in the USSR. The chairman of the State Economic Committee gave the 2.5-tonne figure in an interview with *Mining Magazine* (January 1992, 7), while a supplement to *Mining Journal* (November 29, 1991) referred to gold output approaching 3,000 kilograms.

12. This is an old export trade. Lazurite from the Pamirs was used in the pharaonic tombs in ancient Egypt.

13. A group of foreign experts commented in 1992 on the substantial pollution of the Amudarya River by the aluminium smelter, leading to severe health problems in downstream communities (Chen, Rohde, and Jolly 1992, 1199).

14. Elsewhere aluminium smelters are located where both cheap hydropower and deep-water ocean berths are available, but Tursunzade is several thousand kilometers overland from an ocean port.

15. There was also a "dumping" problem as the old banknotes flooded into Tajikistan in anticipation of and in response to other CIS countries' decisions to abandon the ruble zone.

Chapter 8

1. In this chapter the names Kirghizia and Kyrgyzstan refer to the same geographical entity, with the former (Russian) name being used for the preindependence period.

2. Many Kyrgyz farmers fled the country, but actual loss of life during the collectivization episode was far less than among Kazakhs.

3. The Economist Intelligence Unit estimates that two hundred thousand Russians, Ukrainians, and Germans emigrated from Kyrgyzstan between 1990 and mid-1992. *Country Profile 1992–93*, 72.

4. The gold mines also pose fewer environmental dangers than do the antimony, mercury, and, especially, uranium facilities. A World Bank report stated that "the uranium tailings disposal dump at the Uhzpolymetal facility in Kara Balta poses clear and immediate dangers to the health of workers and residents in proximity to the plant" (internal document sent to author); pollution of the groundwater table and radioactive dust lifted from the tailings pile by winds spread the hazard wider afield.

5. In the USSR, Lake Issyk-Kul was a renowned summer resort, with vacations granted as rewards to cadres from all over the Soviet Union. The facilities from that era, however, are inadequate to satisfy foreign tourists in the 1990s.

6. The rail network connects Bishkek and Osh to the Soviet system, but the track within Kyrgyzstan is small (to travel from Osh to Bishkek by rail involves transiting Uzbekistan, Tajikistan, Uzbekistan again, and Kazakhstan), so most domestic transport is by road. At present the most accessible sea ports are on the Black Sea, but after the Turkmenistan-Iran rail link is completed in 1995 the Gulf will be closer; rail shipments from Kyrgyzstan to an Iranian port will, however, have to pass through at least three other countries.

7. The major external import was cane sugar from Cuba, to be refined in Kirghizia, and then exported within the USSR. According to the International Monetary Fund, Kyrgyzstan's hard currency exports fell to a mere $23 million in 1991, by far the smallest of any Soviet republic. IMF, *Economic Survey: Kyrgyzstan* (May 1992), 24.

8. One of the major adjustments was to turn to opium poppies, which according to some (invariably undocumented) reports had become Kyrgyzstan's most important crop by value. The town of Osh was also becoming a major staging post in drug routes from Tajikistan through the CIS to Europe, especially as old routes through Turkey and Yugoslavia became disrupted by Balkan wars.

9. The figures in this paragraph are taken from the World Bank's November 1992 Country Economic Memorandum for Kyrgyzstan, table 2.2a. At other points (for example, p. 6 of the text) slightly different numbers are given, but the qualitative results are the same.

10. Partly offsetting the good harvest, severe earthquakes and mudslides destroyed production facilities in some areas. The economic aftermath of these disasters continued into 1993 as government spending was required for emergency assistance over the winter to displaced persons in the relatively poor affected districts.

11. The formula was 1,000 rubles plus one-half of the average monthly salary over five consecutive years out of the last fifteen times the number of years in employment. IMF, *Economic Survey: Kyrgyzstan* (1992), 45.

12. In spring 1993 President Akayev proposed a constitutional amendment lifting the ban on private ownership of land, but the legislature rejected the amendment.

13. There is anecdotal evidence of privatization from within occurring in Kyrgyzstan in 1992–1993, but it appears to have been more limited than in other former Soviet republics.

14. The price of a standard loaf was raised from 8 to 22 rubles, whereas the February increases were by 100–150 percent.

15. The first tranche was $25 million, compared to $23 million export earnings for 1991. The second tranche was made available in September 1993.

16. Reported in the *IMF Survey*, October 25, 1993, 323.

Chapter 9

1. The impression is heightened by the location of the capital, Ashgabat. The other Central Asian capitals, Dushanbe, Tashkent, Bishkek, and Almaty, lie on a thousand-kilometer arc of road, which provides a sense of being interlinked, whereas Ashgabat feels about equally distant from Baku, Meshed, and Tashkent.

Completion of the rail link between Turkmenistan and Iran, estimated for 1995, will presumably make Meshed feel closer than anywhere else.

2. As in the other CARs, Russians have emigrated since 1989, leaving Uzbeks as the largest minority. They are concentrated in the Tashauz region, which is home to 220,000 Uzbeks, over two-thirds of the total in Turkmenistan (just south of the Aral Sea, Tashauz suffers from severe environmental problems, especially salinization of the land). The Russian population is concentrated in the capital, Ashgabat, over 40 percent of whose population in 1989 was Russian.

3. The "gas Kuwait" tag has been used by President Niyazov, for example, in a November 1992 speech quoted in *Central Asia Today* 1 (1993):32. "The Kuwait of Asia" is a bizarre slogan, which ignores not only Kuwait's geography, but also Kuwait's troubled recent history, which suggests that it may not be an altogether comfortable situation to be a small, resource-rich country surrounded by large, powerful neighbors.

4. Turkmenistan has also remained neutral in Caucasian conflicts, supplying gas to Armenia, Azerbaijan, and Georgia as long as they paid their bills. Temporary supply cuts were used against all three countries in 1993 to enforce payment.

5. IMF, *Economic Review, Turkmenistan* (May 1992), 70.

6. Turkmenistan holds large reserves of iodine-bromine, sodium sulphate, and various types of salts. One Soviet project to dam a bay in the eastern Caspian Sea to obtain salts turned into an ecological disaster and was abandoned (and the dam destroyed) after independence. In 1993 negotiations were in progress with a French company to invest $12 million in a salt-processing complex at Krasnovodsk.

7. In both Australia and Argentina, governments tried to diversify the national economy by fostering manufacturing sectors, many of which never became internationally competitive and were a cumulative drag on economic performance, but because of their large and politically active labor force, they were difficult to reform. Only when the costs of this strategy had become blatantly obvious in the 1980s were the protective trade barriers and other forms of support reduced.

8. One indication of the lack of commitment to reform is the pace of institutional reform. In all of the former Soviet republics the old State Planning Committee (Gosplan) has had to be reformed (or at least renamed). In Turkmenistan this was not done until the end of 1992, when it was joined to the Ministry of Finance to create a new Ministry of Economics and Finance. When I visited Ashgabat in late March 1993 the post of minister was still vacant, the first deputy minister was away and the second deputy minister was sick. None of this suggests that the main institution responsible for macroeconomic policy was being given high priority.

9. The practical step involved permitting citizens to lease up to fifty hectares of land for thirty–forty years, but the state retained the right to repossess the land if it was not being utilized properly. To launch this "land to the people" campaign, President Niyazov himself leased a plot of land to make a garden.

10. Although some 1993 bills remained unpaid, Turkmenistan continued to make contracts and to supply gas to Ukraine in 1994. A report in *Transition 5* (February/March, 1994, 16) relates that out of $154 million worth of gas deliveries in the early months of 1994, Ukraine had paid for only $3.4 million worth. In late February Turkmenistan turned off the tap on supplies to Ukraine.

11. Work on the rail link began in 1992. A project to build a road from Ashgabat to the Iranian border town of Tajan is under consideration by the Islamic Development Bank. Iran and Turkmenistan also signed a tourism cooperation agreement in 1993, whose main purpose is to facilitate overland travel from Turkmenistan to the Gulf, particularly in the pilgrimage season.

Chapter 10

1. Rosenstein-Rodan 1961; and Chenery and Strout 1966.

2. It does not involve protecting the manufacturing sector to ensure a base for future economic prosperity. All that does is to create an inefficient industrial sector, which will be difficult to reform later—as Argentina, Australia, and New Zealand have discovered in recent decades. The Albertan model of allocating oil revenue to a heritage fund is a better approach, but the outcome depends crucialy on how the fund is used.

3. UN Food and Agriculture Organization (FAO), *Production Yearbook 1988* (Rome, 1989), 70–76. Only the transition economies of Southeast Asia (Vietnam, Laos, and Cambodia) are remotely similar to China by this measure. Pomfret (1995) analyzes the recent experience of other Asian transition economies.

4. One consequence of this has been the difficulty experienced by China in its bid to join (or rejoin) the General Agreement on Tariffs and Trade, which was initiated in 1986 and was still under negotiation in 1994.

5. Jefferson, Rawski, and Zheng (1992) provide positive evidence of state enterprise performance. The literature survey by Wu (1993) emphasizes the far stronger performance by the nonstate sector.

6. Dual pricing was quickly abandoned by other Asian transition economies (Laos, Vietnam, and Mongolia), presumably because they were not prepared to tolerate the cost. It is also not a serious long-term option in the CARs.

7. This feature put off potential foreign stockholders, who were allowed to buy "B" shares in some listed companies after February 1992. Despite much initial fanfare, "B" share prices performed sluggishly, even as all other Asian emerging markets boomed in 1993.

8. This is neither a transition nor a development issue. It is the secret of Italian economic success since the late 1940s, based on efficient and flexible small-scale enterprises.

Chapter 11

1. The international organizations were providing technical advice and training from early in 1992, but it was a slow process to reach all policymakers. My own observation in 1993 was that many senior officials when faced with unpalatable symptoms of policy failure instinctively reacted by suggesting the imposition of controls (for example, when advised that subsidies financed by monetary expansion would lead to exchange rate depreciation, they would suggest imposing exchange controls).

2. The political decision to stand by the ruble received support from Western economists, who argued on the basis of optimal currency area theory that the case

for a common currency was strong for the USSR and especially for the CARs (Corden 1992, 14–15). The IMF's *Economic Reviews* of the former Soviet republics published in spring 1992 also came out in favor of retaining the ruble as a common currency.

3. Interfax/CIS Statistical Committee Report no. 9 (November 12, 1992), 3.

4. The Centre for Economic Policy Research's (1993) collection of studies on new currencies is especially good on events in Estonia and Latvia during 1992 and the first half of 1993. The Slovenian tollar also experienced a period of appreciation, even against the German mark, after Slovenia left the Yugoslavian dinar zone (Mencinger 1993).

5. The formal declaration of monetary independence was no more than a recognition of reality. Printing large numbers of coupons quickly led to people's accepting coupons only at a discount to the ruble, so the two currencies circulated side by side with different values, which changed daily. The government could enforce the use of coupons because it issued them directly as payment to workers. Declaring the coupon to be sole legal tender reinforced its acceptability, but made little practical difference. A similar situation existed in Azerbaijan in spring 1993 after the government had substantially increased the number of manat in circulation. Anybody paying for goods or services in rubles would negotiate a discount, so the manat was de facto an independent currency with its own exchange rate, which was unrelated to the notional par value. The decision to declare the manat sole legal tender was taken in early June but the government was overthrown before the law was enacted and implemented; the monetary situation was unaffected by the failure to make the legal change (Pomfret 1993).

6. The Uzbekistan government paid wages in the Karakalpak autonomous republic with coupons, which circulated locally as a medium of exchange. The currency situation was alleviated after the CBR began printing large-denomination ruble banknotes in summer 1992, although cash shortages reemerged in 1993. Some dollarization was observable, especially in Kazakhstan, but the ruble remained the dominant means of exchange.

7. A problem encountered by Latvia and Lithuania when their initial temporary currencies began to appreciate was that the poor-quality banknotes could easily be counterfeited. Several printing presses operated openly just across the border in Russia. The Lithuanian talonas notes, originally issued as a ration coupon, were known colloquially as zoo tickets, after the bears and other animals featured on the notes.

8. Spencer and Cheasty (1993) describe the evolution, or nonevolution, of these negotiations.

9. The banknotes carried a 1 percent service charge and a 20 percent annual interest charge on banknotes provided on credit. The other republics complained about this exploitation of Russia's monopoly over currency printing, but with four-digit annual inflation, the interest charges were highly negative in real terms.

10. The causes and consequences of Azerbaijan's move to monetary independence are discussed in Pomfret (1994a).

11. Georgia introduced coupons in April 1993, which were made legal tender on August 2, after the Russian note withdrawal.

12. Other ruble assets and liabilities were converted into som at the same rate, apart from deposits with the Savings Bank (Sberbank) which were revalued at 1 som for 150 rubles to compensate savers for the previous low real interest rates.

13. In early July rates ranging from 4 som/$ up to 6.5 som/$ were observable. There must have been some obstacle to arbitragers, but it was not obvious what this was.

14. One internationally syndicated article, featuring an interview (on the Monday) with a trader who stated he would never accept these new pieces of paper, appeared in many newspapers, which did not print follow-up reports (including the *Wall Street Journal*). The same trader was happily accepting som by the end of the week. A similar myopic hyperbole had been visible in foreign press coverage of other defections from the ruble zone; for example, the *Financial Times* (May 15, 1992) had described the introduction of the Latvian ruble as a "suicidal step."

15. The external financing commitments are reported in the World Bank newsletter *Transition*, 4 (April 1993, 2; May 1993, 13). The *IMF Survey* (October 25, 1993, 32) describes the currency conversion.

16. These were the main considerations behind the negative headlines that introduced the som stories in the *Far Eastern Economic Review* ("Out of Steppe") and *The Economist* ("Battle of the Som"), although *The Economist*'s concluding paragraph began, "Inside Kirgizstan, the som has brought little joy either." Six months later, *The Economist* was writing, "Estonia and Kirgizstan, however, have shown that it is possible to introduce an independent currency successfully, even in the turbulence of the former Soviet Union" (November 20, lead story in the Finance section).

17. Political differences between Kyrgyzstan and Uzbekistan continue to be rooted in ethnic disputes in the Fergana Valley, which were simmering in spring 1993. Over the summer the two governments adopted a more cooperative attitude, primarily in response to the situation in Tajikistan and a perceived need for a united CIS front. It should also be noted that "closing the border" is less dramatic than it sounds since the countries are contiguous only in the Fergana Valley, and closing the border really would affect only the city of Osh. Travel between the capitals, Tashkent and Bishkek, is via Kazakhstan.

18. The more independent-minded of these republics were clearly the Achille's heel of Russia. Some, such as Tatarstan, had already made far-reaching declarations of economic sovereignty, adopted a position of tax independence, and even printed (but not yet issued) their own currencies. In sum, their situation was similar to that of the CARs in all respects other than formal political sovereignty, and some of the Russian Federation's Asian republics had very close cultural and ethnic links to the CARs. Interstate links were already developing; a delegation of the Republic of Saha (Yakutia) headed by Prime Minister M. Nikolayev had paid an official visit to Almaty in early June.

19. The market exchange rate for old rubles in Moscow was quoted at 1,500/$ (*Asian Wall Street Journal*, July 26, 1993) and 2,000/$ (*Financial Times*, July 27, 1993). There does not appear to have even been a market in the Central Asian capitals.

20. For this and other bizarre actions, the chairman of the CBR has come under heavy criticism. According to Jeffrey Sachs, "Mr. Gerashchenko may be the worst central-bank governor of any major country in history" (quoted in *The Economist*, October 16, 1993, 82). Prime Minister Victor Chernomyrdin, who signed the decree, also came in for criticism in the West. Ex-Soviet politicians, however, probably saw the action as having deeper roots than a couple of antireform personalities. The USSR had a history of confiscatory currency reforms (Tsapin [1993] describes the 1947, 1961, and 1991 reforms, as well as the July 1993 measures). Yeltsin could have dismissed Gerashchenko and Chernomyrdin, but chose instead to endorse the main features of the decree. Distrust of the top Russian policymakers lay behind Nazarbayev's October 31 announcement and the rapid introduction of national currencies by Kazakhstan and Uzbekistan during the first half of November 1993.

21. By January 1994 the black market rate was 25 manat to the U.S. dollar, but this high discount is partly explained by the thinness of the foreign exchange market in Turkmenistan's highly regulated economy.

22. The timing and nature of the currency reform were laid out for me in some detail by senior government officials in Ashgabat in March 1993.

23. Since transfers could be used only to pay taxes and utilities bills, which are low, the accounts were practically frozen. A previous arrangement by which transfers could be made to, say, the department store on production of a passbook was abolished, which was one reason why the central department store closed its doors for the second half of November.

24. Uzbekistan's trade deficit also pushed the som coupon's value down because of excess demand for foreign currency. Initially, the depreciation overshot with reports of rates of 3,000–6,000 som coupons per dollar. By the end of November the market rate was around 2,700, but the market was imperfect; in the bazaar on the first Sunday in December, the moneychangers were offering 2,200 for dollars and selling dollars at 3,200. The previous Friday the central bank of Russia had announced that it would accept som coupons at a rate of 3 per new ruble (and tenge at a rate of 260, compared to Kazakhstan's official rate of 500).

25. As it turned out, the som coupon was made sole legal tender on 1 January 1, 1994, and introduction of the new permanent currency was postponed.

26. The political situation in both Russia and Belarus was unclear, but in January 1994 unionists in both countries were sufficiently powerful to sign a monetary agreement; the Russian negotiators were Chernomyrdin and Gerashchenko, the men behind the July 23 ruble reform, while the Belarus negotiator, Prime Minister Kebich, was a former Soviet industrialist. The agreement, formalized on April 12, ratified a one-for-one exchange of Belarus coupons for new rubles (the market rate was 5:1) and allowed the Belarus central bank to regulate money creation within Belarus. This would be immediately costly for Russia (*The Economist* [January 15, 1994] estimated the conversion cost at $1.2 billion—and on April 16 increased this estimate to "more than $1.5 billion"), and would recreate the inflationary bias of the 1992–1993 ruble zone. The Russian motives appear to have been entirely political (that is, cementing Belarussian economic dependence), while Belarus was being offered financial aid to alleviate the costs of the economic cul-de-sac along

which it had traveled since independence (the economic crisis in Belarus, as of mid-1993, is analyzed in Lucke [1993]).

27. In Tajikistan itself new and old rubles were not at par. In November the exchange rate was around 2.5 old rubles for one new ruble. On November 26, 1993, an agreement was reached whereby Russia would provide a $100 million loan for Tajikistan to convert its currency from old to new rubles, but as of early 1994, it was unclear whether this would be disbursed and how it would eventually be used if the money did reach Tajikistan.

28. There were also reports in Uzbekistan that Russia was making "excessive" demands on the CARs to provide reserves to back the common currency.

29. The problem with optimal currency area theory, which had guided Western economists to support continuation of the ruble zone after the disintegration of the USSR, was that it weighed the microeconomic benefits of reduced transactions costs against the macroeconomic benefits of policy independence under the assumption that macroeconomic policies would be efficiently implemented. Pomfret (1994a) discusses the demise of the ruble zone in greater detail.

Chapter 12

1. The Soviet intervention in Afghanistan had remarkably little impact on the CARs, which is why there is minimal reference to the Afghan War in this book. Statements by foreign commentators in the mid-1980s that the Afghan War was leading to "deterioration of the political climate" in the CARs and that the December 1986 Almaty demonstrations were "an indirect backlash from the war in Afghanistan" (Bennigsen 1987, 294) appear to be unfounded. Tajikistan was the main exception, but although opposition to the government grew there during the 1980s, there was no strong movement for secession from the USSR (see Chapter 7).

2. Similar security concerns exist in the other western provinces, although explicit separatism appears strong only in Tibet (technically, Tibet, Xinjiang, and Ningxia are autonomous regions, and Gansu and Qinghai are provinces). On October 7, 1993, public security forces attacked the Dongguan mosque (one of China's largest) in Xining, capital of Qinghai Province, to end five weeks of protests by tens of thousands of Moslems; reports did not appear in the foreign press until three weeks later, and the facts were unclear, although the *Far Eastern Economic Review* (November 11, 1993, 15) reported that "Chinese troops killed at least nine Muslims" in the October 7 incident. On August 14, riot police stormed a chemical factory in Lanzhou (Gansu Province) occupied by protesters against the sulphuric acid waste being dumped into the water supply; "several people" were killed by the police (*Asian Wall Street Journal*, November 4, 1993, 1, 24).

3. Although the rail link had been operating since 1990, the change of gauge at the border made it inconvenient. In 1993 the train from Urumqi to Almaty took twenty-four hours, the same journey by bus took twenty hours, and by plane it took ninety minutes.

4. In 1990, with 54.7 million rubles of trade, China was the eighth largest among Kazakhstan's extra-USSR trading partners. In 1992 trade turnover was $433 million, more than double the value of Kazakhstan's trade with any other

non-CIS country. Data from State Committee on Statistics and Analysis of Republic of Kazakhstan, *Statistical Bulletin no. 2* (Alma-Ata 1992).

5. The general Chinese view, held by the governments in both Beijing and Taipei, is that Xinjiang has been part of China for millennia. It is unclear where the eastern border is considered to lie; the PRC government does not recognize the 1881 Treaty of St. Petersburg by which China regained Ili from Russia but surrendered its claim to the Ferghana Valley. The historical basis for China's claims in Central Asia is, in fact, not so strong; Chinese influence was greatest during the Tang dynasty, when lands west of present-day Xinjiang were ruled by Chinese vassals, but this influence diminished after military defeat by Islamic forces in 751. Xinjiang and the Ferghana Valley were only brought back under Chinese rule by the Manchus in the eighteenth century, so continuous Chinese rule in Xinjiang is no longer than Russian rule over Kazakhstan (see Chapter 2).

6. This is in contrast to Azerbaijan, where the United Kingdom is active and Baku has so many green and yellow "I ♥ BP" stickers that it can seem like a company town.

7. Incipient alliances in the new Great Game can already be observed. China supplies military equipment to both Iran and Pakistan. Chinese policymakers, suspicious of pan-Turkism and distrustful of Turkey as a running dog of U.S. imperialism, are improving relations with the Islamic Republic of Iran as a counterweight, despite their fears of Islam's being spread in Xinjiang by foreign agents. When Iranian President Rafsanjani visited China in September 1992, his itinerary included an Urumqi trade fair in which Iranians and Pakistanis were participating. Despite its long-standing alliance with Pakistan, China strongly opposes changes in the Kashmiri status quo, again reflecting concern about Islamic forces in an area bordering Xinjiang (Walsh 1993).

8. When Georgia's President Sheverdnadze signed a decree on October 23, 1993, for Georgia to join the CIS, all of the non-Baltic former Soviet republics were CIS members.

9. Quoted in *The Economist*, August 28, 1993, 13.

10. When Estonia had proposed in summer 1993 a citizenship law that would exclude ethnic Russians, President Yeltsin made a thinly veiled threat of retaliation which was sufficient to prevent the enactment of the law. The threat was as much directed to other former Soviet republics with large Russian populations.

11. In January 1994 Presidents Karimov and Nazarbayev announced an agreement to form a "common economic space" in which Kazakhstan and Uzbekistan would have coordinated policies for credit and finance, budgets, tax, customs duties, and currency until 2000 (*The Economist*, January 15, 1994).

12. The main joint activity by the Caspian Sea states in 1993 was an attempt to establish a caviar cartel to halt the slide in caviar prices that occurred after the collapse of the USSR's central marketing of caviar. Potentially more important is cooperation among the Caspian states to establish oil and gas pipelines to deep-sea ports, although Russia's interests may diverge from those of the other former Soviet littoral states. Existing routes via the Volga-Don Canal cannot accommodate large tankers, with the result that much of the oil and gas from Kazakhstan, Azerbaijan, and Turkmenistan continues to go to Russia and Ukraine; new pipelines would facilitate market diversification.

13. Kazakhstan, with its large non-Moslem population, is the cultural exception, although linguistically Kazakh is very close to the other Turkic languages. The main Islamic group left outside ECO is in Xinjiang Province of China (and Bosnia and Albania in Europe).

14. ECO could also encourage more exports from the three original members to the CARs. In March 1993, for example, Toyota opened a car assembly joint venture in Pakistan, and a senior executive explained in an interview with *Asiaweek* (February 24, 1993, 61), "We are mainly looking at Iran, the newly independent republics of Central Asia, and Bangladesh." An important precondition for Pakistan to participate in Central Asian markets, however, is resolution of the Afghanistan civil war which disrupts the only road connections between Pakistan and other ECO members.

15. Observer status is typically a halfway house in which countries consider making a formal application. By early 1994, Armenia, Belarus, Latvia, Moldova, Russia, and Ukraine had observer status and were negotiating accession. Azerbaijan, Estonia, and Lithuania (like Kazakhstan, Kyrgyzstan, and Turkmenistan) were observers, but had not yet lodged an accession application. Among the former Soviet republics, only Georgia shared the nonobserver position of Tajikistan and Uzbekistan. One added incentive to make a formal application after December 1993 was the successful conclusion of the Uruguay Round of trade negotiations, which increased the benefits of GATT membership (as well as the obligations), and the creation of a World Trade Organization (to replace the GATT Secretariat in 1995), of which Russia in particular wanted to be a founder member (as did China, whose application for reaccession to GATT had been on the table since 1986).

16. Western leaders and opinionmakers appeared to have fallen into the same trap they had fallen into with Gorbachev. Yeltsin was portrayed as the last best hope for economic reform and political stability, even though he had shown no consistent commitment to economic reform and much evidence of instability as a political leader. When Yeltsin endorses imperialist moves in the Caucasus and Central Asia, Western supporters explain that he is drawing the fire of extremists, such as Zhirinovsky.

Chapter 13

1. "Political stability" is used here to indicate continuity of rule by the former Communist political elite, even if it has changed its party name or become nonparty. At the end of 1993 all of the non-Baltic republics had leaders who were in power before 1992 or represent some continuity from that leadership. In Azerbaijan, where a Popular Front government displaced the old Communists in 1992, the new government was overturned by a coup in June 1993, and the subsequent presidential election was won by Geidar Aliev, a former member of the Brezhnev Politburo. Russia and Kyrgyzstan had the most radical leadership, because their presidents had come to power as challengers to the main Communist party candidate, but Yeltsin and Akaev still rose to power through Soviet mechanisms.

2. There had also been no real privatization program or other components

of economic reform in Ukraine, which might create interests in favor of further reform.

3. Other examples are the popularity of German vodka (ironically, with Russian-sounding brand names, such as Rasputin or Petrov, but with un-Russian quality control) and the large number of hairdressers and stalls selling cheap but cheerful jewelry. In some respects, the atmosphere is reminiscent of Western Europe in the late 1940s, where a great desire for a happier life after decades of economic misery provided a foundation for rapid economic growth based on buoyant demand and willingness to work hard for material rewards.

Appendix 1

1. A more comprehensive analysis of Soviet statistical issues is contained in IMF et al. (1991, 1:133–69). Ofer (1987) reviews the Soviet Union's growth record up to 1985. Bergson (1991) discusses estimates of consumption in Gorbachev's USSR, emphasizing conceptual problems of international comparisons.

2. This paragraph and the two that follow are based on "Measuring the Incomes of Economies of the Former Soviet Union," World Bank Policy Research Working Paper, WPS 1057 (December 1992).

3. The CIA estimates referred to above are now generally believed to have grossly underestimated quality differences; for example, U.S. and USSR cars were considered identical for the purpose of calculating PPP exchange rates. The resulting overestimate of Soviet GNP may also have been politically motivated, as the CIA did not wish to understate the Soviet threat, but it should be added that many independent researchers in the 1980s believed the Soviet economy to be healthier than it now seems to have been with hindsight.

4. If the World Bank figures shown in Table 4.1 are used as the base (for example, if for Kazakhstan the base is 2,600/2,870, or 0.9006 of the USSR average), then the official figure for Kazakhstan is only 82 percent of this relativity (that is, 0.74 percent of the USSR average). The corresponding figure for Turkmenistan is 93 percent, and that for Tajikistan is 94 percent; all other republics' figures lie between 95 percent and 101 percent. The U.S. Census Center for International Research has estimated relativities similar to the official Soviet ones, apart from ranking Azerbaijan, Georgia, and Tajikistan higher (World Bank, WPS 1057, 18).

5. This contrasts to the bias toward overreporting by enterprise managers under the central planning system.

6. Koen and Phillips (1993), in a comprehensive analysis of Russian price behavior in 1992, maintain that real income did not fall significantly in Russia in January 1992, and that the large drop in real wages reported in official statistics is spurious. It is probable that prices in Central Asia were tracking those of Russia in 1991–1992, since all the CARs were still in the ruble zone.

7. GDP measures the total amount of goods and services produced within a country while GNP measures the total amount produced by a country's residents. GNE differs from GNP if a country is a net importer or net exporter, in which case it spends more than the value of its product or vice versa.

8. A similar but distinct point has been made in this book about domestic trade. Liberalizing housing markets can increase welfare even if the stock of housing is

unchanged, because occupiers can exchange property to obtain housing better matched to their preferences.

9. For example, for Tashkent schoolchildren, is a poorly taught course in Uzbek history of more or less value than a well-taught course in Soviet (or Russian) history? Were the subsidized opera houses an example of "pure socialist production," with an output which nobody wanted? In 1993, when the relative price of opera tickets was minimal (typically about one-tenth the price of a small Snickers bar), well-produced, good-quality performances played to quarter-full houses in Almaty and Tashkent.

References

Armendariz de Aghion, Beatriz, and John Williamson. 1993. *The G-7's Joint- and Several Blunder*. Essays in International Finance no. 189. Princeton University, Princeton, N.J.

Aslund, Anders. 1989. *Gorbachev's Struggle for Economic Reform*. London: Pinter.

Aslund, A., and O. Sjoberg. 1992. "Privatization and Transition to a Market Economy in Albania." *Communist Economies and Economic Transformation* 4: 135–50.

Bailey, F. M. 1946. *Mission to Tashkent*. London: Jonathan Cape. Originally written as a report to the UK Foreign Office in 1918.

Bailey, Martin J. 1991. "Mismeasurement of Economic Growth." International Center for Economic Growth, Occasional Paper no. 23 San Francisco: ICS Press.

Bennigsen, Alexandre. 1987. "Afghanistan and the Muslims of the USSR." In Rosanne Klass, ed., *Afghanistan: The Great Game Revisited*. New York: Freedom House.

Benson, Linda. 1990. *The Ili Rebellion: The Moslem Challenge to Chinese Authority in Xinjiang, 1944–1949*. Armonk, N.Y.: M. E. Sharpe.

Bergson, Abram. 1991. "The USSR before the Fall: How Poor and Why?" *Journal of Economic Perspectives* 5:29–44.

Boycko, Maxim, Andrei Shleifer, and Robert Vishny. 1993. "Privatizing Russia." *Brookings Papers on Economic Activity*, no. 2, 139–92.

Centre for Economic Policy Research. 1993. *The Economics of New Currencies*. London: CEPR.,

Chen, Kang, Gary Jefferson, and Inderjit Singh. 1992. "Lessons from China's Economic Reform." *Journal of Comparative Economics* 16:201–25.

Chen, Lincoln, Jon Rohde, and Richard Jolly. 1992. "Health Crisis in Central Asian Republics." *Economic and Political Weekly*, June 6, 1197–1202.

Chenery, Hollis B., and Alan Strout. 1966. "Foreign Assistance and Economic Development." *American Economic Review* 56:679–733.

Clem, Ralph S. 1992. "The Frontier and Colonialism in Russia and Soviet Central Asia." In Robert A. Lewis, ed., *Geographic Perspectives on Soviet Central Asia*. London: Routledge.

Corden, W. Max. 1992. "Integration and Trade Policy in the Former Soviet Union." Paper presented for the UNDP/World Bank Trade Expansion Program, Washington, D.C., January.

Dornbusch, Rudiger. 1992. "Monetary Problems of Post-Communism—Lessons from the End of the Austro-Hungarian Empire." *Weltwirtschaftliches Archiv* 128:391–424.

Ellman, Michael, and Vladimir Kontorovich. 1992. *The Disintegration of the Soviet Economic System*. London and New York: Routledge.

Ericson, Richard. 1991. "The Classical Soviet-type Economy: Nature of the System and Implications for Reform." *Journal of Economic Perspectives* 5: 11–27.

ESCAP. 1991. "The Asian Republics of the Former USSR: Current Economic and Social Situation and Possibilities for Closer Economic Cooperation with the ESCAP Region." *Economic Bulletin for Asia and the Pacific XLII*, no. 1/2, June/December, 1–13.

Europa Publications. 1992. *Eastern Europe and the Comonwealth of Independent States 1992*. London: Europa.

Fernandez, Raquel, and Dani Rodrik. 1991. "Resistance to Reform: Status Quo Bias in the Presence of Individual-Specific Uncertainty." *American Economic Review* 81:1146–55.

Fischer, Stanley. 1992. "Russia and the Soviet Union: Then and Now." National Bureau of Economic Research Working Paper no. 4077. Cambridge, Mass.

Fischer, Stanley, and Alan Gelb. 1991. "The Process of Socialist Economic Transformation." *Journal of Economic Perspectives* 5:91–105.

Friedman, L. 1993. "Ethnic and National Composition of Population in Newly Independent Countries of the Middle East and Caucasus." *Central Asia Today* 1:56–60. Moscow State University Institute of Asian and African Studies Information-Analytical Bulletin.

Garber, Peter M., and Michael G. Spencer. 1994. *The Dissolution of the Austro-Hungarian Empire: Lessons for Currency Reform*. Essays in International Finance no. 191. Princeton University, Princeton, N.J.

Garver, John. 1993. "The Chinese Communist Party and the Collapse of Soviet Communism." *China Quarterly* 133:1–26.

Harris, Lillian Craig. 1993. "Xinjiang, Central Asia and the Implications for China's Policy in the Islamic World." *China Quarterly* 133:111–29.

Heller, Mikhail, and Aleksandr Nekrich. 1986. *Utopia in Power: The History of the Soviet Union from 1917 to the Present*. New York: Summit Books.

Hopkirk, Peter. 1990. *The Great Game*. Reprint, Oxford: Oxford University Press, 1991.

International Monetary Fund, World Bank, Organisation for Economic Co-operation and Development, and European Bank for Reconstruction and Development. 1991. *A Study of the Soviet Economy*. 3 vols. Paris: OECD.

Jefferson, Gary, Thomas Rawski, and Zheng Yu Xin. 1992. "Growth, Efficiency and Convergence in China's State and Collective Industry." *Economic Development and Cultural Change*, January, 239–66.

Koen, Vincent, and Stephen Phillips. 1993. "Price Liberalization in Russia: Behavior of Prices, Household Incomes, and Consumption during the First Year." IMF Occasional Paper no. 104. Washington, D.C.: IMF.

Lewis, Robert A., ed. 1992. *Geographic Perspectives on Soviet Central Asia*. Studies of the Harriman Institute for Advanced Study of the Soviet Union. London: Routledge.

Lucke, Matthias. 1993. "Policy Options for Economic Transformation in the Republic of Belarus." *MOCT-MOST* (Economic Journal on Eastern Europe and the former Soviet Union), no. 3, November, 53–71.

McAuley, Alastair. 1992. "The Central Asian Economy in Comparative Perspective." In Michael Ellman and Vladimir Kontorovich, eds., *The Disintegration of the Soviet Economic System*. London and New York: Routledge.

Mencinger, Joze. 1993. "How to Create a Currency?—The Experience of Slovenia." *Weltwirtschaftliches Archiv* 129:418–31.

Morrison, John. 1991. *Boris Yeltsin*. London: Penguin.

Niyazi, Aziz. 1993. "The Year of Tumult: Tajikistan after February 1990." In Vitaly Naumkin, ed. *State, Religion and Society in Central Asia*. Reading, England: Ithaca Press.

Nordhaus, William, Merton Peck, and Thomas Richardson. 1991. "Do Borders Matter? Soviet Reform after the Coup." *Brookings Papers on Economic Activity*, no. 2, 321–40.

Nove, Alec. 1969. *The Soviet Economy: An Introduction*. New York: Praeger.

———. 1976. *An Economic History of the USSR*. Rev. ed. London: Penguin. A third edition was published in 1993.

———. 1986. *The Soviet Economic System*. Boston: Allen and Unwin.

Nyman, Lars-Erik. 1977. *Great Britain and Chinese, Russian and Japanese Interests in Sinkiang, 1918–1934*. Lund Studies in International History no. 8. Stockholm: Esselte Studium.

Ofer, Gur. 1987. "Soviet Economic Growth: 1928–1985." *Journal of Economic Literature* 25:1767–1833.

O'Leary, Brendan. 1989. *The Asiatic Mode of Production*. Oxford: Blackwell.

Pomfret, Richard. 1991. *Investing in China: Ten Years of the Open Door Policy*. Hemel Hempstead: Harvester Wheatsheaf; Ames: Iowa State University Press.

———. 1992. *Diverse Paths of Economic Development*. Hemel Hempstead: Harvester Wheatsheaf; Englewood Cliffs, N.J.: Prentice Hall.

———. 1993. "Monetary Reform in Azerbaijan." *Centre for International Economic Studies (University of Adelaide), Seminar Paper 93–07*, November.

———. 1994a. "The Choice of Monetary Regime in Asian CIS Countries." *Asia-Pacific Development Journal* 1:47–61.

———. 1994b. "The Chinese Model of Economic Reform: Can Eastern Europe Learn from Asia?" Paper prepared for the International Economic History Association Conference in Milano, September 1994.

———. 1995. *Asian Economies in Transition: Reforming Centrally Planned Economies*. Cheltenham: Edward Elgar.

Rosenstein-Rodan, Paul. 1961. "International Aid for Underdeveloped Countries." *Review of Economics and Statistics* 43:107–38.

Rumer, Boris Z. 1989. *Soviet Central Asia: A Tragic Experiment*. Boston: Unwin Hyman.

Sachs, Jeffrey, and Wing Thye Woo. 1994. "Structural Factors in the Economic Reforms of China, Eastern Europe and the Former Soviet Union." *Economic Policy* 18:101–45.

Shome, Parthasarathi, and Julio Escolano. 1993. "The State of Tax Policy in the Central Asian and Transcaucasian Newly Independent States." International Monetary Fund Paper on Policy Analysis and Assessment, PPAA/93/8. Washington, D.C.: IMF.

Sinnott, Peter. 1992. "The Physical Geography of Soviet Central Asia and the Aral Sea Problem." In Robert A. Lewis, ed., *Geographic Perspectives on Soviet Central Asia*. London: Routledge.

Spencer, Grant, and Adrienne Cheasty. 1993. "The Ruble Area: A Breaking of Old Ties." *Finance and Development* 30:2–5.

Stein, Aurel. 1933. *On Ancient Central-Asian Tracks*. London: Macmillan.

Tanzi, Vito. 1993. "Fiscal Policy and the Economic Restructuring of Economies in Transition." International Monetary Fund Working Paper, WP/93/22. Washington, D.C.: IMF.

Tarr, David. 1994. "How Moving to World Prices Affects the Terms of Trade in 15 Countries of the Former Soviet Union." *Journal of Comparative Economics* 18:1–24.

Terzani, Tiziano. 1992. *Buonanotte Signor Lenin*. Milan: Longanesi. English translation entitled *Goodnight, Mr. Lenin*. London: Picador, 1993.

Theunissen, Joop, and Ilkka Kimmo. 1994. "The Status of Food and Agriculture in the Central Asian Republics of the Former Soviet Union." *Agro-chemical News in Brief* (FADINAP, Bangkok), September, 1–18.

Tsapin, Alexander. 1993. "Russia's Withdrawal Syndromes in Currency Reform." *Transition* 4:4–5.

Wallich, Christine. 1992. *Fiscal Decentralization: Intergovernmental Relations in Russia*. Washington, D.C.: World Bank.

Wallich, Christine, and Ritu Nayyar. 1993. "Russia's Intergovernmental Fiscal Relations: A Key to National Cohesion." *Challenge*, November/December, 46–52.

Walsh, J. Richard. 1993. "China and the New Geopolitics of Central Asia." *Asian Survey* 33:272–84.

Williamson, John, ed. 1993. *Economic Consequences of Soviet Disintegration*. Washington, D.C.: Institute for International Economics.

Wittfogel, Karl A. 1957. *Oriental Despotism*. New Haven: Yale University Press.

World Bank. 1993a. *Statistical Handbook 1993: States of the Former USSR*. Washington, D.C.: World Bank.

———. 1993b. *Historically Planned Economies 1993: A Guide to the Data*. Washington, D.C.: World Bank.

———. 1993c. *Uzbekistan: An Agenda for Economic Reform*. Washington, D.C.: World Bank.

———. 1993d. *Kazakhstan: The Transition to a Market Economy*. Washington, D.C.: World Bank.

———. 1993e. *Kyrgyzstan: The Transition to a Market Economy*. Washington, D.C.: World Bank.

———. 1993f. *Kyrgyzstan: Social Protection in a Reforming Economy*. Washington, D.C.: World Bank.

Wu, Yanrui. 1993. "Productive Efficiency in Chinese Industry." *Asian-Pacific Economic Literature* 7:58–66.

Index

Page numbers in italics indicate the chapter reference for that subject.

About the Author

RICHARD POMFRET is Professor of Economics at the University of Adelaide. During 1993 he was affiliated with the United Nations for twelve months, working as regional adviser to the governments of the Central Asian republics Azerbaijan and Mongolia.